# Politics in China Since 1949

Since the victory of the 1949 revolution, the incumbency of the Chinese Communist Party (CCP) has been characterized by an almost relentless struggle to legitimize its monopoly on political power. During the Mao era, attempts to derive legitimacy focused primarily on mass participation in political affairs, a blend of Marxist and nationalist ideology and the charismatic authority of Mao Zedong which was reinforced by a widely propagated cult of personality. The dramatic failure of the Cultural Revolution forced the post-Mao leadership to discard these discredited paradigms of legitimacy and move towards an almost exclusively performance based concept founded on market economic reform.

Whilst this went some way towards resurrecting the popularity of the CCP, the reforms during the 1980s spawned a number of unwelcome but inevitable side effects such as official corruption, high unemployment and significant socio-economic inequality. These factors detracted from the party's legitimacy and culminated ultimately in the 1989 demonstrations in Tiananmen Square and throughout China. Since Tiananmen, the party has sought to diversify the basis of its legitimacy by adhering more closely to constitutional procedures in decision making and to a certain extent reinventing itself as a conservative nationalist party.

This probing study of post-revolutionary Chinese politics sets out to discover if there is a plausible alternative to the electoral mode of legitimacy or if legitimacy is the exclusive domain of the multi party system. Including key analysis of contemporary issues which challenge the authority of the CCP, *Politics in China Since 1949* will be essential reading for scholars of Chinese studies, history and politics.

**Robert Weatherley** is a lawyer with the UK based law firm Mills & Reeve and heads the firm's China group. He is author of *The Discourse of Human Rights in China* and has written a number of academic articles on Chinese politics. He previously lectured on Chinese politics at the University of Newcastle and now teaches part-time at Cambridge University.

# Routledge Contemporary China Series

# Politics in China Since 1949

Legitimizing authoritarian rule

**Robert Weatherley**

Routledge
Taylor & Francis Group

LONDON AND NEW YORK

First published 2006
by Routledge
2 Park Square, Milton Park, Abingdon, Oxon OX14 4RN

Simultaneously published in the USA and Canada
by Routledge
711 Third Avenue, New York, NY 10017

*Routledge is an imprint of the Taylor & Francis Group, an informa business*

First issued in paperback 2012

Typeset in Times New Roman by
Newgen Imaging Systems (P) Ltd, Chennai, India

*British Library Cataloguing in Publication Data*
A catalogue record for this book is available
from the British Library

*Library of Congress Cataloging in Publication Data*
Weatherley, Robert, 1967–
    Politics in China since 1949 : legitimizing authoritarian
rule / by Robert Weatherley.
        p. cm. – (Routledge contemporary China series ; 11)
    Includes bibliographical references and index.
    1. Legitimacy of governments – China – History – 20th century.
2. Authoritarianism – China – History – 20th century. 3. Zhongguo
gong chan dang – History – 20th century. 4. China – Politics and
government – 1949– I. Title. II. Series.
    JQ1516.W43 2006
    951.05–dc22                                        2005028644

ISBN13: 978–0–415–39109–2 (hbk)
ISBN13: 978–0–415–51245–9 (pbk)

To Helen, Alice and Matilda

# Contents

# Figures

# Acknowledgements

Special thanks to Shaun Breslin (University of Warwick), Phil Deans (University of London) and Peter Jones (University of Newcastle) for their thoughts and advice on various parts of this book. Thanks also to Helen Maddocks, Colin Graham, Jennifer Jin, David Clark, Alan Dignam, Amy Wallhead and to the librarians at Rock Road Library for their assistance with my numerous requests for inter-library loans.

# Abbreviations

| | |
|---|---|
| BSAF | Beijing Students' Autonomous Federation |
| BWF | Beijing Workers' Federation |
| CAC | Central Advisory Committee |
| CCP | Chinese Communist Party |
| CDIC | Central Discipline Inspection Committee |
| CMC | Central Military Commission |
| CRG | Cultural Revolution Group |
| CUST | City University of Science and Technology |
| GNP | Gross National Product |
| KMT | Guomindang (Nationalist Party) |
| MAT | Mutual Aid Team |
| NPC | National People's Congress |
| OLVC | Organic Law of the Villagers' Committee |
| PLA | People's Liberation Army |
| PPA | Poor Peasant Association |
| PRC | People's Republic of China |
| PSC | Politburo Standing Committee |
| RMB | Renminbi (currency of the PRC) |
| SARS | Severe Acute Respiratory Syndrome |
| SEM | Socialist Education Movement |
| SEZ | Special Economic Zone |
| SOE | State Owned Enterprise |
| TVE | Town and Village Enterprise |
| VC | Villagers' Committee |
| WTO | World Trade Organization |

Map of the People's Republic of China.

# Introduction

The measure of success for any ruling party is the extent to which it secures the willing obedience of the people it governs. Although obedience can be achieved by resorting to military force or other forms of coercion (e.g. police surveillance or terror), a regime which relies on force alone cannot always be assured of its continued incumbency and may be susceptible to mass public uprisings or challenges from within the political (or military) establishment. Relying exclusively on coercion can also be expensive, as successive administrations in the former Soviet Union discovered. Instead, if a regime wishes to enhance its prospects of staying in power indefinitely, it invariably needs the support of the people it rules; in other words it must be perceived by the populace as *legitimate*. As Rigby explains:

> The expectation of political authorities that people will comply with their demands is typically based not only on such considerations as the latter's fear of punishment, hope of reward, habit or apathy, but also on the notion that they have the *right* to make such demands [my emphasis].
>
> (1982: 1)

So how do governments attain the status of rightful ruler and how do we know when they are genuinely perceived as legitimate in the eyes of the population; in other words, how do people express their consent for those who govern them? The answer depends entirely upon the political system under which the ruler operates. The multi-party system, for example, is characterized by what Beetham (1991: 150–2) defines as the electoral mode of legitimacy. Under the electoral mode, Beetham argues, consent to rule derives from two interrelated beliefs both of which are intrinsically bound to the individualism of the liberal tradition. The first belief is that no person has the right to give consent on behalf of another unless expressly permitted to do so. In many pre-modern societies, consent to rule was transmitted by a small privileged elite whose actions (e.g. swearing an oath of allegiance to the ruler or participating in a consultative council with the ruler) were deemed to represent the views of the wider community. It was this tiny sector of society that comprised what we now call the political community. In contemporary democratic societies, the political community has expanded to include the entire adult population such that consent must be *popular* consent if it is to confer genuine legitimacy on those in power.

The second constituent feature of the electoral mode relates to diversity of choice. For Beetham, consent can only be voluntary if there is a genuine choice between political parties at the polls. This ensures that express consent is bestowed on the government that is elected:

> On the part of the majority, because they have voted for it; on the part of the minority, because by participating in the election they are assumed to have demonstrated their acceptance of the rules by which the government was chosen.
>
> (Beetham 1991: 152)

In sum, therefore, the means by which a government is elected under the multi-party system (i.e. the act of voting) is also the means by which the consent of the populace is expressed: 'elections thus perform two quite distinct functions simultaneously' (Beetham 1991: 151).

Of course, the multi-party system is far from perfect. Critics may argue, for example, that a vote every few years is hardly adequate as an expression of consent and that something more interactive or frequent (e.g. referenda) is required to make the democratic system more legitimate. It may also be argued that under some multi-party systems there is little of real substance to distinguish the policies of the main political parties such that the notion of a genuine choice between parties, so fundamental to the electoral mode, is a misnomer (Robinson 1996). This is especially deemed to be the case in democracies such as Britain and America where the political system is dominated by Labour and the Conservatives and the Republicans and Democrats respectively. Notwithstanding these criticisms, the durability of the multi-party system and its expansion throughout many parts of the world is plain to see and this, it might be argued, is testament to its legitimacy.

The single party system is altogether different. There is no choice between alternative political parties, although the existence of other parties is sometimes permitted (under controlled circumstances), and there is no direct election of the party in power, although most single party regimes insist that they came to power with the support of the majority of the population. Does the absence of direct elections and diversity of choice mean that single party governments are not legitimate in the eyes of the populace? Devout liberals would no doubt argue that it does by pointing out that there is no genuine opportunity for the populace to express its consent (or lack thereof) for the governing party. It is certainly true that without multi-party elections it can be more difficult to gauge whether the party in charge is really accepted by the people because, quite simply, how do we know? Often we do not know and the popular mood may only become evident through outward expressions of discontent (e.g. anti-government demonstrations). Yet, this does not mean that we should automatically dismiss single party regimes as bereft of legitimacy. Whilst single party governments may use coercion to enforce public obedience, alternative modes of legitimacy to the electoral mode have been applied under the single party system. The purpose of this book is to describe and evaluate the principal methods of legitimacy employed by the Chinese Communist Party (CCP), the single ruling party of the People's Republic of China (PRC) since 1949.

One notable advantage that multi-party democracies enjoy over the single party alternative is that the system itself usually remains legitimate even if the government of the day is disliked by the electorate. This is because the legitimacy of the democratic system is dependant not upon the quality of government but upon the procedure for deciding who that government might be; in other words, the ability of the electorate to remove an unpopular government and choose a new one if it so desires. By contrast, the legitimacy of the single party system is inseparable from the legitimacy of the ruling party. If the party experiences a decline in its popularity this is usually accompanied by a decline in the popularity of the system because the system does not contain any procedures for removing the unpopular administration (Zhao Dingxin 2001: 22–3) and the electorate is essentially stuck with this administration. Invariably, therefore, if the people succeed in ousting an unpopular single party government they usually succeed simultaneously in ousting the single party system. This was most evident during the collapse of single party rule in Eastern Europe during 1989.

## Theories of legitimacy

Having established what we broadly mean by the concept of legitimacy, namely (borrowing from Rigby) an acceptance by the populace that a particular government has the *right* to issue directives and make demands, it is necessary to examine some of the key tenets of legitimacy as developed by leading political theorists. In so doing, I focus on theories developed by Western scholars. This is not because of any intrinsic ethnic bias but because I remain unconvinced by models which claim, for example, to be distinctively "Chinese" (Guo Baogang 2003).

### *Contrasting the electoral mode and mobilization mode*

We have already looked at Beetham's electoral mode of legitimacy and its intrinsic relationship with the multi-party system. An alternative to this is what Beetham describes as the mobilization mode of legitimacy. In contrast to the electoral mode, the consent of the people under the mobilization mode is not manifested through the act of voting. Instead, it is expressed through the direct involvement of the masses in the implementation of a particular policy or political objective which is designated by, and ultimately supportive of, the government (typically a single party regime). As Beetham (1991: 155) puts it, popular consent is evinced through the 'continuous mass participation in political activity supportive of the regime and contributory to the realisation of its political goals'. Beetham (1991: 155) also contends that, in most cases, a government which relies on the mobilization mode as a means of legitimacy derives its power through revolutionary means and that the continuation of mass participation into the post-revolutionary epoch 'can be seen as a perpetuation of the revolutionary process'. This is particularly relevant to Mao Zedong's theory of continuous revolution which is discussed later in this book.

In Beetham's view, the majority of the populace under the mobilization mode may not actually participate in policy implementation (contrast this to the Chinese model of *mass* mobilization). However, such inactivity is sufficiently compensated by the vigour and commitment with which the substantial minority gets involved. In addition, since the ruling party often portrays itself as accessible to the entire (or most of the) population and those participating in politics can be identified through their greater dedication 'they can be seen as representative of the people as a whole, and their activity in the regime's cause is demonstrative of the continuing support of society at large' (Beetham 1991: 155–6).

With the focus on the execution of policy, although not, Beetham suggests, its formation, political participation under the mobilization mode does not encompass the election or appointment of those in power. As such, the function of the ruling party under the mobilization mode is fundamentally different to that of a ruling (or any) party under the electoral mode. Put simply, whilst the latter is occupied with making its personnel and policies appealing to the electorate, the former concentrates on fomenting a grass roots enthusiasm for a particular policy such that the masses will be inspired to carry out that policy. Whilst the ruling party under the mobilization mode may offer certain incentives or privileges as an inducement into action, 'the effectiveness of participation as a legitimating process depends on the commitment of those involved to a cause over and above that of their own personal advancement' (Beetham 1991: 156).

The mobilization mode, common to many communist states (Denitch 1979, Lomax 1984), is highly pertinent to our study of regime legitimacy in the PRC. After coming to power in 1949 following a protracted revolutionary armed struggle, the CCP relied heavily on mass mobilization as a means of legitimizing its authority, most notably during what is commonly referred to as the Mao era (1949–76). Although the CCP was founded on a traditional Leninist structure of tight central control through a hierarchy of party-state institutions, Mao believed that political power could usefully be legitimized by immersing the masses more directly into the policy process not only at the level of implementation but also with regard to the formulation of policy (in contrast to Beetham's assessment of the mobilization mode). Mao's logic in espousing such a concept was broadly as follows: the political integration of the masses would engender strong sentiments of worth and belonging; a common perception amongst the masses that their views and input were of considerable value to the party and were indispensable to the future wealth and stability of the country. In turn, this self-worth would generate feelings of loyalty towards the CCP and establish (or perhaps reinforce) the belief that the CCP was the legitimate ruler of China.

Manifesting Mao's belief in the wisdom of mass politics were the dual concepts of the mass line and the mass campaign. The former was developed during the party's formative years (1935–45) in Yanan (Shaanxi province) and was designed to foster close relations between the party and the masses, especially in the countryside where the link between ruler and ruled was traditionally weak. The mass line required the local party cadre to submit himself entirely to his community by living under the same rural conditions as his peasant associates, participating with them in productive labour, encouraging and yielding to their criticisms and, most importantly, canvassing them for their opinions on pressing local issues (Blecher 1986: 24–8). This approach was most apparent during the Great Leap Forward (1958–60) which we will discuss in Chapter 2. Mass campaigns were slightly different to the mass line in that local people were typically asked to implement a policy that had already been determined by the authorities, although often the principles of the mass line would underpin a given campaign. Examples of some of the mass campaigns carried out during the early period of CCP rule (discussed in Chapter 1) were the Land Reform Campaign (1947–51), the Resist America Aid Korea Campaign (1950) and the Campaign to Suppress Counter-Revolutionaries (1951).

Ultimately, the CCP leadership became divided over precisely how much autonomy to grant the masses. For several of Mao's more Leninist oriented colleagues including Liu Shaoqi, Chen Yun and Deng Xiaoping, participation by the non-party masses had to be tightly controlled by centrally-appointed party work teams so as to maintain the focus of a particular campaign and more importantly to keep the masses in order. Conversely, Mao had an almost undying faith in the ability of the masses to understand the implications of a given campaign and to carry it out accordingly. Indeed, during his most radical phases Mao believed that the masses should even be allowed to rectify the institutions of party and state that governed them, an idea that was abhorrent to the Leninists. As we shall see, the ill-fated Hundred Flowers Campaign (1957), the Great Leap Forward and the Cultural Revolution (1966–76) showed that Mao's confidence in the ability of the masses to understand what he wanted from these campaigns was misplaced.

## Weberian concepts of legitimacy

The most celebrated academic study of legitimacy is unquestionably provided by the German social and economic theorist Max Weber. In his book, *The Theory of Social and Economic Organization*, Weber identifies three distinct categories of legitimacy, each of which has had a profound influence on the work of subsequent scholars of legitimacy, although not everyone agrees with Weber's analysis (Schaar 1970, Habermas 1975, Grafstein 1981, Beetham 1991). The three categories are legal rational legitimacy, charismatic legitimacy and traditional legitimacy.

### Legal rational legitimacy

Legal rational legitimacy refers to the established procedures by which decisions are made, laws are enacted and office holders are appointed or dismissed. Although some scholars tend to lump this in with electoral legitimacy (Zhao Dingxin (2001: 22), for example, refers to the concept of legal-electoral legitimacy), electoral legitimacy, as we have seen, is exclusive to multi-party systems and only then to the process of electing governments. Legal rational legitimacy refers to decision making procedures under all types of political system and encompasses more than just the act of electing governments.

According to Weber (1964: 328), legal rational legitimacy derives from a 'belief in the "legality" of patterns of normative rules and the right of those elevated to authority under such rules to issue commands'. For a political system to be legitimate in legal rational terms such procedures must be clearly defined and transparent. For a regime to be legitimate in legal rational terms it must adhere closely to these procedures. Logically, therefore, the personal attributes of a particular office holder are irrelevant (in contrast to the concept of charismatic legitimacy). What matters is that this person has been appointed in accordance with accepted procedures and remains true to these procedures in reaching decisions and making laws without exceeding the parameters of his or her authority. If the office holder obeys the rules then the populace will be more likely to accept his or her authority even if they do not particularly like that person and will obey the decisions he or she makes even if they do not particularly like those decisions. As Weber summarizes:

> Obedience is owed to the legally established impersonal order. It extends to the persons exercising the authority of office under it only by virtue of the formal legality of their commands and only within the scope of authority of the office.
>
> (1964: 328)

Decision making in the PRC is dominated by the CCP and within it by the party leadership. Notwithstanding the detailed hierarchy of government and party institutions that exists from the local township level right up to the national level, key decisions ultimately emanate from a handful of men at the helm of the CCP who comprise the Politburo Standing Committee (PSC). This, in itself, has negative implications for legal rational legitimacy given the presumed separation of powers between party and state in the PRC (see Chapter 1). The procedure for reaching decisions at the PSC level and throughout the party-state apparatus (although my focus is mainly on the highest levels of decision making) is governed by the Leninist rules of democratic centralism. In arriving at a decision, party members are invited to exchange views in a free and open environment without the threat of later reprisals for anyone whose views are in the minority. This is the "democratic" element of the doctrine. The "centralist" element applies once a decision is reached by majority vote. At this point, all members are required to fall in behind the new policy line without dissent and without attempting to overrule the decision through irregular means.

The reality has been something quite different. Although Mao paid lip-service to the sanctity of democratic centralist procedures, he frequently violated them when he could not get the majority of the party leadership to agree with him on a particular issue. Mao's principal tactic on such occasions was to construct a support base *outside* the party leadership (and sometimes even outside the *party*) which he would then use to impose his ideas on his noncompliant colleagues. For example, during the mid-1950s leadership debate over the pace of rural collectivization, Mao acquired the backing of his supporters in the provincial party to force his will on the centre (see Chapter 1). Using identical tactics, Deng Xiaoping (Mao's ultimate, although not chosen, successor) demonstrated that he was equally willing to abrogate the rules of democratic centralism despite strenuous claims that he represented a more legal rational era. Most notably, in successfully reversing the direction of central economic policy after the 1989 Tiananmen crackdown, Deng, like Mao, utilized support from his allies in the provincial party apparatus (see Chapter 6).

In terms of the process of appointing and dismissing office holders, the CCP's record is equally dismal. As we shall see throughout this book, high-level appointments and dismissals have frequently been made without regard to stipulated constitutional procedures, often at the behest of the paramount leader (both Mao and Deng) during a time of political crisis. The more recent initiatives of Jiang Zemin (who succeeded Deng) and more notably Hu Jintao (who succeeded Jiang) have been more promising although China remains a weak legal rational system.

*Charismatic legitimacy*

What is evident from the discussion in the previous section is the very personalized nature of politics in the PRC, dominated (until recently) by the whims of individuals rather than institutions or the black letter of the law. This brings us to the Weberian concept of charismatic legitimacy. The defining characteristic of an individual invested with charismatic legitimacy is the common perception that he is someone very special, and that he has an ability which no ordinary person possesses. As Weber suggests:

> The term 'charisma' will be applied to a certain quality of an individual personality by virtue of which he is set apart from ordinary men and treated as endowed with supernatural, superhuman, or at least specifically exceptional powers or qualities.
>
> (1964: 358)

It is with reference to these exceptional powers or qualities that the populace may, sometimes even blindly, obey the directives of the charismatic leader. From the perspective of the masses, their relationship with the charismatic leader is one of personal devotion.

According to Weber (1964: 363–86), charismatic legitimacy in its "pure" form (as we have just described it) only emerges when the perceived qualities of the charismatic leader are required to resolve a political or national crisis. Once the crisis passes and the situation becomes more stable, charisma becomes "routinized" and the system of leader-led relations moves in a legal rational (or sometimes traditional) direction. The original features of authority relations based primarily on a lack of hierarchy and rules, quickly gives way to a more predictable and familiar structure as the charismatic authority of the leader becomes "depersonalized".

Politics in China, perhaps more than in any other country in the world, is closely associated with charismatic legitimacy, most notably with regard to Mao. Although Mao never ruled the country single-handedly as some observers have suggested (Leys 1977, Li Zhisui 1996, Jung Chang and Halliday 2005), he was unquestionably the most powerful Chinese figure of the modern era, achieving a degree of prestige amongst his colleagues and the masses alike that none of his successors have attained. Mao held the top post in both the party and the government. He was State Chairman until he voluntarily resigned in 1959 and Chairman of the CCP until his death in 1976. But the real source of his power came not from the institutional positions that he held but from who he was. More than anything else Mao was a hero.

In classic Weberian terms, the origins of Mao's charismatic authority derived primarily from his perceived ability to excel during periods of crisis, for example, during the 1935 Zunyi conference when he stood firm on CCP independence from the Soviet Union (see Chapter 1). This allowed Mao to completely dominate the decision making process since many of his leadership colleagues believed (at least initially) that he could do no wrong. On the occasions that Mao could not persuade the party centre of the wisdom of his standpoint he would invariably use his charismatic authority to convince those outside the central apparatus that he was correct. During the rural collectivization debate noted earlier, Mao gathered support from provincial party leaders by appealing to them in person. Most of them had never met Mao before and Mao realized (correctly) that his mere presence as a revered revolutionary leader would have an enormously persuasive impact on them. With the provinces on his side Mao was then able to intimidate the centre into accepting his position on this issue.

The post-Mao era has been less reliant upon charismatic legitimacy and has moved towards a more stable, legal rational system. This is partly to do with the deleterious legacy of the Cultural Revolution which brought the country to the brink of civil war and the party to the brink of collapse (see Chapter 3). But it is also because leading political figures, especially from the post-Deng era (after February 1997), namely Jiang Zemin and Hu Jintao, were not around during the pre-revolutionary Yanan period and as such have not been able to inspire the charismatic authority of Mao, and to a lesser extent Deng. Instead, they have been obliged to rely on institutions and procedures as a means of augmenting their political power.

### Traditional legitimacy

Traditional legitimacy refers to the contemporary application of methods of governing or political ideas that stretch back through the ages and which are familiar to the populace. As Weber (1964: 341) puts it, a regime enjoys traditional legitimacy 'on the basis of the sanctity of the order and the attendant powers of control as they have been handed down from the past, [and] have always existed'. According to this theory, the populace is an inherently conservative entity who feel more comfortable with recognizable ways of doings things rather than enduring a complete overhaul of the system under which nothing is familiar. But it is more than simply a question of habit. Political ideas or governance techniques are accepted on the grounds that they embody the accumulated wisdom of successive generations of leaders.

Conceptually, traditional legitimacy lies somewhere between charismatic legitimacy and legal rational legitimacy (Teiwes 1984: 58). Leaders (or governments) derive authority on the grounds of their traditional status, but whilst this authority is usually grounded in a charismatic predecessor who may be responsible for the established tradition, such tradition will impose constraints on the arbitrary actions of the leader. The populace will obey the leader's directives but only if he or she does not flout the traditional order. If the leader does so, this will jeopardize his or her incumbency and may be used as a justification for popular revolt (Weber 1964: 341–5).

At first glance, it might appear that traditional legitimacy is anathema to PRC politics given the anti-Confucian rhetoric of the communist revolution. According to the then party line, Confucianism, China's state ideology for almost two millennia (206 BC–1911), was a feudal and backward tradition responsible for the country's political and socio-economic under development and for the exploitation and suffering of its predominantly rural population. Yet, the party was careful not to push the anti-Confucian line too far. Whilst the peasantry may have been optimistic about the prospect of a new era which would allow them to cultivate their own land and produce enough grain to feed their families, they were also suspicious of their new communist rulers who were an unknown quantity. For many, therefore, a complete break with the past was a daunting prospect. Although the old Confucian system may not have treated them well it was at least familiar.

In seeking to alleviate concerns about the unfamiliarity of the new communist system, the CCP carefully retained certain elements of the past to which the people were accustomed. As discussed in Chapter 1, the party frequently alluded to (and continues to allude to) the long-term objective of restoring China to its "rightful" place in the world as a leading international power. This drew heavily on the entrenched Confucian conception of China as the centre of all civilization. In addition, Mao was often depicted (although not expressly referred to) as a new and "wise" Emperor – the natural successor in a long line of figurehead rulers.

Claims of traditional legitimacy do not always apply to the prevailing patterns of the pre-modern era (Lane 1984). In a PRC context, such claims have also drawn on the CCP's own traditions, built up since its formation in 1921. As we shall see in Chapter 4, during the late 1970s' struggle between Deng Xiaoping and Hua Guofeng to succeed Mao as paramount leader, both men sought to bolster their legitimacy by presenting themselves (in very different ways) as the obvious successor to Mao's legacy. Likewise, as Deng Xiaoping sought to legitimize a new post-Mao era of economic reform and political stability, numerous analogies were drawn with the early post-revolutionary period (roughly 1949–57). After the failure of the Great Leap Forward and the Cultural Revolution, Deng's reforms were widely heralded as the restoration of this halcyon era.

### Ideological legitimacy

Outside the scope of Weber's study, but crucial to any understanding of CCP legitimacy is the question of ideology. In general terms, ideology is usually defined by reference to a unified or systematic set of ideas and values which govern a given society (or dominant group within that society) such that they shape the way in which people behave and perceive events around them. In his book *Ideology and Utopia*, Mannheim (1949: 5) suggests that the unity of these values is not manifested in the ideas themselves, but in the collective or individual unconscious. Thus, 'a class or an individual may express a range of ideas which phenomenally appear to be diverse, yet noumenally have a unity in an underlying spiritual matrix'. In his celebrated volume on Chinese communist ideology, Schurmann (1968: 18) focuses more specifically on the ideology of organizations, suggesting that ideology in this context is 'a systematic set of ideas with action consequences serving the purpose of creating and using organization'.

Reliance on ideology as a mode of legitimacy is common place under the single party system and the organization which disseminates ideology and seeks to unify society's value system or world view is the ruling party, in China's case, the CCP. In the absence of a multi-party system with its plurality of political parties and diversity of views, the ruling party presents itself as the sole bearer of the "truth" as encompassed by ideology. The content of ideology is often highly utopian (e.g. Fascism or Marxism) and the ruling party exists in order to implement ideology and bring about this utopia. To the extent that the party progresses society towards this goal, it theoretically derives legitimacy from its people. The articulation of ideas which challenge or oppose the "truth" constitute a threat to the legitimacy of the ruling party since they may contradict the very claims upon which the party's authority is grounded. Whilst it may be permissible to express dissenting views in private, an ideology-dependant regime will invariably seek to block the public expression of such views, usually through a system of police surveillance or repression.

As a communist state since 1949, the formal ideology of the PRC is Marxism, a scientific doctrine which prioritizes the interests of the proletariat or working class as the most progressive force in society and sets out the historical and social conditions that will lead inexorably towards a communist future. The representative of the working class is the Dictatorship of the Proletariat, or in modified Chinese terms the People's Democratic Dictatorship, an organization carefully schooled in Marxism (Harding 1983). In theory, only the Dictatorship of the Proletariat is qualified to rule on behalf of the proletariat because only it understands the intricacies of the Marxist doctrine which embodies and protects proletarian interests. Although in China the masses were invited to put forward their views on certain issues, only the CCP was qualified to rule China because only the CCP could understand and interpret the intricacies of Marxism.

We will see in later chapters how the CCP has revised Marxism especially since the death of Mao, and how nationalism has often been used as a supplement or more recently as an *alternative* to Marxism. We will also examine the detailed propaganda process by which the masses are indoctrinated with ideology. For the purposes of this introductory chapter, it is instructive to examine how the CCP itself is ideologically indoctrinated. As the body which propagates ideology to the non-party masses, the party has to believe in what it is saying. It does this, according to White (1993: 148–9), by absorbing ideology at three basic levels. At a cognitive level, ideology acts as a language which defines the key concepts of political thought. On a value based level, ideology provides party members with a set of moral beliefs about 'what is good or bad, right or wrong' (White 1993: 148). Finally, on an instrumental level, ideology sets out the principles which guide 'the action of political leaders and the operation of political institutions' (White 1993: 148). In theory, it is only once the party has absorbed ideology in these three ways that it is fully equipped to lead the masses.

Logically, therefore, the impact of ideology on party members is far more entrenched than it is on the masses, particularly in terms of depth of commitment to the communist cause. This difference, White suggests, is mirrored in the paternalistic nature of party–mass relations within communist states in general. Whilst the CCP's long term objective is to convince the masses of the wisdom of Marxism and 'to incorporate the mass of the population into the ideological world of the political elite', in the short term it is hoped that there will at least be a mutually advantageous relationship between the party and the people so that:

> On the one side, the political elite is better able to lead because the Ideology provides it with the intellectual clarity and moral authority which in turn affects the 'masses' through good example and effective leadership; on the other side the 'masses' are more willing to accept leadership to the extent that they have been socialised into accepting reigning values and they perceive that the leadership is living up to their ideological pretensions.
>
> (1993: 149)

What we have then is a kind of virtuous cycle of party–mass relations, with the party ruling through righteous example (intrinsic to its role as the Dictatorship of the Proletariat) and the masses prepared to accept this authority because of the righteous example of their rulers. This clearly places a responsibility on the party to maintain an exemplary and upright approach to leadership and means that problems inevitably arise if the party is perceived as incompetent, divided or corrupt. Crucially, this is enough to disrupt the cycle of relations between ruler and ruled and create a situation in which the masses become disillusioned with the party and no longer perceive it to be a legitimate force (White 1993: 149). As we shall see in Chapter 3, this is precisely what happened during the Cultural Revolution, a campaign which effectively destroyed the CCP's ideological legitimacy.

### Performance based legitimacy

Perhaps the most obvious criteria for measuring the strength of a regime's legitimacy relates to the record in power or performance of that regime. Putting it simply, to what extent has the government in question lived up to popular expectations by fulfilling the promises that it made on coming to power? Has it achieved all (or any) of the objectives that it set out to achieve? Whilst this may be a common test of legitimacy for any government, it is especially pertinent to Marxist ruling parties since they invariably set long term social and economic goals (White 1986). Rigby (1980, 1982) defines this type of legitimacy as goal rational. The ultimate goal is communism which, as Teiwes (1984: 51) notes, 'is a sufficiently vague concept to allow successive leaderships great leeway in giving it content'. Yet, ruling communist parties usually set more tangible and measurable targets within this utopian vision (often contained in five year plans for economic growth) and this allows the populace to judge for itself how successful the party has been in attaining these targets.

The CCP's record within a performance based context is mixed to say the least. Whilst the early post-revolutionary period was successful in performance terms (most notably, in relation to agricultural and industrial reform), the Great Leap Forward, which succeeded the party's "honeymoon" period, was catastrophic. Designed to rapidly and simultaneously accelerate agricultural and industrial production, output targets, especially for grain and steel, were set unrealistically high and were pursued at any cost as the party leadership became obsessed with catching up with the West. The end result was the stagnation of the economy and the starvation of millions of rural inhabitants. Despite common assumptions to the contrary, the Cultural Revolution (which followed the Leap) was less calamitous in economic terms than the Leap, as China achieved average growth rates of about 4 per cent per annum during this period. This modest success, however, was completely overshadowed by the destruction reaped by the student Red Guards.

The post-Mao era is closely identified with performance based legitimacy as the party, led by Deng Xiaoping, sought to recover from the Cultural Revolution by implementing a far reaching programme of economic reform. Farmers were re-allocated individual plots of land and permitted to sell some of their produce in the market place. Urban workers were offered material incentives to increase production. International companies were invited to trade with, and invest in, the Chinese economy as part of what became known as the open door policy. Whilst the success of economic reform in China is unprecedented with the economy growing at near double digit rates for most of the past two decades, the reforms have created as many problems for the party's legitimacy as they have solved (see Chapters 5 and 6). In pure economic terms, growth has been uneven often benefiting those from the cities over the countryside and those from the coastal regions over the hinterland. In addition, a massive rise in unemployment and official corruption has caused a rapid increase in small-scale protests and rioting.

## Chapter outline

My analysis of CCP legitimacy follows a broadly chronological pattern comprising six chapters. Chapter 1 looks at how the party sought to establish its legitimacy during the early post-revolutionary era. Here we examine, amongst other things, the emphasis on mass mobilization as the party attempted to integrate the populace into the process of national reconstruction through a series of mass campaigns. We also assess the legal rational procedures (and Mao's breaches thereof) associated with the newly established apparatus of party and state and the attempt to propagate Marxism (and to a lesser extent nationalism) as China's new state ideology, and Mao as China's charismatic leader. The chapter concludes with a study of the Hundred Flowers Campaign, the first of Mao's radical (and unsuccessful) projects to strengthen party legitimacy by inviting the public (in this case intellectuals) to criticize party rule.

Chapter 2 examines the Great Leap Forward. In keeping with Mao's commitment to mass participation as a mode of legitimacy, the Leap drew heavily on the productive capacities of China's peasant population in an effort to boost industrial and agricultural output. Policies were largely devised at the local commune level where residents, mainly farmers, were canvassed by party cadres for their opinion on local conditions in keeping with the principles of the mass line. Due to a culmination of factors, one of which was an over-reliance on the masses, the Leap ended in mass starvation and economic stagnation. This precipitated a sharp decline both in the party's legitimacy amongst the masses and Mao's charismatic legitimacy amongst his leadership colleagues.

Undeterred by the failure of the Leap and convinced of the wisdom of his own radical ideas, Mao initiated the Cultural Revolution, the focus of Chapter 3. Perennially concerned about the legitimacy of Chinese socialism in the context of what Mao perceived as non-socialist domestic policies (including the post-Leap economic retrenchment programme) and the apparent decline of socialist attitudes at home and abroad (most notably, in the Soviet Union), Mao devised the Cultural Revolution as a means of re-invigourating (or re-legitimizing) the Chinese revolution by once again immersing the masses (principally the Red Guards) into political life and allowing them to carry out their own revolution from "below" against the remaining vestiges of revisionism within the party-state (primarily Mao's opponents in the leadership). Here we will see how the Cultural Revolution represented the pinnacle of Mao's cult of personality, as Chinese youth flocked in their millions to see the paramount leader and carry out his every word. The end result, however, was a deepening in the decline of CCP legitimacy (especially in ideological terms), as law and order collapsed completely (including any adherence to legal rational procedures) and the country teetered on the edge of civil war.

Chapter 4 analyses the rise of Deng Xiaoping as China's new paramount leader following the death of Mao and the eclipse of Hua Guofeng, skilfully outmanoeuvred by Deng during a power struggle in which both men sought to draw on the traditional legitimacy of the deceased leader. In this chapter, we will discuss how Deng's emergence offered the only real hope of resurrecting the CCP's credibility following the calamity of the Cultural Revolution. No longer perceived as a genuine political and moral force in Chinese society, Deng "de-politicized" the image of the party by moving away from the failed Maoist notions of mass mobilization and the cult of personality towards a more predictable system in which economic reform and modernization were brought to the fore. In simple terms, the promise of economic advancement for the masses became the cornerstone of CCP legitimacy.

Notwithstanding the increase in personal wealth that characterized the 1980s, the reforms gave rise to a number of new problems, each of which detracted from the party's legitimacy. These are identified in Chapter 5. For example, the reliance on Marxism as a justification for party rule became increasingly tenuous as the economy moved in a distinctly capitalist direction. The acceleration of economic reform also increased pressure on the party (mainly from the student and intellectual population) to reform the political system, an extremely thorny issue given the party's monopoly on political power. The growth of unemployment, inflation and corruption raised questions about the party's ability to implement economic reform competently and led ultimately to the ill-fated Tiananmen demonstrations of spring 1989.

The final chapter of this book examines the efforts made by the party to diversify the basis of its legitimacy. The Tiananmen protests showed just how risky it was for the CCP to rely too heavily on economic legitimacy. Although the principal focus of party work has remained on the economy, greater attention has also been paid to legal rational matters (particularly under Hu Jintao) and electoral issues with the implementation of reforms to village and township elections. A more recent phenomenon is the emergence of stability as a means of legitimacy, with the party presenting itself as the only political institution capable of providing political stability and personal safety during the difficult and uncertain period of economic transformation.

But the main basis of legitimacy (outside economic legitimacy) has been nationalism. With the continuing decline in its Marxist credentials in light of the deepening of market reforms, the CCP has increasingly sought to identify itself as a nationalist force, transforming China into an economic superpower and standing firm against attempts by foreign governments to undermine this process. Although this approach has found a sympathetic ear amongst China's fourth generation of nationalists (men and women in their thirties), many have complained that the CCP is not doing enough to protect the dignity of the Chinese nation, particularly against America and Japan. Ironically, the growth of nationalism has become something of a double-edged sword in that it challenges rather than boosts party legitimacy.

# 1 Legitimizing the new regime
## The early post-revolutionary years

The establishment of the PRC in 1949 was the final step in an astonishing rise to power by the CCP (Wilson 1982, Saich 1996). Formed less than three decades earlier by a handful of men on a lake in Shanghai, the CCP overcame a number of seemingly insurmountable obstacles during its ascendancy. In 1927, the party's fragile urban base was virtually wiped out by the nationalist Guomindang (KMT). On retreating to the rural province of Jiangxi, the party soon found itself under threat again by the KMT as well as aggressive regional warlords. During the ensuing search for a new base known as the Long March (1934–5) the party was repeatedly attacked by hostile minority groups and faced arduous terrain and severe weather conditions that accounted for well over 90 per cent of its membership. After travelling for over a year through 11 provinces and covering over 8,000 miles, the remnants of the party finally set up camp in the northern region of Yanan but with the KMT closing in once again the likelihood of survival appeared remote.

The threat of foreign imperialism also loomed large, mainly in the form of Japan which had colonized the whole of north east China (or Manchuria) and looked set to make further territorial advances. Although the eventual defeat of Japan in 1945 offered a temporary respite to the CCP, civil war between the communists and the nationalists broke out almost immediately, and with the United States providing financial and military support to the KMT, it seemed unlikely that the CCP could survive, especially in the absence of any support from Stalin and the Soviet Union. Against the odds, however, it was the CCP that triumphed four years later thanks mainly to a combination of KMT military incompetence and shrewd CCP military strategy (Eastman 1984, Pepper 1999).

Notwithstanding the impressiveness of the CCP's ascendancy, outright victory was far from complete. The preceding decades of civil and foreign war, inept KMT administration and warlord factionalism, not to mention the absence of any central authority since the late nineteenth century, had inflicted deep wounds on China's political and socio-economic system. To make matters worse, the ethnic minority provinces of Tibet, Xinjiang and Inner Mongolia had not succumbed to CCP control and pockets of KMT resistance continued in south western China for some months after the revolution. The scale of the task ahead was monumental.

If the CCP was to rebuild China much was required from a party with little experience in local administration and none at all in national government.

But the party had another pressing issue to deal with as it emerged victorious after the revolution – that of how to legitimize its new-found authority. Whilst the success of the communist armed struggle did much to enhance the popular support (or revolutionary legitimacy) of the CCP especially amongst the peasantry who comprised over 80 per cent of the population, the party was in no position to become complacent. The euphoria of the revolution would not last for ever and if the party intended to retain its monopoly on power for any meaningful period of time, new and more durable sources of legitimacy were required. This chapter examines some of the principal modes of legitimacy employed by the CCP during the early period of its incumbency (1949–57).

## Administrative control and legal rational legitimacy

One of the most pressing tasks of the early post-revolutionary period was the establishment of central administrative control over the entire country. Given the incompleteness of CCP rule in 1949, this needed to be a staged process which meant that for the first few years the PRC was governed by six regional administrative bodies (north west, north, north east, east, south west, central south). In the north and north east, civilian governments were set up without much difficulty due to the strength of the CCP in these areas and the successful completion of the various military campaigns. But in the other four regions where the party was not in full control it was necessary to temporarily accede administrative power to the party's military wing, the People's Liberation Army (PLA) until the conditions were ripe for the local party-state to take over.

It was during this transitional period that the legal rational procedures of democratic centralism were first applied at a governmental level. As explained in the Introduction, in reaching a decision, party members are encouraged to discuss their opinions in an open and democratic manner without fear of retribution should they hold a minority view. A decision is reached by majority vote and once this is achieved all participants are expected to conform to the party line without dissent and without resort to irregular methods of overturning this line. We shall see later in this chapter how Mao was quick to violate this fundamental principle.

The hand over from military to civilian institutions occurred much sooner than expected and was relatively seamless. Although the military authorities (known as Military Control Commissions) enjoyed considerable autonomy as policy-making units during the transitional phase, their role was soon scaled down to that of co-ordinating the establishment of local civilian administrations, and by 1952 fully centralized institutions of party and government (or state) were put in place. Each was to be governed by its own constitution (1954 for the state, 1956 for the party) which set out, amongst other things, a detailed hierarchy of congresses (i.e. decision-making bodies) and a legal rational system of procedures for reaching decisions and for appointing and dismissing office holders.

## The state structure

The structure of government, which remains in place today, comprises congresses at five ascending levels: national, provincial, prefectural, county and township (Schram 1987) (see Figure 1). During the early period, in accordance with the 1953 Election Law, representatives at the national down to the county level were elected indirectly (i.e. by congress members from the level immediately below them). So, for example, deputies at the national level, known as the National People's Congress (NPC), were elected by members of provincial congresses,

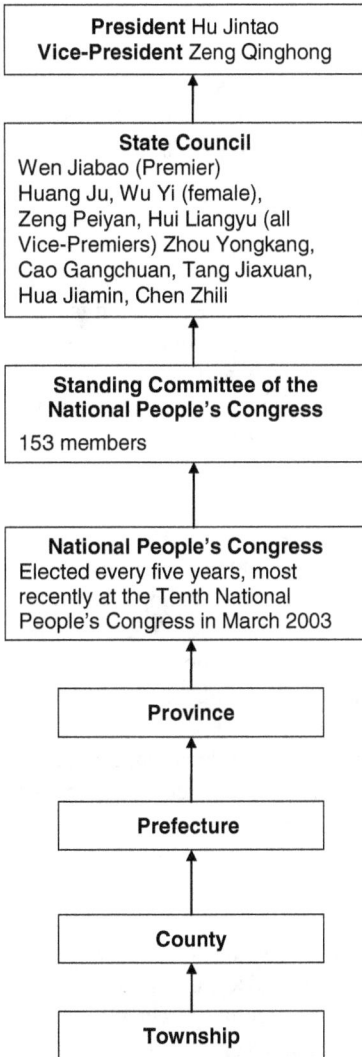

```
┌─────────────────────────────────────┐
│        President Hu Jintao           │
│   Vice-President Zeng Qinghong       │
└─────────────────────────────────────┘
                  ▲
┌─────────────────────────────────────┐
│            State Council             │
│   Wen Jiabao (Premier)               │
│   Huang Ju, Wu Yi (female),          │
│   Zeng Peiyan, Hui Liangyu (all      │
│   Vice-Premiers) Zhou Yongkang,      │
│   Cao Gangchuan, Tang Jiaxuan,       │
│   Hua Jiamin, Chen Zhili             │
└─────────────────────────────────────┘
                  ▲
┌─────────────────────────────────────┐
│   Standing Committee of the          │
│   National People's Congress         │
│   153 members                        │
└─────────────────────────────────────┘
                  ▲
┌─────────────────────────────────────┐
│   National People's Congress         │
│   Elected every five years, most     │
│   recently at the Tenth National     │
│   People's Congress in March 2003    │
└─────────────────────────────────────┘
                  ▲
       ┌──────────────────────┐
       │       Province       │
       └──────────────────────┘
                  ▲
       ┌──────────────────────┐
       │      Prefecture      │
       └──────────────────────┘
                  ▲
       ┌──────────────────────┐
       │        County        │
       └──────────────────────┘
                  ▲
       ┌──────────────────────┐
       │       Township       │
       └──────────────────────┘
```

*Figure 1* Simplified structure of the Chinese government (2005).

deputies to provincial congresses were elected by representatives of prefectural congresses and so on. By contrast, representatives at the township level were elected directly (i.e. by residents of that township).

According to Jacobs (1991: 173–4), in the state elections which took place during 1953–4 (the first in the PRC), 97 per cent of the population aged 18 and over were registered to vote and of them 86 per cent actually cast their vote. In the direct elections to the township congresses, votes were cast in large public meetings by a show of hands. In the indirect elections, lower level people's congress members used secret ballots to vote for higher level people's congress members. Yet, irrespective of which voting method was applied, there was no genuine choice of candidate because in every election the number of candidates always equalled the number of positions available.

The NPC is (theoretically) the supreme organ of legislative power. Comprising up to 3,000 delegates at any one time, its role is constitutionally defined as devising laws, amending the state constitution, ratifying international treatises and nominating or appointing senior state officials. The NPC is elected for a term of five years and holds one plenary session (or Plenum) each year. The unwieldy size of the NPC and the infrequency with which it meets means that it is unable to fully exercise its powers. It therefore elects a Standing Committee comprising about 150 members and this body acts on behalf of the NPC when it is not in session. Convening every two months (since 1987), the Standing Committee has gradually seen an increase in its law making powers and powers of supervision over the enforcement of the constitution. It also functions as an examination and approval authority for any proposed adjustments to the state budget and the fixed term plan for the national economy.

Yet, ultimate governmental authority lies with the State Council, officially the executive organ of the NPC but in reality also the state's principal legislative body. Consisting of a small number of senior officials who meet frequently but secretly, it is the State Council rather than the NPC or the Standing Committee that formulates government policy and administrative measures. The State Council's proposals are submitted to the Standing Committee for modification and then to the NPC for "consideration" (i.e. approval). The State Council also supervises the numerous policy commissions and ministries that now exist such as the State Economic and Trade Commission and the Ministry of Education. During the Mao era, the State Council was headed by a Chairman and a Vice-Chairman who were advised by a Premier and a number of Vice-Premiers. Following the 1978 state constitution, the posts of Chairman and Vice-Chairman were abolished and the government is now formally led by a President (currently Hu Jintao) and a Vice-President (currently Zeng Qinghong).

The dominance of the State Council means that the function of the NPC is largely superficial in that it ratifies State Council decisions rather than devises any policies of its own; in other words, notwithstanding a recent increase in its powers, the NPC was and remains little more than a rubber-stamp. This has done little to strengthen the legal rational legitimacy of the Chinese government. Despite the official rhetoric about the supremacy of the NPC in government decision making, all important government decisions are made behind closed doors by a handful of men. The annual plenary sessions of the NPC, which are heavily publicized throughout the country, are just for show. They are, in truth, an outward attempt to provide a veneer of procedural uniformity and demonstrate a commitment to a legal rational system of decision making.

## The party structure

The party structure mirrors that of the government with a hierarchy of congresses from the township level up to the national level (Lieberthal 1995) (see Figure 2). The system of selection is also the same with delegates from each level elected by those members belonging to the congress immediately below with the exception of the township level where members are nominated by the next highest level up. In theory, the party is headed by the National Party Congress (not to be confused with the National People's Congress) which comprises approximately 2,000 members and convenes once every five years for approximately one week. The National Party Congress (theoretically) acts as a forum for debate on important party matters, but in reality this function is carried out by its Central Committee which comprises about 350 full members (including alternate members) and holds five annual plenary sessions before being reconstituted.

As with the state, party policy is ultimately decided by a much smaller group of people in the form of the Politburo (about 20 members) and within that group the PSC which is made up of about six men. Like the State Council, the PSC is a secretive organization which meets in private to formulate party policy (usually at the seaside resort of Beidaihe, not far from Beijing). At the Eighth National Party Congress in 1956, the PSC was led by a Chairman and under him were five Vice-Chairmen and a General Secretary. The posts of Chairman and Vice-Chairman have since been abolished and the party is now led by a General Secretary (currently Hu Jintao) who is also head of the Secretariat, a body that was resurrected in 1982 to take care of routine party work.

Like the NPC, therefore, the National Party Congress and its Central Committee are primarily rubber-stamping bodies. Although the Central Committee enjoys certain formal powers such as the power to "elect" (i.e. approve) the composition of the Politburo and the PSC, and is a much more active debating chamber than it was during the Mao era, its principal purpose is to ratify draft documents that are handed down by the PSC. The National Party Congress is even more toothless than the Central Committee. As Saich (2001: 86) points out, in meeting once every five years its role is restricted to 'providing a display of power and unity, and more important "milestones" in party's history'. As with the state apparatus, this makes for a very weak legal rational system in China.

One important point to remember about the institutions of party and state in China is that they are largely one and the same entity. As Zheng Shiping (1997) has shown, although official theorists maintain that the state is separate from the party, the party has always dominated the state by consistently staffing its key decision-making bodies with senior party personnel; in other words, those who

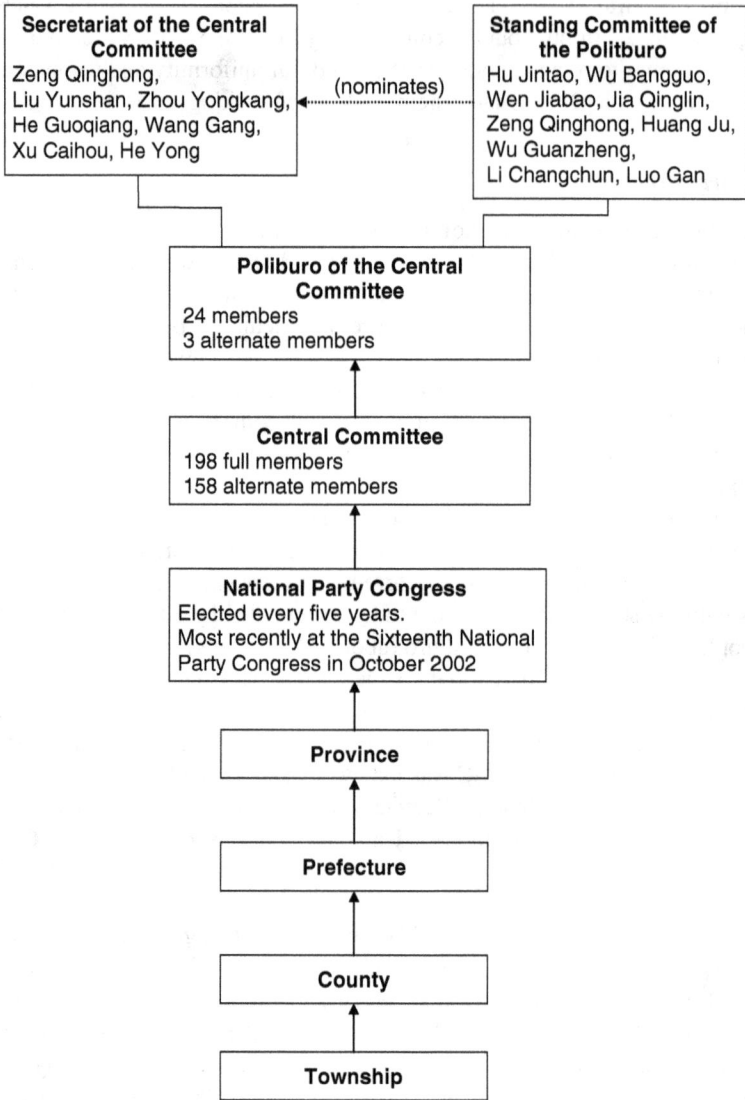

*Figure 2* Simplified structure of the Chinese Communist Party (2005).

have occupied leading positions within the State Council have usually occupied leading positions within the PSC. So, for example, in 1956 (after the Eighth National Party Congress) Mao was Chairman of both the party and the state, Zhu De was Vice-Chairman of the two institutions, Liu Shaoqi was Vice-Chairman of the party and Chairman of the NPC (effectively third-in-command of the state) and Zhou Enlai was a party Vice-Chairman and Premier.

Consequently, all important government decisions were (and have continued to be) made by leading party members. There is no genuine separation of powers in Chinese politics.

The secretive and elitist nature of decision making in China and the domination of the party over the state has been matched over the years by the neglect of other legal rational procedures (Teufel-Dreyer 1996: 90–1). For example, on no occasion during the years 1956–77 did any National Party Congress see out its statutory five year term. Conversely, the Eighth Central Committee (constituted in 1956) served a 13 rather than a 5 year term. The reliability of government procedure is no better. During the 30 years from 1949 to 1979, the NPC did not convene for 13 of them, including one entire 8 year period from 1966 to 1974. Dismissals and appointments of senior office holders have also been arbitrary. As Chairman of the state, Liu Shaoqi's term in office was scheduled to end in January 1969. However, he was deposed three months earlier and not by the NPC (the only body constitutionally empowered to do so), but by the Central Committee, a *party* organ (see Chapter 3). Similarly, the appointment of Hua Guofeng as Premier (a government post) in 1976 and the simultaneous removal of Deng Xiaoping as Deputy Premier were carried out by the Politburo during a *party* conference (see Chapter 4).

### The military

Any discussion of China's power structure would be incomplete without examining the integral role of the PLA, which includes a standing army, navy and air-force (Whitson and Wang Chen-hsia 1973). Although the military relinquished administrative control a few years after the revolution, it continued to participate in party-state affairs. This was born out of tradition. During the revolutionary years, the relationship between the party and the military (then known as the Red Army) was virtually impossible to differentiate. Non-military men often advised on tactics for guerrilla warfare whilst the military frequently implemented policy (e.g. land reform) in areas where the party was not well represented.

The military retained its administrative role in several ways. One way was through the transfer of military personnel into civilian jobs such as Deng Xiaoping who moved from Political Commissar of the Second Field Army to Vice-Premier (in 1954) and member of the PSC (in 1956). Inevitably, Deng and others like him did not simply sever their loyalty to the military on assuming their civilian positions. In fact, in many cases, they retained extremely close ties with former military colleagues from their old military units. According to Whitson (1969), Chinese politics during the early period (and beyond) was characterized by policy disputes between representatives from the different field armies of the old Red Army.

Some scholars have suggested that the transfer of military personnel into civilian administration posts was often made at the expense of "party-only" personnel. Mozingo (1983) suggests that whilst many party members did not play a leading role in actually fighting the revolution, they were far better qualified as technocrats to run the affairs of state. Mozingo concludes from this that if there had not been such a massive shift of personnel from military to party-state, the party would have found it much easier to control the military.

The link between military and party-state was also maintained through the appointment to civilian posts of people who kept their military positions. This was the case at all levels of the hierarchy all the way to the very top with several leading military officials appointed to powerful positions in the party and the government. Zhu De (Vice-Chairman of the party and the state) and Lin Biao (party Vice-Chairman and Vice-Premier) were high-ranking military officials, as were Peng Dehuai and Li Xiannian who both became full Politburo members and Vice-Premiers under the new political order. Perhaps most significantly, a new state post of Minister of Defence was set up and assigned to a serving military leader (the first incumbent was Peng Dehuai). Although formal control over the military lay with the Military Affairs Commission which was a party-run body (of which the Minister of Defence was a member), the Minister was given considerable autonomy on all the key areas of military affairs. In effect, the military was controlled by one of its own.

The blurring of the boundaries between the military and the civilian administration has given rise to the perennial problem of who controls who? According to a famous Mao dictum, "the party must always control the gun". However, in allowing the military to play such a prominent role in civilian matters, the CCP has often found it difficult to adhere to this principle, as was particularly evident during the aftermath of the Cultural Revolution when the military functioned as *de facto* ruler following the collapse of the government (see Chapter 3). The military overlap into civilian affairs has also had a negative effect on legal rational proceedings in China. By allowing for such an incestuous relationship to exist between the party, the state and the military, it has often been hard to tell precisely which institution is making the decisions and whether they are constitutionally entitled to do so.

## Ideology and legitimacy

A more definite form of regime legitimacy during the early period was ideology. As discussed in the introductory chapter, the official ideology of the PRC in 1949 was (and remains) Marxism, a doctrine which prioritizes the interests of the proletariat or working class through the leadership of the CCP. So what were the proletarian interests that the CCP sought to represent? In accordance with orthodox Marxism, CCP rhetoric focused on the necessity of eliminating the exploitation inherent in the capitalist system (the penultimate stage of human society). Under capitalism, it was argued, the ruling bourgeois class exploited the proletariat by forcing it to sell its means of production (i.e. its labour) for a pittance and often under oppressive working conditions. The new regime vowed to extinguish all vestiges of private ownership upon which such exploitation rested and build a society based on the socialist principles of equality and freedom in which the proletariat were not only equal in terms of their personal income, but also in terms of their wider opportunities in areas such as education, employment and even leisure. This was the utopia (i.e. communism) that the CCP claimed to be working towards; its ideological legitimacy depended on the extent to which the utopia was realized.

### Chinese Marxism and Maoism

But much like Lenin and the Bolsheviks, Mao and the CCP *reinterpreted* Marxism. Despite adhering to the basic Marxist principle of overthrowing the bourgeoisie and liberating the proletariat, the CCP did not conceptualize these two classes within an urban based framework as Marx and Lenin had done (Shum Kui Kwong 1988: 6). Given that over 80 per cent of the Chinese population lived in the countryside, the party developed a more agrarian understanding of class so that the bourgeoisie was predominantly made up of the landlord class and the proletariat was predominantly made up of the poor peasant class. Indeed, the Chinese term for proletariat translates directly as "the class without property".

Marx had little faith in the revolutionary potential of peasant society and envisaged the communist revolution occurring in wealthy industrialized countries like Britain and Germany rather than under developed peasant countries like China. In this sense, therefore, the CCP was "leapfrogging" the penultimate stage of Marxist development (i.e. capitalism) to arrive at communism early (as the Bolsheviks had done, although the October Revolution was urban based). On the other hand, proponents of the Chinese Marxism would probably argue that the underlying principle of the Chinese revolution could still be described as Marxist in that the class that had previously owned the means of production (i.e. the landlord class) was eliminated to the advantage of the class that for centuries had been forced to sell its means of production (i.e. the peasantry).

Another variation of the Marxist canon, and something quite unique to Mao, was the conception of class in post-revolutionary China. For Marx, a person's class status was defined in terms of his relationship to the means of production so that those who owned it were members of the bourgeoisie and those who were forced to sell it were members of proletariat. Whilst Mao did not dispute this simple binary, he also examined class within the context of a person's class origins or class background. This conceptualization was especially prominent during land reform when landlords were identified and stripped of their land (see later discussion). In categorizing just who was a landowner Mao did not only concentrate on those people who owned land. Many former landowners who no longer owned land and who were, on the face of it, proletariat, were also designated as bourgeois by virtue of their landowning *past*. This even extended to those people who may *never* have owned land but whose parents or grandparents had been landlords, such that class became determined by a person's ancestry.

So why did Mao conceive of class in this way? Ultimately, it was for the practical purposes of weeding out not only real opponents of the new regime but *potential* opponents. Despite no longer owning land (or maybe never having owned land), the individual in question, it was felt, may nevertheless (perhaps innately) harbour feelings of superiority over his poor peasant associates and seek to exploit them once land reform was over. Remarkably, therefore, what Mao appeared to be espousing was class as a state of mind. This and other departures from "pure" Marxism have led many scholars to question whether Mao really was a Marxist after all (Knight 1983, Starr 1986).

Of further note is Mao's theory of continuous revolution (Schram 1971). In contrast to the doctrine developed by Marx and Lenin, Mao believed that revolution was a permanent phenomenon and must continue well after the victory of the armed struggle and the establishment of the communist state. In this regard, Mao proposed a series of "mini-revolutions" to be carried out at the grass roots level by the ordinary masses. This would ensure that the masses retained their fervour and enthusiasm for revolution whilst at the same time keeping party members on their toes, preventing them from becoming complacent about their positions of authority. The alternative, Mao insisted, was the ossification of the revolution leading to a situation in which the ruling party turned into a ruling *class* and the masses became a *ruled* class. The mass campaigns of the early 1950s (including land reform), the Hundred Flowers, the Great Leap Forward and the Cultural Revolution are all examples of the application of continuous revolution.

### Nationalism

It is difficult to gauge precisely how effective Marxism was as a means of legitimizing the CCP during the early period (and indeed subsequently). This is partly because of the overlap between Chinese Marxism and a more informal mode of legitimacy in the form of Chinese nationalism (Johnson 1962). The unquestionable popularity of the CCP following the success of the revolution was officially credited to the superiority of Marxism as a revolutionary concept. At the same time, the party also presented itself as a progressive nationalist force. Under the old system, it was claimed, China was a backward and feudalistic society facing the increasing possibility of outright colonization by the imperialist powers of Europe, America and in particular Japan. Thanks to the CCP the Chinese people could now look forward to a bright new future in which the nation would be strong enough to compete economically and militarily with its erstwhile imperialist oppressors. The party's communist message, therefore, was not easily divorced from its nationalist message since Chinese Marxism and Chinese nationalism were essentially promising to do the same thing, namely make China strong. This was neatly reflected in the ubiquitous slogan "only communism can save China". (After the collapse of communism in Eastern Europe and the Soviet Union, Chinese satirists reversed the slogan to read "only China can save communism".)

This not unfamiliar blend of communism and nationalism (many other communist states have drawn on both forms of ideology) was further developed by the xenophobic Maoist doctrine of economic autarky which held that China could only survive and flourish as a nation if it steadfastly avoided economic interaction with the outside world (at least the imperialist parts of it). According to such a view, foreign trade was synonymous with foreign imperialism so that if

China began to trade with the wealthy imperialist nations (having spent decades fighting them off) the country would quickly find itself once again under imperialist control.

Yet, some scholars have insisted that the role of nationalism during and immediately after the revolution was not as pronounced as is often portrayed. Indeed, if anything, appeals to nationalism may have hindered the CCP's cause. One such exponent of this view is Gillin (1964) who suggests instead that land reform was fundamental to the popularity of the party, a view supported by Thaxton (1983). Similarly, Selden (1971) argues that, despite the party's post-1935 anti-Japanese propaganda campaign, the really important issue of the day was the elimination of landlord control over the countryside.

## Indoctrinating the people

Constructing a state ideology is a fairly meaningless exercise unless it is effectively communicated to its intended audience and this brings us to another (albeit interrelated) technique for legitimizing political power during the early period, namely propaganda, the means by which a particular message (be it an ideology or a policy) is disseminated to the population (Houn 1961, Landsberger 1995, Cheek 1997). In a country as large as China, achieving this objective was a phenomenally difficult task. How, for example, would the new orthodoxy be conveyed to peasant farmers living in remote Chinese villages thousands of miles from China's capital or to every pupil in every classroom in every school?

### *The Propaganda Department*

The first and most important step in the mass indoctrination process was the establishment of strong central control over all possible sources of public information. The responsibility for this task was entrusted to the Propaganda Department (of the Central Committee) which was given strong supervisory powers over key government ministries (e.g. the Ministries of Education and Publication) and ultimate authority over the entire nexus of the mass media. So, for example, all forms of national and local press were brought under the control of the Propaganda Department. This saw the introduction of new communist oriented newspapers such as the *People's Daily* and the *Guangming Daily* in which every printed word was carefully vetted to ensure that it conformed to the correct party line. Simultaneously, all independently owned (and hence dissenting) newspapers disappeared from circulation. According to Lynch (1999: 243), in mid-1930s China there were about 1,800 newspapers in circulation but by 1956 there were just 655.

The content of all theatre and film productions was heavily prescribed by the Propaganda Department to make certain that the correct revolutionary images were portrayed. But the most effective mechanism for disseminating propaganda was probably the Central People's Radio Network. In the absence of television (until the 1980s), this new network was able to broadcast propaganda to every corner of the country through a nationwide system of loudspeakers which were set up in just about every location imaginable including workplaces, schools, residential areas and even on public transport.

To ensure that absolutely no-one evaded the message, every spare inch of wall space was daubed with simple but direct political slogans such as "socialism is good" or "uphold the socialist system". Countless monuments to the revolution and statues of revolutionary heroes (often Mao) were erected all over the country. The reach of the party became all-encompassing. As Frederick Yu (1964: 155) points out, within a few years of coming to power the party 'succeeded in bringing more people into direct and close contact with the central government than ever before in Chinese history'.

### Study groups

A more personalized method of indoctrination were small study groups. Meeting at least three times a week and daily during political campaigns, every Chinese adult was required to belong to at least one group and sometimes several depending on personal circumstances. So, for example, a worker was made to join a study group in his or her work unit whilst the unemployed, the elderly and housewives joined study groups in their residential area. The groups comprised between 8 and 15 people and were invariably led by a party member (often the only literate member of the group) who was responsible for encouraging the study of the political literature, all of which was provided by the authorities (Lynch 1999: 21).

The literature usually focused on the history and ideology of the party or the objectives of a given campaign and in almost every case it would be heavily laden with the thoughts, achievements or quotations of Mao as the party leadership attempted to build a cult of personality around the new paramount leader (see later). Although the agenda was controlled from above, attendees were regularly invited to contribute to proceedings by offering their opinions on certain (often non-controversial) issues. Ultimately, as Whyte (1979: 116) explains, 'the ideal is that all members of the group should state their understanding of the message in their own words and give their reaction to it, so that higher authorities can be sure the message is getting across'.

### The young

The party also focused its efforts on indoctrinating the young (Chan 1985). This was especially important given that the younger generation would eventually inherit the legacy of the Chinese revolution and the party needed to be sure that this heritage would be safe in their hands. The classroom was the most logical forum with which to begin this process. Accordingly, education curricula at all levels were re-written in order to promote revolutionary ideals and party ideology. Children's nursery rhymes were about tales of admirable socialist camaraderie or the wisdom of Mao such as the ubiquitous "protect Chairman Mao". Storybooks featured romantic accounts of the Long March or the struggle against the KMT and the Japanese. Sentences praising Mao became commonplace in school texts including "we must be obedient to the words of Chairman Mao and be good children of Chairman Mao" or "the grace of Chairman Mao is the most precious thing in the world". Descriptive terms applied to Mao included "the sun of new China", "our great leader" and "the glorious glitter of Chairman Mao" (Fu Zhengyuan 1991: 264).

Political education classes were also introduced to the classroom and it was here that students learned more directly about the principles of socialism and the works of Mao. Although participation was encouraged, pupils were only expected to articulate views that conformed to the party line and supported the objectives of the revolution. The overall aim was to instil into the youth an attitude of acceptance and obedience rather than free thought and expression.

## The role of tradition

Another useful source of legitimacy for the new regime and one that is closely linked to the party's attempts to build up its ideological legitimacy at this time (be it communist and/or nationalist) were frequent, albeit selective, references to China's Confucian past (Franke 1963, Gong Wenxiang 1989, Fu Zhengyuan 1991). As part of the CCP's declared long-term objective of making China strong, official sources alluded to the notion of restoring China to its "rightful" place in the world. On the face of it, this was a nationalistic message aimed at persuading the masses of the party's nation-building potential. Yet, it also bore a deliberate resemblance to the ancient Confucian tenet that China was the Middle Kingdom, the centre of all civilization to which the rest of the world should pay homage.

This use of the old to complement and bolster the new is a clear example of what Weber calls traditional legitimacy. As noted in the Introduction, traditional legitimacy derives from the perception that long established and time-honoured political ideas and methods of governing are legitimate because the populace is accustomed to them. They and a long line of ancestors before them have grown up with these ideas and methods and have come to believe that they are an acceptable way of doing things. In early post-revolutionary China it may have seemed strange (even hypocritical) to draw favourably on traditional Confucian concepts given that the communist revolution was built upon a fierce repudiation of the old feudal order. The logic, however, was clear. The continuation of certain of these concepts was beneficial to party legitimacy and would help soften the transition from two millennia of entrenched tradition to a new, radical and highly unfamiliar social order.

Another example of traditional legitimacy is related to the role played by the CCP. The CCP presented itself as the People's Democratic Dictatorship, an essentially selfless organization which ruled exclusively in the interests of the people through its unique understanding of Marxism. In so doing, it not only drew on Marxist ideology but on Confucian tradition. Under the old system, the ideal form of government was benevolent, ruling virtuously by example and functioning only to safeguard the welfare of the people (Weatherley 1999: 126–8).

The party also drew on the ancient Confucian concept of the Mandate from Heaven. This held that the Emperor was appointed by Heaven on account of his ability to understand and represent the will of the people. If the Emperor failed to carry out this divinely ordained duty he automatically forfeited the Mandate which then passed to a prospective new ruler (selected by Heaven) who was charged with the sacred task of overthrowing the old regime, often described (arguably incorrectly) as the "right to rebel" (Weatherley 2002: 262). Accordingly, Chiang Kai-shek, leader of the KMT, was depicted as the disgraced and corrupt former ruler who had relinquished the Mandate to the virtuous Mao Zedong, head of a party which had shown a genuine concern for the needs of the peasants and thereby justified its incumbency. By using slogans like "may Chairman Mao live ten thousand years" and extolling Mao as the "sun" and the "saviour" in the new revolutionary anthem *The East is Red*, party theorists successfully portrayed Mao as the new communist equivalent of the Emperor.

## Mobilizing the masses

The most characteristically Maoist technique for legitimizing CCP rule was through the participation of China's masses (Townsend 1967, Pye 1971) or what Beetham calls the mobilization mode of legitimacy (see Introduction). Applying a concept which he called "big democracy", Mao believed that the party could only become genuinely legitimate if it gave the masses a direct role in Chinese politics, specifically in the formulation and implementation of policy. By so doing, Mao believed, the gulf between ruler and ruled that was characteristic of the old Confucian order (when politics was the traditional preserve of the minority literati) would be broken down and for the first time in China's history the masses would come to feel integrated into the political system and valued by the new regime. The net effect, it was felt, would be an increased faith in the party's ability to rule. As Breslin explains:

> The party thought that if the people were encouraged to participate in political action, it would create a closer relationship between the party and the people. The masses would gain a better understanding of the party's goals and ideas through participating in attaining them. The people would also feel that they had a stake in the new political system, and would be more prepared to defend it against external and internal threats.
>
> (1998: 111)

Although Mao was sincere in his advocacy of a mass role in Chinese politics, there was clearly an instrumental element to his perspective on the subject. Mass participation may well have been a morally acceptable approach to politics in Mao's view, but it was also a means to a higher end, that of legitimizing party rule.

Mao's logic was at least partly influenced by the views of radical late Qing (nineteenth century) non-Marxist scholars such as Yan Fu and Liang Qichao who championed the need for a system of participatory democracy (based on the

Western European model) as a means of generating popular support for the Qing government in its struggle to resist the imperialist powers (Schwartz 1964, Hao Chang 1971). Whilst Mao was by no means espousing the adoption of multi-party democracy in China, he was greatly persuaded by the underlying principle that greater mass involvement in the system could be beneficial to the legitimacy of the regime.

## The mass line

One manifestation of the mobilization mode was the mass line. The mass line was intended to draw the party closer to the masses through the submersion of party cadres into the local rural community. This saw cadres working the fields with their peasant associates, embracing peasant criticisms of party working methods and ascertaining their views on important issues of local concern. Given that the vast majority of the peasantry were illiterate, they often expressed themselves in a manner that was difficult to decipher. The role of the cadre, therefore, was to interpret these views and use them as a starting point from which to construct new policies. Once these policies were formulated, the cadre was then required to go back to the people and explain to them how their ideas formed the backbone of these new policies. As Mao suggested at his Yanan base in 1943:

> All correct leadership is necessarily from the masses, to the masses. This means: take the ideas of the masses (scattered and unsystematic ideas) and concentrate them (through study turn them into concentrated and systematic ideas), then go to the masses and propagate and explain these ideas until the masses embrace them as their own, hold fast to them and translate them into action.
>
> (Schram 1989: 98)

## Mass campaigns

It was not unusual for the principles of the mass line to feature as an intrinsic part of the many mass campaigns that took place during the early period. Invariably, though, mass campaigns directed people towards supporting or implementing a given policy rather than actually devising it. So, for example, following China's entry into the Korean War in October 1950 (Whiting 1960), the CCP launched the Resist America Aid Korea Campaign which called on millions of people throughout the country to participate in supporting activities such as collecting funds for the families of Chinese soldiers, signing "patriotic pacts" for increased production and cutting links between Chinese Christian churches and their Western counterparts (Dietrich 1998: 70). Whilst the objective of the campaign was to generate support for the war effort in Korea, it was also designed to bring the masses closer to the party and political system as a whole.

Shortly afterwards three interlinking campaigns were launched with the aim of radically transforming urban society (Teiwes 1997: 37–40). The Campaign to

Suppress Counter-Revolutionaries which began in February 1951 targeted people with links to the old KMT regime and those with an independent local support base (e.g. religious leaders) who were seen as a threat to the CCP. This was followed by the Three Antis Campaign in September 1951 (anti-corruption, waste and bureaucracy) which concentrated on ridding the party of "opportunists" who joined up to further their own careers or to exploit the financial opportunities that party membership or administrative office might offer. The Five Antis Campaign (anti-bribery, tax evasion, fraud, theft of government property and theft of state economic secrets) launched in early 1952 saw the focus shift to the national bourgeoisie (small-scale factory owners and shop-holders) who were accused of corruption.

The masses played an integral role in each of these campaigns. As well as assisting central party work teams in identifying those involved in corrupt or "counter-revolutionary" activities, people participated in small groups to force confessions from accused individuals. Once the confessions were extracted, tens of thousands of people attended mass trials at local stadia. The nature of these campaigns was brutal. Stavis (1978: 29) notes that up to 800,000 people may have died in the counter-revolutionary campaign alone. But unlike Stalin's public security style purges of the 1930s (known as the Red Terror), the "Antis" campaigns were genuinely participatory affairs integrating the people further into the system and giving them a sense of inclusion in the fundamental reshaping of the urban social environment.

### Land Reform Campaign

Perhaps the most successful campaign in terms of bolstering CCP legitimacy was the Land Reform Campaign of 1947–51 (Hinton 1996). The principal objective of the campaign was to destroy the tenancy system which existed for millennia prior to the revolution. Under the old system, rural land was owned by a minority of wealthy landlords many of whom exploited poor peasants by renting out land and farming equipment at extortionate prices or hiring workers under punitive conditions. As a consequence, peasant suffering was acute and starvation common place. Land reform changed all this by stripping rich peasants (i.e. those with substantial landholdings) of their property and redistributing it to the poor. But in contrast to the Soviet equivalent (of the 1920s) which was enforced exclusively (and brutally) by the authorities, Chinese land reform was much more of a grass roots process.

The first stage of the campaign involved setting up Poor Peasant Associations (PPAs) in each village. These were usually led by local non-party activists with fierce anti-landlord sentiments and an ability to articulate their grievances and persuade others to join them in the struggle. Under the tutelage of CCP work teams sent down from urban areas, the PPAs organized large public meetings that all inhabitants of the village were expected to attend. During these mass meetings, appropriately known as "speak bitterness meetings", the disenfranchized of the community were encouraged to identify their landlord oppressors, expose the extent of their exploitation and subject them to mass criticism. This was followed by the confiscation of landlord holdings which were redistributed to those who needed them most.

The ambitious nature of the policy meant that implementation was not always smooth. In some of the more politically conservative areas party work teams found it hard convincing peasants to identify and criticize landlords, whilst in areas with a much stronger CCP base (e.g. the north east) the difficulty was *controlling* the poor peasant population who were only too keen to settle old scores. Stavis (1978: 25–30) notes, for example, that of the 800,000 landlord fatalities, a considerable proportion were the direct result of mob rule. Problems also arose during the redistribution process. There were often disputes, for example, over whether PPA activists should get more or better quality land than non-activists by virtue of their leading role in organizing land reform. This often led to open conflict when corrupt party cadres sought to help themselves to available land. Furthermore, in some areas (mainly in the north) there was simply not enough confiscated land to go round.

Notwithstanding these (and other) problems with the implementation of land reform, and not forgetting many of the practical successes of the policy (Blecher 1986: 44–5), the actual *process* of land reform was immensely positive for the popularity of the CCP. Not only did the party succeed in radically transforming a deeply unpopular and inequitable system of land ownership, but it did so in a manner that *included* the peasantry. Through the PPAs, landless peasants were directly involved in a process which would affect their every day lives. In this sense, the peasants were made to feel as though they were active participants in the land reform process rather than passive recipients of it.

## The charismatic legitimacy of Mao Zedong

Of fundamental importance to the legitimacy for the CCP was the notion of charismatic legitimacy, specifically with regard to Mao. For Weber, a person who is bestowed with charismatic legitimacy is perceived by his colleagues and the population as a whole as having exceptional abilities and it is on this basis that they adhere, almost slavishly, to the directives of the charismatic leader. Not surprisingly, the qualities attributed to this type of individual means that only a handful of political leaders have ever exercised genuine charismatic authority. South Africa has Nelson Mandela, Palestine had Yasser Arafat and China had Mao Zedong.

### Charisma within the party

So what was it about Mao that inspired such respect? In terms of his charismatic authority within the party, the answer to this question was not initially apparent. Unlike Lenin, who as founder of the Bolsheviks quickly assumed the position of charismatic leader, Mao was very much one amongst equals during the early years of the CCP's existence. Indeed, if anything, it appeared that Mao might *not* possess the right qualities needed to lead and inspire the party. Mao was the principal (although not only) exponent of the concept of revolutionary guerrilla warfare in which he proposed countering enemy attacks by luring the enemy deep into CCP strongholds and ambushing it from within. Yet, his initial application of this tactic was disastrous and was blamed for the near eradication of the party's Jiangxi base by the KMT in the early 1930s. Nor was Mao admired as a great Marxist intellect within leadership circles (again in contrast to Lenin). Indeed, it was widely felt that Mao's understanding of ideological matters as well as his abilities as an administrator were limited.

Pye (1976: 23–4) has suggested that admiration for (leading to deference towards) Mao derived from a distinct and almost unnerving political presence, one feature of which was his aloof remoteness in the presence of his contemporaries. Others have highlighted Mao's apparent willpower as a defining characteristic of his charismatic authority. On meeting Mao during the famous US state visit to Beijing in 1972 (accompanying then President Nixon), Henry Kissinger (1979: 1058) remarked 'I have met no one, with the possible exception of Charles de Gaulle, who so distilled raw, concentrated willpower'. Whilst traits such as these may well have enhanced Mao's prestige amongst those around him, Teiwes (1984: 48) notes that in revolutionary societies such as China, a leader's charisma is grounded in 'demonstrated success at a time of revolutionary crisis'. Although, strictly speaking, charismatic legitimacy is all about *perceptions* of greatness rather than the reality, amongst colleagues at least it is imperative that some of these characteristics are demonstrated.

Mao did so. Under intense pressure to adhere to Moscow's directives on constructing an urban proletarian rather than a peasant support base, Mao, unlike a significant number of others in the leadership (e.g. the so-called 28 Bolsheviks) determinedly resisted. At the party's 1935 conference in Zunyi his unyielding stance on independence from the Soviet Union saw him emerge as the foremost member of the leadership group, although as Teiwes (1984: 143) notes it was not until late 1938 (following his defeat of leadership rival Wang Ming) that Mao was acknowledged as head of the party. By 1943, Mao's control over the party was complete when he was elected as Chairman of both the Central Committee and the Politburo. It was also around this time that Mao's theoretical works attracted favourable attention from leadership colleagues who began to refer to Mao Zedong Thought. Add to this, the success of Mao's guerrilla warfare tactics in defeating of the KMT and there was no questioning Mao's charismatic leadership of the party as he famously stood above the Gates of Heavenly Peace to declare the establishment of the PRC (Teiwes and Sun 1995).

In office Mao's charismatic authority enabled him, at times, to dominate the decision making process, although, at least initially, he favoured a more consensual approach to government. As the party moved from one policy success to another during the early period, Mao's prestige as China's paramount leader became even more entrenched. Of particular note was the success of those policies in which Mao essentially "went it alone". For example, China's entry into the Korean War was at Mao's behest, and whilst the PLA suffered heavy casualties,

Mao showed (unlike Stalin) that he was prepared to stand up for a communist ally in the face of American aggression. This made people inside and outside the communist world sit up and take note of Mao.

The net effect of Mao's enhanced cachet within the party was to convince most of those around him that when it came to the really big decisions, Mao was invariably right. As we shall see in Chapter 2, despite the wildly ambitious objectives of the Great Leap Forward, Mao's colleagues had learned to trust his judgement, and although several leading members of the party expressed mis-givings about this radical programme, they rallied behind Mao because of the charismatic authority he exerted over them. Arguably, even when it became apparent that the Leap was spiralling out of control (during late 1958), many of Mao's colleagues refused to contemplate that he may have been wrong.

### *The cult of personality*

Of course, most of the population had never met Mao and so were never in a position to witness his apparent qualities. In order, therefore, to "educate" the masses in the "genius" of Mao and thereby extend Mao's charismatic authority over the whole country, the party constructed a cult of personality around Mao, a method familiar to authoritarian regimes (Wylie 1980, Gill 1982, Martin 1982). Employing techniques learned from the cult of Stalin, and with the assistance of Mao loyalists such as Kang Sheng, Chen Boda and Lin Biao (who began devel-oping the cult in the early 1940s), Mao was portrayed as a mystic, almost super-human figure who liberated the Chinese people from feudalist and imperialist oppression and created a new era of socialist equality and opportunity.

We have already seen how the glorification of Mao was an integral feature of the propaganda process, particularly during the ubiquitous small study sessions and in the classroom. The press also played a key role in this process. In 1951 the *Southern Daily* portrayed Mao as 'the great leader and helmsman on whom the Chinese people can rely', whilst other sources described Mao as an 'earth god' for his role during land reform and claimed that the subsequent improvement in living standards were 'the good fortunes given to us by Mao Zedong'. In 1950 the *Shenyang Daily* described Mao as the 'venerable Heavenly ruler' who was 'better than the Red Sun' and 'more enduring than Heaven'. In this way, as Sullivan (1986–7: 610) points out, 'long before the fanatical idolizing of the Red Guards, "our Chairman Mao" had already become more than just the formal head of party and state. He was China's representative individual'.

In Chapter 3 we will examine how the Mao cult was intensified during the Cultural Revolution through the use of emulation campaigns when people were required to study and emulate the PLA who were portrayed as model Maoists. But how was the cult of one man deemed to enhance the legitimacy of an entire party? This was never clear. Perhaps it was thought that if the masses saw Mao as a great leader of the party then they would likewise perceive the party itself as great. It may be that for this reason Mao's leadership colleagues were initially enthusias-tic about the cult of personality, although as Sullivan (1986–7: 608) notes the

Mao cult was considered to be a useful device in defeating Wang Ming, Mao's key opponent in the leadership. It was probably also useful in diverting public attention away from some of the more "unsocialist" policies that were being implemented at that time, most notably imports of grain from Canada, a country that was unquestionably a member of the capitalist fold.

Yet, there was also an inherent danger for the leadership in encouraging Mao's cult of personality. If the cult was allowed to develop too far it might generate an uncontrollable dynamism of its own creating a situation in which the individual charismatic status of Mao became bigger or *more legitimate* than the collective status of the party he represented. In fact, there was already a growing concern within the leadership that this was occurring as peasants were seen kowtowing before Mao in Tiananmen Square (Sullivan 1986–7: 613).

## Breaching the principles of democratic centralism

An important point to note about charismatic legitimacy is its fundamental incompatibility with legal rational legitimacy. In his interpretation of Weber, Teiwes suggests that a rise in the charismatic authority of a single leader will often coincide with a decline in legal rational legitimacy because the former is invariably made at the *expense* of the latter (Teiwes 1984: 54). This transpires because the process of exerting charismatic authority invariably involves a violation of prescribed rules of decision making as the charismatic leader seeks to achieve his ends by applying whatever means are at his disposal. Mao did this throughout his entire time in power, the first instance of which took place during the mid-1950s leadership debate over rural collectivization (Blecher 1986: 59–65).

By way of background, the debate surfaced a year or so after the implementation of land reform which had unexpectedly created class cleavages in the countryside. In order to combat this trend the party adopted a policy of agricultural collectivization with the establishment of Mutual Aid Teams (MATs) as the first step in this process. The MATs comprised between five and ten households who shared land and exchanged labour and farming resources for mutual benefit. Initial signs suggested that the MATs were successful and this convinced party leaders that China should embrace the next stage of collectivization in the form of larger co-operatives encompassing about 30 households.

But Mao soon found himself outnumbered on the question of how fast and how far collectivization should go. The majority of the leadership, including key figures such as Liu Shaoqi and Chen Yun, favoured the gradual implementation of the co-ops. Given the age-old tradition of individual farming in China, they argued, there was a real possibility of mass peasant rebellion if there was a sudden lurch towards unfamiliar collective farming methods. Instead, the peasantry should be given time to adapt to the new system. It was also argued that the goals of the co-ops should be moderate. At this early phase of post-revolutionary development, the emphasis should be on providing enough grain and basic food stuffs to feed the growing population and enough raw materials and capital to assist in the industrialization process.

Mao and a minority of the leadership (including allies such as Chen Boda) espoused a much faster transition towards the co-ops. This, they argued, would ensure rapid self-sufficiency allowing farmers to concentrate on producing "cash crops" (e.g. cotton and silk) which could then serve as the backbone of China's new textile industry. In response to concerns over peasant resistance to the co-ops, Mao argued that the vigour with which the peasants had participated in the revolution and land reform demonstrated an insatiable popular enthusiasm for socialist transformation. Rather than acting cautiously and "tottering along like a woman with bound feet" (as Mao accused his opponents), the party should take advantage of this grass roots enthusiasm by pushing ahead quickly with the co-ops.

The decision went against Mao in March 1955 as a majority of the leadership voted in favour of a gradualist approach to the co-ops and it was at this point that Mao used his charismatic authority to override established legal rational procedures. Instead of adhering to the will of the majority in accordance with the principles of democratic centralism, Mao sought to overturn the new party line by going outside the central party-state apparatus. Embarking on an extensive tour of the countryside, Mao appealed directly and emphatically to local party leaders to back his minority stance on the co-ops in the hope of building enough local support to overrule the official policy. As Sullivan (1986–7: 630) notes, 'Mao skirted formal policy-making channels at the party centre by issuing direct orders to party and non-party personages and stressing that he directly represented rank-and-file and popular interests'. In adopting this personalized, one-to-one approach, Mao calculated that his charismatic presence as a revered revolutionary leader and Chairman of the party and state would have a persuasive impact on local party opinion.

This is precisely what happened. By the end of 1955 almost two million co-ops were organized throughout China as local leaders enthusiastically implemented Mao's stance. Based on the combined Marxist principles of "each according to his ownership" and "each according to his labour", peasants were remunerated partly on the basis of how much property they contributed to their co-op and partly on the amount of work they put in. In the meantime, Liu and Chen were left espousing an official policy line to which few cadres at the ground level were adopting. Outflanked by Mao's political cunning, the majority leadership had little alternative but to fall into line.

Yet, Mao's success was short lived. A rapid push towards rural collectives (comprising between 100 and 300 households) caused production to falter and this led to a gradual reversal of collectivization. Mao's prestige was further damaged by the much-publicized "secret speech" given in February 1956 by Nikita Khrushchev, Stalin's replacement as Soviet President. Amongst other things, the speech was fiercely critical of Stalin's personality cult and this was widely regarded as an indirect attack on Mao and those responsible for the development of the Mao cult.

Opponents of collectivization used Khrushchev's speech to marginalize Mao and by the time the Eighth National Party Congress was convened in September 1956, a more moderate second Five Year Plan (the first being from 1953–7) was implemented. Mao then suffered another set back following the deletion from the new CCP constitution (1956) of Mao Zedong Thought as part of the party's guiding ideology. As such, not only had Mao's vision of agrarian socialism been rejected, but his position as China's leading Marxist theoretician had been downgraded. Arguably, these setbacks may have led Mao to initiate the Hundred Flowers Campaign, although as we shall see, it might also be suggested that the campaign was a bid to restore the party's waning legitimacy.

## Restoring legitimacy: the Hundred Flowers Campaign

Deriving its name from an ancient Chinese adage entitled "let a hundred flowers bloom, let a hundred schools of thought contend", the Hundred Flowers Campaign, launched in June 1957, gave Chinese intellectuals a rare opportunity to express themselves publicly (MacFarquhar 1974). Previously, intellectuals had been tightly restrained, both by the directives of the 1942 Yanan Conference on Art and Literature which held that all forms art and literature should focus exclusively on matters of a socialist nature and by the Thought Reform Campaign (1951–2) which attempted to force intellectuals into a Marxist straight-jacket (MacDougall 1980). During the Hundred Flowers and under Mao's strict instruction (significantly, given *before* formal party approval), scholars from all academic disciplines were invited to articulate their views openly on the policies and work-style of the CCP during officially-organized conferences and large public forums. The emphasis, it appeared, was on constructive criticism of the party, although the precise meaning of "constructive" was not initially clear.

Many of the opinions expressed during the campaign were not directly critical of the party, targeting instead the undefined and ambiguous role of intellectuals within the communist system. Numerous demands were made for amendments to the state constitution which would help clarify and strengthen the legal position of intellectuals, especially in relation to freedom of speech and academic expression. Proposals for institutional reform were also put forward such as the establishment of an independent upper chamber of the NPC, an idea which certain quarters of the official media and party leadership had been espousing for some time.

Whilst views such as these were not deemed by Mao to be threatening other views were, most obviously calls for the complete abandonment of the socialist system expressed by a handful of outspoken intellectuals. Yet, of perhaps greater concern was the more widely held assertion that local party cadres were inept and obstructive in their day-to-day dealings with intellectuals. As Teiwes (1997: 80) explains, 'by focusing on the shortcomings of Party cadres in the everyday affairs of their work units, intellectuals were in effect raising the issue of the Party's competence to guide China in the new period of socialist construction'. The reaction of China's student population also caused alarm amongst party leaders. Whilst many students expressed their dissatisfaction with the party by pasting wall posters that were critical of the party's record in office or by writing incisive articles for underground newspapers, some groups of students took to the streets in protest and in certain areas (e.g. Wuhan) these protests turned to riots.

As the Hundred Flowers began to slip from the party's control, urgent measures were taken to abandon the campaign after just five weeks of "blooming and contending". The party backlash was formidable and took the form of the Anti-Rightist Campaign. Anyone who had spoken out against the party, including over 500,000 (party and non-party) intellectuals, was branded a rightist, the majority of whom were then subjected to an intensive programme of "re-education" through labour, a long period of forced manual labour under gruelling rural conditions. According to the official line, this helped to break down the barrier between mental and manual work, especially for many urban based intellectuals who had never even been to the countryside. In reality, of course, it was simply a way of meting out punishment to those who had earlier dared to voice their opinions. Party intellectuals were dealt with particularly harshly. This was because they were expected to demonstrate more loyalty to the party than non-CCP members. They were also considered to be potentially more dangerous since they were effectively on the inside.

### A Maoist coup?

So what was Mao's rationale for the Hundred Flowers? Why was the campaign launched and then curtailed within such a short space of time? For some scholars (Han Suyin 1976, Teufel-Dreyer 1996: 92–4, Lynch 1998: 26–8), the Hundred Flowers was little more than a trap to weed out CCP opponents. Mao was convinced all along of the existence of class enemies even within party ranks and was determined to expose and then silence them. With this objective in mind, Mao assumed the guise of a tolerant, liberal leader so that opponents would feel confident enough to express their true anti-party feelings. Once they had done so, Mao quickly reverted to his naturally autocratic self and determined that those who had spoken out were appropriately dealt with during the Anti-Rightist Campaign.

Exponents of this view draw particular attention to Mao's February 1957 speech entitled *On the Correct Handling of Contradictions Amongst the People* which set no obvious limits to what people could and could not say. Yet, when Mao's Contradictions paper was officially published in the immediate aftermath of the Hundred Flowers, it was conveniently revised to include six criteria imposing clear restrictions on the freedom of expression. This left many intellectuals stranded outside the parameters of permissible debate.

There is also the related question of Mao's declining position within the party leadership, as noted earlier. Defeat over the issue of rural collectivization, Khrushchev's "secret speech" and the deletion of Mao Zedong Thought from the party constitution left Mao personally embarrassed and politically sidelined. In an effort to re-gain some control over the party and over the direction of Chinese socialism in general, Mao devised the Hundred Flowers closely followed by the Anti-Rightist Campaign.

The notion of Mao the Machiavellian is engaging. There is little doubt that throughout his career Mao was motivated by considerations of power and was, at times, prepared to act with ruthlessness and guile to achieve his political objectives. As we shall see in later chapters, Mao's purge of Peng Dehuai during the Great Leap Forward and his willingness to use and then abandon Lin Biao and the Red Guards during the Cultural Revolution are occasions when Mao resorted to shrewd political tactics to get what he wanted. The Machiavellian argument is further strengthened by the fact that Mao did indeed restore his authority over the party following the Hundred Flowers, although this may have had more to do with the fact that people were consequently scared to oppose him rather than a genuine belief that Mao's political agenda was correct.

### Legitimacy crisis

Yet, it is not enough to argue that Mao was only motivated by considerations of power when he launched the Hundred Flowers. Whilst he may well have been angry with those colleagues who rejected his stance on agricultural collectivization, neither Mao nor anyone else could have *foreseen* that the campaign would put him so firmly back in control. Instead, Mao launched the Hundred Flowers because he was genuinely convinced that party legitimacy was in decline. From the beginning of 1956, Mao began to express grave concerns about the process of bureaucratization that was enveloping the party, especially at the local level. Smug about the party's early post-revolutionary success and complacent about the responsibilities of office, local party cadres, Mao believed, were more concerned with the perks of bureaucratic life than with the needs of their constituents. If this situation was allowed to continue, the CCP would degenerate into a self-serving elite, distant and aloof from the people that it once claimed to represent. These fears were compounded by signs of ideological revisionism within the party, as reflected by the increasing reliance on expertise in decision making rather than ideology or "redness". As Mao saw it, CCP policy makers were now only interested in obtaining the assistance of technocrats, managers and intellectuals and had no time for the views of the revolutionary masses.

The apparent alienation of the population was manifested by the significant number of demonstrations that took place during 1956–7 (Perry 1994). Although some of the unrest was due to food shortages (in rural areas) and job demands (in urban areas), many protesters were angered by the increasingly bureaucratic work-style of party cadres and enterprise managers and the reluctance of those in charge to listen to the ideas put forward by ordinary people. For Mao, the CCP was facing the daunting prospect of a national uprising. Events in Eastern Europe during 1956 fuelled Mao's fears with both Poland and Hungary witnessing spontaneous uprisings against inept communist rule. Mao also drew parallels to the situation in the Soviet Union. For some years, Mao had been lamenting the growth of an unwieldy and unaccountable Soviet bureaucracy which had caused the Soviet regime to lose touch with its revolutionary origins. In Mao's view, this culminated in the rise of Khrushchev who was attempting to revise communism by reforming the Soviet economy along market-based lines and aligning with the United States as part of a softer approach to Soviet foreign policy.

The urgent need to rectify the party in order to prevent a national rebellion in China led Mao towards the Hundred Flowers. As the party drifted further away from its revolutionary roots, Mao used the Hundred Flowers as an attempt to bring it back down to earth. In classic Maoist fashion, however, rectification would not be carried out internally as some party leaders hoped. If the party was to restore its waning legitimacy amongst the population it had to be rectified publicly using ordinary people (albeit in this case only a small section thereof). Although some opinions might be hard to swallow, only a full public examination of the party's record would ensure that the party was properly rectified because only the people (in this case, mainly intellectuals) could really judge how well (or badly) the party was doing. In the end, of course, the Hundred Flowers did not proceed in the way that Mao desired and this forced him to jettison the campaign altogether. But it was the need for party rectification and the need to involve the public in this process that caused Mao to initiate the Hundred Flowers in the first place.

## A Halcyon era?

The early period of CCP rule is often described as a halcyon era in post-revolutionary Chinese politics. A fully centralized apparatus of party and government was set up after decades of administrative disunity. A radical programme of land redistribution was carried out in the countryside marking the end of a deeply unpopular era of landlord domination. The party established and successfully disseminated its new Marxist ideology as well as a cult of personality devoted to Mao. Millions of opponents and potential opponents of the party were flushed out during the radical reform of urban society. In just a few years, the party registered a number of notable domestic successes that went a considerable way towards establishing its performance based legitimacy.

Further bolstering the regime's legitimacy was its all-embracing approach to policy matters. Despite the party's undoubted authoritarian instincts, several of its key policies were devised and implemented with substantial assistance from the masses. None more so than land reform which directly involved millions of disenfranchised peasants in the process of identifying and criticizing landlords. This and some of the other mass campaigns of the time immersed the populace into politics for the first time in China's history, engendering feelings of inclusiveness and public worth in the new era.

But not everything went smoothly for the party. Bitter divisions emerged over the pace and extent of agricultural collectivization which, some have argued, were never resolved. On this issue, Mao demonstrated an alarming contempt for the legal rational rules of democratic centralism, rallying support at the local level in order to overturn established party policy. The Hundred Flowers proved an embarrassing failure for the party and Mao in particular, exposing dissatisfaction with the party from significant sections of intellectual and student society. Mao's response was to spearhead the Anti-Rightist Campaign which put him firmly back in control of party policy. This domination of the political agenda led China hurtling disastrously towards the Great Leap Forward.

# 2 Mass participation and mass legitimacy

## The Great Leap Forward

One of the defining characteristics of Mao's style of politics was mass participation. We saw in Chapter 1 how the masses were directly involved in a number of nationwide campaigns during the early 1950s when they were instrumental in the radical transformation of both urban and rural society. Although Mao was convinced of the revolutionary potential of the masses and possessed an almost undying faith in their ability to change society for the better, his espousal of mass politics was also motivated by the issue of legitimacy. For Mao, the assimilation of the masses into the political system was not only the right way of doing politics but also the best way of enhancing the legitimacy of the CCP since, in Mao's view, legitimacy would inevitably flow from such mass assimilation.

The Great Leap Forward saw a continuation of Mao's commitment to mass mobilization, only this time on a much larger scale. Originally conceived as an ambitious attempt to rapidly and simultaneously increase agricultural and industrial production in order to catch up with the levels of developed Western nations, the Leap relied exclusively on the productive capacities of China's rural millions who were asked to turn their hands to almost any task from the construction of dams and irrigation canals to the production of steel. Decision making was decentralized to the local commune level where policies were derived from the first hand experience of local residents (especially farmers) rather than the more "abstract" theoretical input of specialist academics who were denigrated during this period. In theory, the Leap was an exercise in the mass line with a view to furthering the mass legitimacy of the party. In practice, it turned out to be something quite different.

## Assessing the economic alternatives

So why did the CCP embark on the Leap? Why was such a radical policy seen as the best route to Chinese economic development? In order to answer these questions, it is necessary to begin by assessing the alternatives available to the party leadership in 1957 and explain why none of them were chosen. According to Lippit (1975: 95–6), there were four options: aid from the Soviet Union, trade with the outside world, a second Five Year Plan or an increase in state investment for the agricultural sector.

The Soviet aid option was not really an option at all. Given that Soviet credit for new investment in China made up just 3 per cent of total state investment (much of which were loans not grants), it was implausible for the leadership to base its economic strategy on Soviet money since it was clearly nothing like the amount that China needed. Moreover, as Sino-Soviet relations continued to sour following the appointment of Khrushchev as Soviet President (Zagoria 1962, Salisbury 1969), it became more and more likely that China would not want to accept or borrow money from the Soviet Union and that the Soviet Union would not want to give or lend money to China.

The foreign trade option was equally unlikely. In keeping with Maoist prescriptions for economic development, the Chinese economy was largely geared towards autarky. In 1958, for example, imports (US\$ 1.86 billion) and exports (US\$ 1.97 billion) were just a fraction of China's GNP (Gross National Product) (US\$ 43.56 billion). Moreover, even if the party wanted to pursue the foreign trade alternative, few countries were willing to reciprocate. The Soviets were increasingly unlikely trading partners for the reasons already considered whilst the United States expressed its hostility towards the communist regime by imposing a trade embargo against China and encouraging other developed nations to follow suit.

On the face of it, a second Five Year Plan was a much more plausible option given the success of the first Five Year Plan (1953–7) which yielded an increase in heavy industrial output of over 15 per cent per annum (Blecher 1986: 53–8). Yet, growth in this sector was achieved at the expense of agricultural output which rose at only 2 per cent per annum, a rate which barely exceeded population growth at this time. Not only did this raise obvious concerns about insufficient food supplies, but ironically it also posed problems for the industrial sector. Agriculture is a vital source of raw materials, markets and foreign exchange for industry which meant that any under-performance in the agricultural sector would have a negative impact on industrial growth. In the end, therefore, it was concluded (principally by Mao) that maintaining a sectoral imbalance for the sake of achieving high industrial growth rates could in the long run be counter-productive to industrial development and it was on this basis that proposals for a second Five Year Plan were rejected.

So why not simply increase state investment in agriculture to redress this imbalance? For Chen Yun this was the most logical approach, but for Mao it was unattractive both politically and economically. From a political perspective, the impressive pace of industrialization during the early period showed the outside world that Chinese communism was working. An increase in agricultural investment would inevitably be made at the expense of industrial investment which would slow down industrial output. This, Mao feared, would damage China's "shining" international image. From an economic perspective, Chen's solution might even be *detrimental* to the agricultural sector. Although, in the short term, extra investment in agriculture would be useful (especially in terms of feeding the population!), in the long term China needed a strong industrial base in order to *facilitate* agricultural growth. A fully industrialized China would be able to provide agriculture with essentials for production such as tractors, water pumps and chemical fertilizers. What Mao wanted, therefore, was the best of both worlds: an economic policy that would rapidly increase both industrial and agricultural output without involving a major shift in state investment from one sector to the other. The answer, or so it was thought at the time, lay in the Great Leap Forward.

## Domestic and security issues

Other considerations pushed China towards the Leap. One was the pressing issue of how to maximize the potential of China's huge labour force. Given the country's very basic levels of agricultural and industrial development, it made sense to fully utilize the one resource that China had plenty of, namely people. In fact, according to Gray (1990: 306), China had more than it realized. As part of a 1953 census, demographers estimated the Chinese population to be around 450 million. The results put the figure at 582 million. So, for example, in agriculture where there was a severe shortage of tractors with which to farm crops, the problem could be overcome, it was thought, by drawing on the vast reservoir of local labour so that crops were farmed primarily by hand. This mass labour approach reinforced Mao's fervent conviction that correctly mobilized, the people could overcome any structural impediment to economic development. High unemployment in China made the Leap seem like an even better idea. With unemployment (and under-employment) particularly pronounced in the countryside, the Leap would act as an inexpensive way of providing urgently needed jobs.

Issues of national security also dictated the need for an economic policy based on the principles of the Leap. With the United States supplying ballistic missiles to Chiang Kai-shek and the KMT in the neighbouring island of Taiwan, the party leadership was concerned about the possibility of an American-sponsored invasion of the mainland, especially in light of American aggression in North Korea which threatened to spill over on to Chinese territory. Compounding these fears was the uncertainty over Soviet support in the event of an American invasion in light of Khrushchev's push towards rapprochement with the United States. To test out Soviet loyalty, the PLA shelled the Taiwanese islands of Quemoy and Matsu near the eastern province of Fujian to see what the response would be. As feared, the United States re-affirmed its military support for Taiwan but there was no equivalent response from Moscow in support of Beijing. This only came *after* the Taiwan crisis was over confirming the CCP's belief that the Soviets were moving dangerously close to the Americans (Gray 1990: 313–14).

Relations with India (on China's western border) were also tenuous following Beijing's suppression of anti-CCP protestors in Tibet, a region with which India traditionally had strong ties. As such, with China seemingly surrounded by hostile foreign powers there was a perceived urgency to build a strong, modern nation, capable of defending itself against sudden military attack. This made the Leap an attractive option for Chinese leaders given its dual focus on rapid agricultural and industrial growth. In addition, since the communes were designed to be self-sufficient (see later), the Leap, it was hoped, would ensure that China could survive even if its major cities and industrial bases were destroyed by foreign attacks.

The Leap was also popular because it was based on the tried and tested formula of the Border Regions decade of the 1930s. As Gray (1990: 307–9) explains, it was during this period that rural industrial co-operatives were established, similar to those that were proposed for the Leap. Run by young professionals who had fled from industrial areas controlled by the Japanese, the co-ops were both self-sufficient and profit-making. Using semi-mechanized technologies, production was diversified to include consumer goods for outside sale and urgently needed raw materials for the Red Army such as uniforms, medical supplies and weapon accessories. Co-op members also helped to improve local agricultural production by advising on farming techniques and providing intermediate farming equipment. Furthermore, the co-ops functioned as social communities, offering education and welfare services to members (and often non-members) who lived in neighbouring villages. Management was carried out democratically. In some co-ops, decisions were only reached on a unanimous basis. In other co-ops, the role of officer was rotated on a daily basis. Perhaps most importantly as far as legitimacy was concerned, the co-ops employed the mass line approach of listening to the suggestions of local people and devising policies accordingly.

## Organizing the masses

In an effort to realize the ambitious goals of the Leap, China's massive work force was organized into communes so that decision making could be carried out more efficiently and workers could be organized more effectively (Donnithorne 1959, Lippit 1977). The communes were much larger than the collectives of the mid-1950s, averaging around 1,600 households (scaled down from an initial figure of about 5,000 households). They were also much broader in scope, combining agriculture and industry so that each commune had its own factories and workshops as well as its own farmers. All managerial, financial and planning functions were closely integrated so that agriculture could provide inputs for industry and industry could provide the necessary materials for agricultural development. In addition, the communes embraced social and political life by merging township governments with local party organizations and by expanding social services to include the provision of health facilities, child care, education and food.

The communes were less numerous in the cities mainly because of the difficulty in finding suitable land for farming. Although many suburbs did contain arable land, travelling to these areas was far too time-consuming for city dwellers. Consequently, most of this land was allocated to rural communes. However, the cities did undergo some radical changes during the Leap. Economic decision making was decentralized allowing each locality more freedom to spend funds and allocate resources. Workers' rights were increased allowing greater participation in managerial activities whilst managers were required to work on the shop floor. Collectivist methods of distribution were prioritized ahead of individual material incentives and mini-campaigns were carried out which stressed the equality of workers, managers and cadres and the inherent dangers of social stratification.

Given the enormous size of the communes, it made sense to break them down into a more manageable level. This was done by establishing production brigades comprising about 160 households which took control of the organization and management of daily affairs in a given area within the commune. Each production brigade was further divided into smaller work teams of about 30 households which were sent out to perform designated tasks. The nature of these tasks was varied. As well as the customary farming duties which were intensified to increase production, teams worked on infrastructure projects such as building dams and irrigation canals and improving China's transportation system so that produce and materials could be moved around the country more quickly. Rural communes were furnished with their own industrial bases in order to increase industrial output and enable the communes to operate without having to rely on outside areas for industrial supplies. Particular emphasis was placed on the production of steel which led to the establishment of back yard steel furnaces where commune members were encouraged to make their own steel. Bizarrely, as the Leap gathered pace, people were expected to melt down personal items such as pots and pans in the rush to produce steel.

With the focus on rapidly increasing production, every effort was made to free workers from any duties that might detract from their availability for work. Creches were set up to release parents from child care and special homes were created for the elderly so that offspring could be relieved of their filial responsibilities. Most famously, huge communal kitchens were established so that workers could eat together. This ensured that women did not have to spend (or waste) time cooking meals and gave local officials an opportunity to monitor the length of time that workers spent eating.

## Mass legitimacy

But the Leap was not only about increasing production. Mao, in particular, was keen for the Leap to be devised and implemented in a manner which would enhance the legitimacy of the CCP. The success of land reform earlier in the decade derived primarily from the inclusive and participatory role afforded to the masses and for this reason the Leap was constructed along similar lines. In keeping with Mao's notion of the mass line, party cadres were instructed to listen carefully to the ideas of local people in each commune and to formulate policies around these ideas. Although the party would take a leading role in, for example, setting production targets and organizing the work force, local people were often far better equipped to advise on certain areas of policy given their intimate knowledge of local conditions. So, for example, a peasant farmer who had lived and worked in the same village for decades was an invaluable source of information on matters such as soil quality, appropriate farming methods and likely weather conditions and knew much more than a party cadre sent down from the city.

By consulting with local "experts" in this way, the Leap was intended to further integrate the masses into the communist system and serve as a vital legitimizing force for the party, an organization that was, in theory, truly *of* the people.

A number of mass campaigns took place during the Leap as large groups of workers were set to work on a particular task and encouraged to attain ambitious production targets. In industry, for example, slogans appeared on factory walls urging workers to produce enough steel to "overtake England's steel production in 15 years". Remarkably, this time-scale was reduced as the Leap gained momentum. Similarly, in agriculture, huge teams of farmers were urged to double or even treble production of grain for their area compared to the figure for the previous year's harvest. In every sector workers were implored to produce "more, better, faster and cheaper".

One of the most well documented campaigns of the period was a nationwide campaign to exterminate sparrows in an attempt to rid farmers of this notorious crop-eating menace. Under the slogan "support the patriotic campaign against sparrows", which was part of the Campaign Against the Five Pests, millions of peasants spent whole days standing by trees hitting pots and pans together or any other metal object they could find. The aim was to make as much noise as possible so that any nearby sparrows would be too scared to perch and eventually fall to the ground in exhaustion. The first stage of the campaign was successful. Not only were all sparrows wiped out, so too was virtually the rest of the bird population leaving the crops free to grow without the impending threat of hungry birds. What the organizers failed take into account, however, was the dual threat posed by insects. With the bird population extinguished there was no natural predator to prevent plagues of insects from taking up where the birds had left off. In terms of agricultural output, therefore, the campaign achieved nothing because it was now insects rather than birds that ate China's crops.

Yet, this was not necessarily important. Of more significance, according to Breslin, was legitimizing the *process* of the Leap. A goal was set by the party and the masses participated in achieving this goal. This in itself was a means of legitimation:

> Simply being involved in the political process was seen as being a legitimating force, and one that tied the people much more closely to party policies and goals. Indeed, in some cases, the result of the participation was perhaps less important than the process of participation itself.
>
> (1998: 112)

## Ideological legitimacy

The Leap also sought to bolster the party's ideological legitimacy in that the principles underlying the policy conformed closely to the doctrine of Marxism. So, for example, in the communal kitchens that were set up to feed the country's work force, the distribution of food was initially organized so that each member ate according to the amount of work he put in, as measured by the number of work points he was allocated by party cadres. Later, when it was (mistakenly) thought that there was an abundance of food, the principles of distribution were adjusted so that each member ate according to how much food he *needed*. Amidst a fanfare of propaganda, the party declared that China was rapidly moving towards the higher stage of socialism as prescribed by Marx in his famous dictum "from each according to his ability to each according to his need". In due course, however, the party was exposed as having acted prematurely in removing all limits from the distribution of food since in reality there was nothing like enough food to go around.

The diversification of labour during the Leap was also heralded as a significant advance towards a truly Marxist society. Throughout the course of the Leap, people were encouraged to participate in new areas of employment. Farmers were required to work in the new rural industrial bases during non-harvest seasons to help produce the industrial machinery that was necessary for the development of the agricultural sector. Similarly, urban workers (many of whom had never been to the countryside) were encouraged to work side-by-side with peasants in the fields. Although the principal objective was to maximize production, the party was also keen to break down the mental and manual differences between the city and the countryside and engender a new and positive attitude towards work. According to official propaganda, this closely mirrored Marx's own vision of communist society in which man would no longer be restricted by the narrow confines of one type of work but would have the opportunity to broaden his horizons by working in several different areas. As Teufel-Dreyer (1996: 95) explains 'in the communist society he envisioned, someone could be a craftsman part of the day and by turns a fisherman, hunter, and literary critic at other times'.

The strengthening of the party's nationalist legitimacy was also a key factor during the Leap. The rationale for the Leap was presented very much in terms of making China strong, resisting foreign aggression and catching up with the West, as reflected in the spate of ambitious target setting that took place. In addition, each of the campaigns launched during the Leap were carefully couched using nationalistic language such as the "patriotic campaign against sparrows" noted earlier.

## The failure of the Leap

Early indications suggested that the Leap was a roaring success. Notwithstanding certain unusual circumstances noted by Lieberthal (1997: 98–9) (e.g. good weather conditions and the fruition of the First Five Year Plan), 1958 was a phenomenally good year for the Chinese economy. Industrial growth rates rose by an unprecedented 55 per cent whilst grain production for that year reached 200 million tons, breaking all previous Chinese records. In the four years that followed, however, the only records to be broken were those relating to the number of people who perished from starvation as China suffered the worst famine in its history (Becker 1996). Precisely how many people died as a result of the famine is difficult to gauge since official estimates are unreliable and scholarly estimates tend to vary wildly. Coale suggests that 16.5 million people perished from 1958–61, Aird estimates that 23 million people died from 1960–1, whilst Mosher puts the figure at 30 million for 1960 alone (Kane 1988). Numerical differences aside, it is clear that peasants suffered the most, especially in central and western provinces where up to 20 per cent of the population died of hunger. In Qinghai province, it is estimated that almost half the population died of starvation. The ferocity of the famine also forced people to do the unthinkable. Instances of prostitution and slavery in exchange for food were rife, and in recent years cases of cannibalism have been uncovered.

Economic statistics for the period say it all. In 1959 grain production fell to 170 million tons and in 1960 the figure dropped even further to 143 million tons, the lowest it had been for 10 years. This left China with no alternative but to spend its scarce foreign currency reserves on importing grain from foreign sources (e.g. Canada). Indeed, more than 50 per cent of all imports during the Leap comprised imports of grain. Industrial output also dropped by 38 per cent in 1961 and by a further 17 per cent in 1962. GNP fell by approximately 15 per cent from 1958–61.

Environmental degradation was prominent during the Leap, especially deforestation. In areas with a paucity of available coal (often due to the huge amounts squandered on mass steel production), workers cut down forests in an effort to provide fuel. Forests were also destroyed in the search for arable land on which to grow crops so as to meet pressing grain production targets. The emphasis on grain production led to ill-conceived farming techniques. In order to increase the areas on which grain could be sown, farmers often ploughed up and down hillsides. Consequently, when the rain came it simply washed away the grain and soil causing soil erosion problems which still exist in China today (Shapiro *et al.* 2001).

China's foreign relations also suffered during the Leap, especially with the Soviet Union. Although a schism with the Soviets had been developing throughout the second half of the 1950s, the Leap brought relations to a new nadir culminating in the withdrawal of Soviet technical assistance in June 1960. In many respects, the Leap was an attempt to break away from the old Soviet model of central planning and this irked Khrushchev who still saw China as a relative newcomer to the communist fold. In the propaganda war that erupted, the Soviets accused China of small-minded idealism (especially in relation to the communes) whilst the Chinese denigrated Khrushchev as a revisionist ally of the United States. The withdrawal of Soviet technicians was partly the fault of the Chinese who did their utmost to drive the Soviets out of the country. As MacFarquhar (1983: 279) notes, Chinese technicians often ignored or dismissed Soviet advice whilst the authorities frequently spied on Soviet advisers and opened their post. But in truth Khrushchev probably withdrew from China because he wanted to bring the Leap to a halt and make the point that China *needed* the Soviet Union and could not survive without it.

## Causes of the failure

So why did the Leap fail so dramatically after the apparent economic successes of 1958? The reasons are numerous and will be examined shortly, but before doing so it is important to set out some of the factors outside the party's control which appear to have intensified the extent of the suffering. Firstly, 1959–60 were the worst two years of weather in China for centuries. According to Lippit (1975: 93–4), drought in the south and flooding in the north meant that over half of China's farmland was seriously damaged by adverse weather conditions. Although this does not relinquish the CCP from all blame for the famine, the bad weather would probably have caused some starvation in China even if the Leap had not been implemented.

The crisis was compounded in mid-1960 by the withdrawal of Soviet technicians. As Soviet personnel departed they took with them all the blueprints that Chinese technicians had been using. This was followed by the cancellation of all Soviet equipment for projects that were under construction in China. As a consequence, a number of large scale industrial and infrastructure projects were abandoned and it took some years before Chinese experts were able to design and produce the equipment that was necessary to complete these projects.

Irrespective of these mitigating factors, there can be little doubt that the failure of the Leap and the causes of the subsequent famine stemmed principally from the flawed nature of the policy itself. From the outset, the Leap was implemented without carefully considering the economic feasibility of such a bold plan. Although there was some experimentation at the local level (as is traditional under CCP rule), the results of these experiments did not provide a convincing case for long-term success. But this did not deter the leadership who pushed ahead with the policy anyway.

To this extent, the leadership was a victim of its earlier domestic successes. In the minds of Mao and his colleagues, the 1949 revolution, land reform and the socialist transformation of the economy (amongst other policies) showed that communism was working in China and this gave party leaders an air of invincibility, a feeling that they had a "Midas touch" when it came to policy making. This led the leadership to rush headlong into a wildly ambitious and ill-considered programme in the naive belief that they could not fail because they had not yet. As the 1981 *Resolution on Certain Questions in the History of our Party* conceded in its analysis of the Leap, 'comrade Mao Zedong and many leading comrades, both at the Centre and in the localities, had become smug about their successes [and] were impatient for quick results' (Joseph 1986: 424).

The naivete of the party leadership at this time was most clearly manifested by the over-reliance on the masses to plan and carry out the policies of the Leap at the expense of Chinese experts. Did the leadership really believe that, correctly mobilized and politically motivated, the masses alone could successfully bring about a sustained and simultaneous growth in industry and agriculture *without* input and advice from people who were specially trained in these areas? (Baum 1964). Perhaps not all of the leadership did, but it was Mao who was in the ascendancy and it was Mao's belief (based on his Yanan experience) that the masses could achieve the seemingly impossible provided they were properly mobilized. This was not borne out by the events of the Leap. Instead, Mao's misguided faith in the masses led to ridiculous situations such as the back yard steel campaign referred to earlier. In the absence of any technological instruction, vast quantities of the steel that was produced was of such low quality that it was simply unusable. Moreover, in the frantic rush to make steel, vital natural resources were squandered such as coal and iron ore (not to mention pots and pans!).

Many of the other mass campaigns were also ill-advised, most notably the campaign to eliminate sparrows. Although the campaign may have helped to legitimize the party by allowing the masses to participate in the political process, its practical effects on the rural economy were disastrous as huge amounts of crops were ruined by insects. To make matter worse, the party followed this up with a mass campaign against insects (part of the "Five Pests" campaign) which involved millions of people digging up the ground and destroying bugs. This proved to be highly damaging to the fertility of the soil and contributed considerably to the more long-term problem of agricultural under-production.

That experts were largely ignored during the Leap was a direct consequence of the hostile political environment created by the Anti-Rightist Campaign. As we saw in Chapter 1, the Anti-Rightist Campaign was launched in reaction to the outpouring of intellectual criticism of the party during the Hundred Flowers. Although it was initially directed at "cultural intellectuals" (e.g. writers and artists), the focus quickly broadened to encompass scientists, technicians and engineers. This category of intellectuals would normally have played an integral role in the planning and implementation of economic policy, but they were frozen out of the Leap because they allegedly espoused bourgeois scientific methods.

The Leap also failed because it over-estimated the political consciousness (or "redness") of the masses. After the vigour with which the peasantry had implemented land reform, Mao convinced himself that the masses were now ready to embrace a higher phase of socio-economic development and one which would involve a greater degree of communal living. He was wrong. When commune members were offered a seemingly inexhaustible supply of food in their communal kitchens they did not eat in a circumspect manner with an eye on maintaining food reserves for future periods of austerity. Instead, they consumed at will while they still had the chance. Similarly, when asked to pool their private property for the benefit of the commune many people simply refused. Why should they share their hard-earned resources with people they had never met before or knew but did not like? This attitude was especially prevalent with regard to grain which many peasants chose to hoard and livestock which many peasants preferred to eat. Consequently, when the famine began to bite in 1959 there was nothing left in reserve to alleviate the hunger. In addition, forced communality acted as a disincentive to work, particularly in those communes where previously rich co-ops were merged with poorer co-ops, leading to gross under-production in certain areas. As Blecher (1986: 73) explains, 'the poor felt less need to work since they had profited from a windfall by being thrown together with the rich, while the rich saw little point in working since they were being dragged down by the poor anyway'.

Whilst this rejection of communal living was clearly undesirable to the leadership and ultimately disastrous for the country, it should not have been surprising. Chinese socialism was still in its infancy in the late 1950s and the peasantry was still more accustomed to the traditional non-collective way of life. The huge and unwieldy communes that accompanied the Leap imposed a mode of thinking on the peasants for which they were simply not ready. In this respect, Mao was guilty of forcing his political will on to a population that did not understand the Leap and did not really want it.

Another reason for the failure of the Leap was the preponderance of false reporting of output figures by local cadres. Caught up in the optimistic fervour of the time, local cadres tried to demonstrate their "redness" by grossly exaggerating output figures in an effort to demonstrate that the Leap was working in their region. Central party inspection teams who went down to the communes to assess the situation were often presented with a completely false picture of agricultural production. For example, in Endicott's (1988: 44–67) study of communes in Sichuan province, grain was taken from neighbouring fields and replanted in a field that was under inspection to give the impression that it was yielding 2,000 kilos of grain per unit of land when in fact the correct figure was just 500 kilos. Once the inspectors left the village, the grain was taken back to where it came from and replanted there. This kind of deception created a dangerous vicious circle. Unaware (at least initially) that output figures were being fabricated, the provincial authorities set higher targets for the communes to achieve. When these figures were exceeded by once again using fabricated figures, central targets went up even further and so on. The reality, of course, was quite different. Production was dropping sharply and people were beginning to go without food. By the time the central government realized what was going on it was too late. The bad weather struck and there was no contingency plan to alleviate the enormous suffering that prevailed.

But it was not just over-zealous local cadres that perpetuated the collapse of the Leap. Unrealistic production quotas set in Beijing also contributed. An especially prevalent form of "high target syndrome" was the linking of Chinese production targets to unachievable international standards. This occurred in the steel industry where the 1957 target to overtake England's steel production in 15 years was gradually reduced to just 3 years, whilst the target to surpass America's steel production was reduced to just 10 years. Even when it became obvious that these fanciful targets could not be met, the party continued to prioritize steel production in a vain attempt to catch up with the West and prove to the world that China was a force to be reckoned with. The end result, as Joseph (1986: 434) suggests, 'was a complete disregard for quality and efficiency because the production of steel had become a "political question" rather than an economic one'.

Worse still, the obsession with steel meant that agricultural production was neglected as manpower was diverted away from the fields and into steel making. This often left inexperienced or incapable agricultural workers (e.g. women or the elderly) in charge of agricultural projects that they did not understand. As a result, potential sources of food were either left to rot or were not farmed properly. Ultimately, "high target syndrome" undermined the mass line principles upon which the Leap was based. With mounting political pressure from above to meet unrealistic production targets, local cadres coerced workers by forcing them to work long hours often under dangerous conditions. Any notion that cadres should listen to the advice of local people and implement policies accordingly was quickly abandoned.

## Apportioning blame

So who was to blame for the catastrophic failure of the Leap? For the most part, public resentment focused on local cadres who were accused of bullying people into joining communes, working excessive hours and pooling their private property. In fact, the strength of public feeling at this time was so pronounced that in several regions groups of angry citizens took to the streets in search of those cadres who had coerced them. According to official reports translated by Chester Cheng (1966: 13 and 190–1), during the immediate post-Leap period there were numerous instances of mob rule against party cadres resulting in mass criticism sessions and sometimes even public beatings.

Whilst the party leadership was probably relieved that local cadres bore the brunt of the public's outrage, it is unfair to place the blame squarely at the local level. Although it appeared to local people that the cadres in their locality were to blame for the suffering inflicted during the Leap since it was they who had acted coercively, it is important not to forget the pressurized political environment under which local cadres were working as created by the Anti-Rightist Campaign. Given the vehemence of the campaign, especially against dissenting party members, cadres lived in genuine fear of being branded rightists for any perceived deviation from the official Maoist line, no matter how minute that deviation might be. Not surprisingly, this frightened some cadres into pressing forward aggressively with the Leap even when it became clear that the Leap was failing. Who can really blame them for this? Faced with the very real prospect of social exclusion, loss of political rights or even banishment to forced labour camps, many cadres simply acted to protect their own skins.

The leadership finally acknowledged the unacceptable degree of blame borne by local cadres in its 1981 *Resolution on Certain Questions in the History of our Party* which concluded that responsibility for the failure of the Leap lay ultimately at the very top from whence the policy derived. Although Mao, in particular, was singled out for criticism for his leading role in devising the policy, the leadership was held collectively culpable. As Deng Xiaoping noted:

> We should not speak only of Comrade Mao, for many other leading comrades in the Central Committee made mistakes too. Comrade Mao got carried away when we launched the Great Leap Forward, but didn't the rest of us go along with him? Neither Comrade Liu Shaoqi, nor Comrade Zhou Enlai for that matter objected to it, and Comrade Chen Yun didn't say anything either.
>
> (Joseph 1986: 441–2)

Spreading out the blame in this way was done out of political necessity. As we will see in Chapter 4, whilst the primary purpose of the Resolution was to criticize Mao's failings so that the party leadership could push ahead with a new programme of economic modernization based on the negation of Maoist principles, it was careful not to go too far in case by damning Mao it unwittingly damned itself (see Chapter 4).

In truth, it is probably fair to single Mao out for criticism over and above his leadership colleagues due to the circumstances relating to his ruthless purge of Peng Dehuai at the Lushan conference in July 1959. Convened by Mao in order to rectify the excesses of the Leap which were becoming increasingly apparent at the time, the conference gave party leaders an opportunity to express openly their reservations over the Leap in accordance with the legal rational principles of democratic centralism. But when Peng Dehuai did just that, he quickly discovered what it meant to incur Mao's wrath. Peng wrote a strongly worded letter to Mao setting out his doubts about the Leap and criticizing it as a manifestation of "petit-bourgeois fanaticism". Mao responded by circulating copies of the letter within the party leadership, waiting nine days and then launching a scathing counter-attack in which he condemned Peng as a right opportunist, threatening to split the party if other leaders did not support his call to oust Peng from his position as Minister of Defence. As Mao remarked:

> I will go to the countryside to lead the peasants to overthrow the government. If those of you in the Liberation Army won't follow me, then I will go and find a Red Army. But I think the Liberation Army would follow me.
>
> (Schram 1979: 139)

The Machiavellian angle on Mao's purge of Peng is intriguing. Did Mao deliberately initiate an "open forum" conference knowing that Peng would speak out so passionately and give Mao an opportunity to remove him? Certainly Mao was aware of Peng's consistent opposition to the Leap which made it at least *possible* that Peng would voice his concerns, especially since there was a history of animosity between the two men over the correct model for military development in China (Mao favoured a fully politicized "revolutionary" army whereas Peng wanted a well equipped professional army with minimal involvement in political affairs). It is also significant that shortly before Peng's fall, Mao manoeuvred his close military ally Lin Biao into a higher-ranking CCP position than Peng, suggesting that Mao was planning all along to replace Peng with Lin as Minister of Defence and was simply waiting for an opportunity to execute this plan (which he did immediately after Peng's dismissal). Finally, why did Mao wait nine days from receipt of Peng's letter before launching his devastating riposte? One possibility is that he wanted to give those who sympathized with Peng's view enough time to ally themselves to Peng so that he could purge them all collectively, which is precisely what he did.

Events immediately after Peng's purge also lead us to the conclusion that Mao should probably be held culpable for the failure of the Leap. As discussed, the Anti-Rightist Campaign (as initiated by Mao) had already created an environment of fear amongst local cadres, many of whom resorted to lying and coercion during the Leap to avoid the prospect of being branded rightist. Mao then accentuated this volatile situation by launching a new campaign against rightist opportunism which threatened to implicate anyone in the party (especially at lower levels) who dared to dissent from the Maoist party line. This left local cadres in an even higher state of anxiety such that they simply exacerbated the excesses of the Leap in order to protect themselves.

The campaign against rightist opportunism also signalled the end of the earlier drive towards the rectification of the Leap initiated by Mao himself in mid-1959. By early 1960 Mao re-launched a "second Leap" despite being aware that there were serious problems with the policy. By prolonging the Leap in this way, Mao ultimately increased the suffering of many peasants and was probably responsible for more deaths than would have occurred if the Leap had been properly rectified (or abandoned) in 1959. In sum, as MacFarquhar (1983) suggests, 'it was Mao's butchery of Peng Dehuai that re-launched the Leap on its erratic course towards disaster'.

The *Resolution on Certain Questions in the History of our Party* is sanguine about the intentions of the Leap. Whilst the extent of the famine is not disputed, the Resolution concludes that the mistakes leading up to the famine were made out of a sincere, albeit misguided desire to build a bright new future for China. According to Bo Yibo (Vice-Premier at that time), 'the masses excused us for doing wrong because our intentions were good' (Joseph 1986: 425). For the majority of the party leadership this was probably true in that the Leap was nothing more than a "tragedy of good intentions" as Joseph describes it. But for Mao, the Leap became something more than this. After his Lushan showdown with Peng, Mao re-launched the Leap not because he thought it would be good for the country but because he wanted to re-assert his challenged authority. On this occasion, Mao was guilty of putting his wounded pride before the needs of the country and it is for this reason that he was primarily to blame for the disastrous consequences of the Leap.

## The power of Mao's charisma?

The next logical question is this: why, as Deng Xiaoping asked during the Resolution (see earlier), did no-one else challenge Mao at Lushan? After all, there is little doubt that several influential members of the leadership were unconvinced by the logic of the Leap. We have already noted Chen Yun's preference for an alternative economic policy based on increased state investment in the agricultural sector. Zhou Enlai was also thought to be unenthusiastic about the Leap on the grounds that the State Council, which was under his control at the time, was sidelined during the Leap in favour of greater party control. Even Liu Shaoqi had doubts about the wisdom of the Leap despite his open display of support for the policy during key party meetings (Lieberthal 1997: 100). So why did none of them join Peng in criticizing the Leap?

One answer might be that they were all acting tactically in order to safeguard or even advance their positions within the leadership. This was certainly true of Liu Shaoqi. In 1958 Mao made it clear that he intended to retire as Chairman of the state in order to concentrate his efforts on party matters. Given that Liu was his most obvious successor it would not be unreasonable to conclude that Liu's support for the Leap was intrinsically related to the question of his imminent succession (which duly occurred in April 1959). As Lieberthal (1997: 100) explains, 'Liu probably had the succession very much on his mind, and personal support for Mao's plans would have been important in his strategy for obtaining the Chairman's blessing as the next in line'.

Another possibility (not unrelated to the one mentioned above) is that Mao's colleagues were simply frightened of him. The Anti-Rightist Campaign showed just what could happen to anyone who criticized Mao, and although that campaign was directed mainly at urban intellectuals and lower level party cadres, party members at the very top must surely have wondered whether the focus of a new political campaign might suddenly turn on them if they openly opposed Mao's proposals on the Leap. This fear was subsequently confirmed by the fate that befell the unfortunate Peng Dehuai.

Perhaps the most convincing explanation as to why key party leaders conformed to Mao's wishes during the Leap, even after Lushan, relates to the strength of his charismatic authority. According to Teiwes (1984: 67), the compliance of Chen, Zhou and Liu demonstrated that 'to a large extent Mao's authority was being acknowledged. Over and above those aspects of tradition which called for obedience, this was largely charismatic authority'. The following observation by Politburo member Ye Jianying (given during the Resolution) seems to confirm Teiwes' assertion. In explaining why it was that no-one joined Peng Dehuai in criticizing Mao over the Leap, Ye noted that:

At the beginning, I, Comrades Liu Shaoqi and Deng Xiaoping, and Premier [Zhou Enlai] all felt that what Peng Dehuai had said was right. But later, after the Chairman had written a letter, issued an instruction, and talked for an hour or so, we all changed our attitude and came to side with Chairman Mao to attack the hapless Peng.

(Teiwes 1984: 66)

Noticeably, however, Mao's charismatic influence on this occasion did not derive from ongoing policy successes (the theory espoused earlier by Teiwes). In contrast to the early 1950s when Mao's status as leader was boosted by his apparent ability to move from one policy success to another, Mao encountered clear difficulties in the latter part of the 1950s not only during the Hundred Flowers debacle, but also during the Leap which was clearly faltering by the time the Lushan conference was convened. Instead, the roots of Mao's charismatic authority during the Leap remained firmly grounded in the inspirational and enigmatic role he played in masterminding the victory of the revolution, which firmly established him (in the minds of his colleagues) not only as a great communist but also as a great nationalist. As Teiwes remarks, policy failures such as the Hundred Flowers and the Leap:

> Paled by comparison with the dual victory of communist revolution and national liberation. However serious his policy errors and violations of official norms [e.g. democratic centralism] in 1959, Mao's colleagues could not separate him from the Party or the nation.
>
> (1984: 67)

Mao's treatment of Peng at Lushan demonstrates again how charismatic and legal rational legitimacy are often incompatible. In Chapter 1, we saw how Mao openly violated the legal rational rules of democratic centralism during the debate over rural collectivization by persuading local leaders to ignore central policy and implement his favoured approach at the provincial level. In so doing, Mao willingly exploited his charismatic status amongst local leaders, many of whom would never have met Mao and were in awe of him. Similarly at Lushan, Mao used his charismatic influence this time over central party leaders to gather allies in ousting Peng Dehuai for simply exercising his democratic right to free speech during an open party session. As he had done in the mid-1950s, Mao applied his charismatic legitimacy to the detriment of legal rational procedures.

## Legitimacy in decline

How did the failure of the Leap impact on the legitimacy of the CCP? As we have already seen, public resentment initially focused on those local party members who were required to implement the unpopular policies of the Leap, so at the local level there was clearly a decline in legitimacy. Whilst this may have deflected some of the blame away from the leadership, it seems incredulous to imagine that the leadership escaped completely unscathed in the wake of such a huge disaster. Although there was no obvious popular movement calling for the overthrow of the CCP, much of the local anger which erupted after the Leap was not just directed at local party officials. The party leadership and Mao in particular were also held responsible. According to Chester Cheng (1966), local people realized that the ideas behind the Leap derived ultimately from Mao and the CCP leadership even though they may have been hundreds of miles away in Beijing. In response, instances emerged of aggrieved local residents tearing down pictures of Mao from public places in anger at what had happened and there were several reports of statues of Mao being vandalized during spontaneous rural outbursts. With millions dead from starvation and no obvious solution to the suffering, some sections of the peasantry appeared to question Mao and the party's right (and ability) to rule China. After the heyday of the early post-revolutionary era, the party's legitimacy was in a state of decline, a process which was ultimately hastened by the Cultural Revolution.

Mao's legitimacy amongst his leadership colleagues also suffered as a result of the Leap notwithstanding his ability to rally allies in the ousting of Peng Dehuai. In 1959, Mao resigned from his post as state Chairman and handed the position over to Liu Shaoqi. It was widely expected that Liu would also succeed Mao as party Chairman when the time came and in preparation Mao began to cut back on his party-related duties. But as the full effect of the Leap became apparent, Mao found that he was increasingly sidelined from party and state affairs. Several of Mao's erstwhile allies before and during the Leap (e.g. Liu Shaoqi, Deng Xiaoping and Chen Yun), no longer held him in such high esteem. Indeed, during the Cultural Revolution, Mao complained bitterly that he had been treated like a "dead ancestor" in the years after the Leap, especially by Deng Xiaoping. As Mao put it, 'whenever we are at a meeting together, [Deng] sits far away from me. For six years, since 1959, he had not made a general report of work to me' (Chen 1970: 40). In fact, anecdotal evidence suggests that Deng *literally* did not hear Mao. Deng was deaf in one ear and rumour has it that during party meetings Deng always sat with his deaf ear facing Mao and with his hearing aid turned off!

As China took the necessary steps towards economic reconstruction in the aftermath of the Leap, divisions between Mao and his colleagues became ever more apparent. Deng and Liu Shaoqi, who had been loyal Maoists in the years before the Leap, allied themselves more closely to Chen Yun in implementing a recovery programme based on individual material incentives, managerial control and market forces. This cut deep into Mao's vision of socialist development by creating a society in which class differences once again became apparent. In a desperate attempt to combat this trend, Mao began planning yet another political campaign that would lead him eventually to the Cultural Revolution. It is to this era that we now turn our attention.

# 3 A crisis of legitimacy

## The Great Proletarian Cultural Revolution

The Cultural Revolution is the most extraordinary event in China's post-revolutionary history. Conceived by Mao as a radical campaign to reverse the tide of revisionism in Chinese politics and society, the Cultural Revolution quickly spiralled out of control until in 1967 China came to the brink of civil war. The main aggressors were the Red Guards, millions of youths drawn primarily from China's schools and universities. The main victims came from a much wider sector of society including intellectuals and government and party officials from the most junior level right up to the very top. Even parents were persecuted on the grounds that they were symbols of authority and oppression. Methods of punishment were diverse. Some of the victims were verbally abused and paraded in public wearing dunces caps or placards bearing insults. Many were beaten, tortured or incarcerated. Some were executed and some simply gave up hope and committed suicide.

The complexity and drama of the events that unfolded during the Cultural Revolution makes it very difficult to understand precisely why Mao launched the campaign in the first place. This is why academic interpretations have tended to differ. Some dismiss the Cultural Revolution as nothing more than a devious plot by Mao to overthrow those members of the party leadership (e.g. Liu Shaoqi and Deng Xiaoping) who were intent on blocking his radical policy initiatives (Leys 1977, Jung Chang and Halliday 2005). According to this view, the Cultural Revolution was simply a smokescreen behind which Mao hid his sole objective which was to regain the power and authority he lost following the failure of the Leap. Another interpretation puts the movement down to a two-line struggle between Mao on one side and Liu Shaoqi on the other (Dittmer 1974). Exponents of this view point out that the two men held fundamentally different, albeit sincere, ideas about the Chinese road to socialism with Mao representing the radical wing of the party and Liu representing the more moderate wing.

Both of these interpretations have merit. There is clear evidence of a divergence of opinion between Mao and Liu during the Cultural Revolution, although a strictly two-line construal over-simplifies the matter. Likewise, whilst Mao did not originally conceive of the Cultural Revolution as a power struggle, his quest for power certainly *became* an important feature of the campaign in that he eventually used it to get rid of his opponents at the top.

Yet, the thinking behind the Cultural Revolution goes well beyond the rather black-and-white explanations given here and can be traced again to concerns about legitimacy. Convinced that the legitimacy of the party and of Chinese socialism as a whole was gradually being eroded by the growth of revisionism within China, Mao launched the Cultural Revolution as a means of reinvigorating both the party and the people with the spirit and energy of the Chinese revolution. Once again, the party was to be immersed into the masses only this time with even more dramatic consequences.

## Revisionism and the erosion of legitimacy

The origins of the Cultural Revolution can be traced to the social and political consequences of the post-Leap economic recovery programme implemented by Liu, Deng and Chen Yun (Baum 1975). Although Mao initially concurred with the general direction of the new policy line, he soon became concerned by the effect it was having on the countryside. Chen Yun was the principal architect of the rural retrenchment policy and he moved quickly to scale down the communes, relax organizational controls and introduce material incentives by allowing peasants to farm their own individual plots and sell a limited amount of produce in the market place. Whilst this succeeded in stabilizing the rural economy and precipitated a gradual rise in grain production, it also allowed some people to turn the situation to their advantage. At the heart of the problem were corrupt local cadres who exploited their authority by monopolizing production contracts and by allocating the most (or best quality) land to themselves, their families and their associates. Some of these associates were former rich peasants under the pre-land reform system, who, in return for these favours, provided cadres with the benefit of their business acumen. This created a situation that was intolerable to the party leadership; a coalition of supposedly communist cadres and former rich peasants joining together to exclude poor peasants from the material benefits of rural de-collectivization and limited market reforms.

Although the leadership was united in its revulsion at these developments, differences emerged over their precise implications and the methods required to deal with them. In the eyes of more moderate leaders such as Liu and Deng, it was simply a case of unprincipled local cadres making the most of economic trends to increase their personal wealth and power. Any rectification should be carried out by designated party work teams who would focus on re-educating the party's rural grass roots. For Mao the situation was much more serious. The unholy coalition of corrupt rural cadres and former rich peasants signified a dramatic lurch towards capitalism or even worse towards the restoration of feudalism and showed that class cleavages still existed in China despite the victory of the communist revolution over a decade earlier. Party rectification was required for sure but this could only be carried out by the *non-party* masses.

But this crisis for Chinese socialism extended well beyond the countryside. As China moved into the 1960s, Mao began to see a similar pattern in just about *every* sphere of Chinese society from education and the arts right through to the party itself. The focus of Mao's unease was the spread of what he called revisionism, a trend in which China gradually drifted away from its revolutionary Marxist origins towards a society that had more in common with capitalism. In education, Mao believed that socialist principles were being eroded by curriculum changes which concentrated on academic excellence rather than commitment to the socialist cause. If the situation was allowed to continue, Mao argued, the longevity of the revolution would become endangered because the next generation would grow up without a revolutionary perspective and with little interest in safeguarding the legacy of the revolution. In addition, as Gray (1990: 330–1) points out, Mao was concerned that education, along with proper medical services, housing, transport and entertainment, was becoming the exclusive domain of the privileged urban classes to the detriment of those who lived in the countryside.

In industry, Mao believed that the post-Leap introduction of material incentives for workers was creating a nation of capitalists and he deeply distrusted the increased role and influence of non-party technocrats who were more interested in output and economic efficiency than socialism. The direction of art and literature in China was also a concern. Back in Yanan Mao had prescribed that art and literature should serve the needs of the party and the people by focusing on matters of a purely socialist nature. Yet, as Mao saw it, art and literature had returned to traditional, pre-revolutionary themes which were dangerously retrogressive. To make matters worse, much of the subject matter appeared to be indirectly critical of Mao's role during the Leap and of his autocratic leadership style in general.

Perhaps of most concern to Mao was the condition of the party. As well as corruption in the rural party apparatus, the party at all levels appeared to be undergoing a degenerative process of bureaucratization, akin to that which was occurring in the Soviet Union. Consistent with his stance during the Hundred Flowers, Mao believed that the CCP had become woefully inefficient due to an unhealthy pre-occupation with bureaucratic procedure. This was mainly because of an over-abundance of staff, many of whom lacked the requisite skills of office or were complacent about their positions of authority. Mao also expressed misgivings about the commitment levels of new party members. Although the party enjoyed an increase in membership from 1.5 million in 1949 to 17 million in 1961, many people were joining to advance their career prospects and enhance their personal contacts. So, for example, people often found that if they joined the party they stood a better chance of sending their children to a good school or getting the apartment that they wanted. But any belief in revolutionary socialism came a distant second. This meant that a party which was supposed to be "of the people and for the people" was rigidifying into the kind of self-serving elite that featured predominantly in capitalist countries. In effect, the ruling party in China was turning into a ruling class, distant from the people and divorced from their needs.

It was not just the attitude of party members that needed to change, but also that of the masses. Although China was a post-revolutionary society, the populace was still marooned in the past in that they were still *thinking* in a backward and feudalistic manner. This was sufficiently demonstrated, Mao suggested, during the Great Leap Forward. Presented with a seemingly unlimited supply of food in the communal kitchens, the peasantry did not possess the foresight to realize that stocks might not last for ever and that it would be wise to be circumspect in consumption. Likewise, their refusal to share private property with other commune members betrayed an alarming distrust for the communal way of living that was meant to underpin socialist society. If China was ever to become a *genuinely* socialist country, Mao argued, the masses needed to shed these outmoded ways of thinking and start analysing every situation in a revolutionary socialist manner. Only this would herald the victory of Chinese socialism.

In sum, therefore, Mao sensed the emergence of a crisis of legitimacy that stretched well beyond the party to the very principles upon which the revolution was founded. Although Liu and Deng's economic plans were intended to re-establish popular faith in the party by alleviating the acute financial hardship suffered during the Leap, Mao believed that these plans would have the reverse effect. Introducing a form of capitalism would not restore socialist legitimacy but destroy it altogether. Likewise, policy changes in education, industry and the arts were pushing China away from its revolutionary roots, and combined with an over-bureaucratic and corrupt party and a population that was politically naive and increasingly ostracized from the political process, Mao feared that China, like the Soviet Union, was abandoning socialism altogether.

## Rectification by the masses

As he had done before, Mao turned to the masses for a solution. During a series of highly charged party meetings that took place throughout 1962, Mao suggested, in a document entitled the *Former Ten Points*, that corruption in the rural party should be dealt with not by pre-selected party work teams, as Liu and Deng proposed (Hinton 1980), but by the masses themselves, and most importantly by those people who had suffered most at the hands of corrupt local officials. As part of what became known as the Socialist Education Movement (SEM), Mao advocated the resurrection of the PPAs, used so effectively during land reform. As before, Mao argued, these non-party village organizations should take the lead in exposing those responsible for local injustices during mass public meetings. Although party work teams should be involved in the organization and activities of the PPAs, their role should be strictly supervisory.

Mao opposed party control of the SEM for two reasons. First, as "outsiders", work team members had no personal experience of the suffering endured by poor peasants and could not hope to understand their needs. Second, the work teams were on the same side as the people who were meant to be the focus of the rectification campaign and could not be trusted to pursue the objectives of the campaign with any real vigour. Conversely, those peasants whose interests had been prejudiced by the cadre–landlord coalition would be much more willing to become actively involved in the SEM.

Beyond this, Mao sensed the need for greater mass participation in Chinese politics. As the perceived gap between ruler and ruled continued to widen during the 1960s and as people began to feel more and more isolated from politics and from the party, the SEM, Mao believed, would be an ideal tool for restoring popular faith in the institutions and methods of the CCP. Instead of relying exclusively on central party diktat, the SEM would re-integrate the masses into the political system by giving them a direct role in social and political affairs. Like land reform, the Hundred Flowers and the Great Leap Forward, the SEM and ultimately the Cultural Revolution was another mini-revolution, aimed at maintaining the momentum of revolutionary socialism in China.

Liu and Deng were staunchly opposed to another mass movement. The failure of the Hundred Flowers and more particularly the Leap convinced them that mass mobilization was a relic of a discredited Maoist past. Although the masses played a key role in the implementation of land reform, Liu and Deng believed that mass involvement in the rectification of the party was undesirable because it risked disrupting the post-Leap process of economic recovery. They also argued that the poor peasant class, in which Mao had such faith, were disillusioned with mass politics following their experiences during the Leap and would not willingly adapt to the demands that Mao wanted to make of them.

As a result, Liu and Deng did their best to sideline Mao's proposals for the SEM in a series of blocking initiatives that resulted ultimately in the unleashing of the Cultural Revolution *against them*. As part of a counter-proposal to Mao's *Former Ten Points*, Liu, Deng and Peng Zhen (Mayor of Beijing) implemented the *Later Ten Points* in September 1963 which instructed party work teams to go down to the countryside and control the rectification process by weeding out and dismissing errant cadres. This ensured that the PPAs played no meaningful role in the SEM. After Mao reiterated his position more firmly in June 1964, Liu responded with another document entitled the *Revised Later Ten Points*. First impressions suggested that Liu and his colleagues had finally fallen into line. The PPAs were given a much broader role in the rectification process and more punitive measures were taken against wayward party cadres. But Mao was still not convinced, arguing that these proposals failed to deal with capitalist elements amongst the peasantry (not just amongst the party) and were actually too severe on party cadres. Moreover, despite Mao's efforts to the contrary, the SEM was *still* dominated by party work teams. In this most recent proposal, Liu espoused that work teams should spend six month periods in selected rural areas where they would strip each administration down to the bare bones and rebuild it. But precisely where the PPAs fitted into this process was difficult to see. As Lieberthal points out:

> The Socialist Education movement had been twisted around to the point where it no longer served as a vehicle for propagating Mao's ideas about revisionism but, rather, had become a relatively savage effort to re-impose discipline in the rural party organs.

(1997: 139)

Frustrated at repeated attempts to stifle his plans, Mao attempted to drag the campaign into the central political arena. In a document entitled the *Twenty-Three Articles* published in January 1965, Mao abruptly redefined the SEM so that it focused not only on rural party corruption but on corruption at *all* levels of the party, including the very top. Furthermore, Mao proposed that just as the non-party masses should rectify the rural party apparatus, they should likewise rectify the urban party elite:

> Where leadership authority has been taken over by alien class enemies or by degenerate elements who have shed their skin and changed their [class] nature, authority must be seized, first by struggle and then by removing these elements from their positions.
>
> (Blecher 1986: 80)

It was at this point that the SEM became an all-out power struggle against those at the top who had consistently blocked Mao's initiatives and who were now being blamed for corruption throughout the entire party (see Figure 3). Without naming them directly, Mao's remarks implicated Liu and Deng as the chief culprits and when the Cultural Revolution exploded into life 18 months later, these two men became the main focal point of Red Guard hostility. To this extent, the *Twenty-Three Articles* was the precursor for the launch of the Cultural Revolution.

## Legitimizing the Cultural Revolution

Before we examine the key events of the Cultural Revolution, it is important to understand precisely *how* Mao was able to launch the campaign given the opposition he faced from the party centre. What groups did Mao use to get the Cultural Revolution off the ground and how was he able to legitimize the campaign within these groups? One of the defining characteristics of Mao's reign was his willingness to flaunt the legal rational rules of democratic centralism. In Chapter 1, we saw how Mao went outside the central party apparatus to enforce his agenda for the rapid collectivization of the countryside and reference should again be made to Mao's violation of Peng Dehuai's legitimate right to speak out at Lushan. The build up to the Cultural Revolution was no different in this respect. Ostracized by his party colleagues in the aftermath of the Leap, Mao once again circumvented the party centre in order to implement his vision of socialism, building an unlikely coalition of the military, the radical intellectual elite and the Red Guards.

### Military

The military was probably the most crucial component part of Mao's Cultural Revolution coalition (Gittings 1966–7, Domes 1968). In simple terms, this was because with the gun on his side Mao could *force* his political will on to others. For example, when Mao sensed that he might be outvoted during important meetings of party or state, the military would physically intervene by preventing

**Major figures of the Cultural Revolution**

| Cultural Revolutionaries | Mao Supporters | Victims |
|---|---|---|
| Mao Zedong | Zhou Enlai | Liu Shaoqi |
| Lin Biao | Li Xiannian | Deng Xiaoping |
| Chen Boda | (Vice-Premier) | Peng Zhen |
| Kang Sheng | | Luo Ruiqing |
| Jiang Qing | Ye Jianying | Yang Shangkun |
| Zhang Chunqiao | (PLA Marshal) | Peng Dehuai |
| Yao Wenyuan | | Lu Dingyi |
| | | (Propaganda Chief) |
| | | Tao Zhu |
| | | (Lu's successor) |

**The Two Cultural Revolution Groups**

| Five Man Group | Cultural Revolution Small Group |
|---|---|
| (set up June–July 1964) | (set up 28 May 1966) |
| Peng Zhen | Chen Boda |
| Lu Dingyi | Kang Sheng |
| Kang Sheng | Jiang Qing |
| Zhou Yang | Zhang Chunqiao |
| (Vice-Director Propaganda Department) | Yao Wenyuan |
| Wu Lengxi (*People's Daily* editor) | Wang Li |
| | Guan Feng |
| | Qi Benyu |

*Figure 3* Major figures of the Cultural Revolution.

potential opponents from attending. In addition, the military provided transport for the Red Guards to travel to Beijing to attend mass rallies or to scour towns and cities in search of class enemies. But there was more to the military's role than pure coercion. It was also an important source of political support for Mao in his battle against the party centre as well as a convenient conduit for the dissemination of Maoist propaganda which went a considerable way towards legitimizing the Cultural Revolution amongst the masses. In both these respects, the role of Lin Biao was crucial.

The appointment of Lin Biao as Minister of Defence in 1959 was not only a testament to his military expertise. Lin was a born-again Maoist and his rise to the apex of the military was intended to bolster Mao's waning political status, although as Mao later discovered, Lin had an eye on his *own* political career.

Accordingly, Lin quickly set about politicizing the PLA along Maoist lines. As a sign of his intent, Lin ensured that the application of Mao Zedong Thought to all aspects of military affairs became official PLA policy. He followed this up with a series of measures which augmented the role of the military in party politics. These included increasing the number of party members in the military, reviving the assorted network of political departments of the military that had fallen into disrepair during Peng Dehuai's incumbency and overseeing the promotion of several loyal Maoists to high-ranking regional party positions (Harding 1997: 155).

Perhaps most significantly, greater emphasis was placed on the political indoctrination of the military. This was achieved by expanding the number of compulsory political education classes for soldiers and revising the content of these classes so that they focused exclusively on Mao rather than on the party as a whole. Indeed, soldiers were encouraged to study Mao's writings to such a degree that they could recite them verbatim. Lin later collected these writings together to publish the Little Red Book which became a symbol of popular devotion to Mao at the height of the Cultural Revolution.

The benefit for Mao of enhancing the political power of the military was obvious. With more and more of his followers assigned to powerful party posts, the political impetus behind Mao's policies became stronger. Although this support base was more central than local, Mao was not averse to calling enlarged Politburo meetings where, in breach of legal rational procedures, he would invite his provincial military followers to attend and vote in his favour (as discussed later). The benefit for Mao of creating an indoctrinated military was a little more subtle. Whilst at one level, a Maoist military could be relied upon to carry out Mao's directives during the Cultural Revolution, at another level the military was a vital means of extending the word of Mao and the cult of personality to the entire country. This proved to be crucial both in launching and legitimizing the Cultural Revolution.

One of the principal ways that the military was able to indoctrinate the masses was through the use of emulation campaigns. The subject matter of such campaigns was often, although not always (e.g. the campaigns to learn from Dazhai and Daqing), a PLA platoon or an individual soldier portrayed as being endowed with an unrivalled degree of political rectitude to which the public were encouraged to aspire (Powell 1965). A number of these campaigns were launched during the prelude to the Cultural Revolution, such as the Good Eighth Company of Nanjing Road and the Shanghai Number One Brigade. The most popular and widely disseminated was the campaign to learn from Lei Feng. Lei Feng was the antithesis of what we might envisage as heroic (Ding Yi 1990). He was not brave or daring and did nothing of individual distinction by which to be remembered. Instead, as Chan (1985) notes, Lei's greatness lay in his ordinariness, particularly in his willingness to put others before himself in carrying out his duties as a soldier and a citizen. Indeed, according to his diaries (which were fortuitously found and published *after* his death), Lei was accidentally killed as he was helping an elderly lady cross the road. Of particular utility to the Mao cult was Lei's seemingly insatiable appetite for Mao's theoretical writings. Not only would he lie awake in his dormitory all night reading Mao's works, but more importantly he would put Mao's words into practice, both in solving day-to-day problems and in understanding the world. In turn, since the masses were expected to learn from Lei Feng's example, the message intended by the Lei Feng campaign was simple: everyone must study and apply Mao's thoughts if they were to become good socialists like comrade Lei.

A degree of scepticism now surrounds the story of Lei Feng. Any mention of Lei Feng is received with faint amusement by the general public and some intellectuals have suggested that Lei's diaries were not only published by the party's Propaganda Department but *written* by it too. Nevertheless, in the early 1960s there was no disputing Lei's existence and the fact remains that the campaign to learn from Lei Feng was an extremely useful tool for enhancing Mao's cult of personality and for legitimizing the Cultural Revolution in general. Ultimately, it was campaigns such as this that elevated Mao to a position in which he was perceived to be superior to the party he represented.

As a final point, it is important to note that the military was far from united in support of Mao. The main source of conflict at the centre came from Chief of Staff Luo Ruiqing and the issue that brought matters to a head was the Vietnam War. As Yahuda's (1972) research reveals, Luo wanted China to assist the North Vietnamese communists in the war against the United States, a stance which would have necessarily involved forming an alliance with the Soviet Union who were already supporting their Vietnamese counterparts. Moreover, like Peng Dehuai, Luo was in favour of modernizing the military along Soviet Red Army lines. Only this type of military, Luo believed, would be capable of defending China against US anti-communist expansionism. But Luo's stance was anathema to both Mao and Lin's position. After the withdrawal of Soviet experts from China in June 1960, relations with the Soviet Union plummeted to a new low. This meant that any prospect of joining forces with the Soviets was out of the question. More importantly, the Soviet-style Red Army that Luo proposed for the PLA cut deep into the Maoist model of a heavily politicized military that relied on commitment to the socialist cause rather than expensive machinery. Eventually, Mao and Lin managed to insinuate that Luo (like Peng) wanted China to follow the Soviet road to socialism, and by December 1965 Luo had disappeared from public view. Arguably, Luo was the first victim of the Cultural Revolution.

Although Luo's demise allowed Lin Biao to consolidate his grip on the military centre, Lin and Mao still encountered opposition from some of the PLA's regional units. The military was set up in a way that accorded regional leaders with considerable autonomy. Consequently, as Domes (1970) points out, Mao's call for the implementation of the Cultural Revolution was ignored by some regional commanders and opposed altogether by others who instead took the side of the party establishment by defending the status quo against marauding Red Guards. Only 5 out of the 29 regional military leaders supported the Cultural Revolution from the outset, 8 gave the movement their nominal support once the Red Guards in their area were under their control and 16 were opposed to the movement throughout. Such opposition at the regional level led to situations such as the Wuhan incident (see later) where different regiments of the PLA fought each other for control of the city.

Notwithstanding this and other pockets of regional military resistance, Mao still found that he had enough military allies to enable him to launch the Cultural Revolution in 1966. Crucially, he enjoyed the support of the 8341 Division lead by Wang Dongxing (Mao's close friend and former bodyguard in Yanan) which guarded the party leadership headquarters in Beijing. This meant that when the time came, the unit was prepared to enter the leadership compound and arrest or detain Mao's opponents. Wang Dongxing was rewarded for his loyalty in May 1966 when he replaced Yang Shangkun as Staff Director of the CCP Secretariat and in April 1969 he became a member of the Politburo.

### Radical intellectuals

The second component part of Mao's Cultural Revolution coalition comprised the radical intellectual elite of Shanghai and Beijing. At the helm of this group was Jiang Qing who Mao married in 1939 and who later became a member of the infamous Gang of Four (see Chapter 4). Like Lin Biao, Jiang closely aligned herself to Mao in the build up to the Cultural Revolution, and like Lin, her motives were as much out of personal ambition as out of any genuine commitment to the Maoist cause. But whereas Lin was driven by political succession, Jiang was just as interested in revenge.

The target of Jiang's retribution were those members of the Yanan party leadership who disliked her (e.g. Zhou Enlai and Deng Xiaoping) and who made sure that she was excluded from any involvement in politics after she married Mao. Indeed, according to Terrill (1984: 154), shortly after marrying Mao, Jiang was forced to make a promise (which she subsequently broke) to refrain from political activity for 30 years. Jiang also had an axe to grind with members of the cultural establishment, especially Lu Dingyi who was Director of the Propaganda Department. Lu regarded Jiang's genre of revolutionary opera (i.e. the promotion of modern revolutionary themes through traditional Beijing opera) with contempt and ensured that her productions never made it to the big stage. By 1966, however, and as a result of her loyalty to Mao, Jiang was appointed to the Cultural Revolution Group (CRG), a powerful central body in charge of cultural affairs. This gave her the perfect opportunity to avenge those who had slighted her over the years.

Serious illness restricted Jiang's access to live theatre, but as she began to recover in the late 1950s she was able once again to attend showings of Beijing opera. To her dismay she found that pre-revolutionary themes were back in vogue and that important socialist issues were being ignored. In keeping with Mao's directives at the 1942 Yanan Conference on Art and Literature, Jiang believed that the arts should "serve politics and the people". What this dictum meant was that art and literature should always have a socialist content so that its mass audience would come to understand and grow to appreciate the wisdom of socialism. In this sense, art and literature were instruments for the indoctrination of the politically ignorant and impressionable masses, nothing more than tools for legitimizing socialism and the party, a means to a higher end rather than an end in itself.

Jiang's subsequent attempts to radicalize Beijing opera brought her directly into conflict with the established acting elite in Beijing as well as party officials in charge of cultural affairs. This led her into an alliance with a group of relatively unknown intellectuals from Beijing and Shanghai who shared her views on the role of art and literature (Goldman 1981). The Beijing clique worked for the Institute of Philosophy and Social Science of the Chinese Academy of Sciences and included Marxist scholars such as Guan Feng, Qi Benyu and Wang Li. The more prominent Shanghai group worked for the Municipal Propaganda Department and included two future members of the Gang of Four, Zhang Chunqiao and Yao Wenyuan. In contrast to their counterparts in Beijing, the Shanghai group specialized in literary and artistic affairs and were particularly adept at journalistic criticism.

One of the key functions of Jiang's clique at this time was to promote and legitimize Mao through art and literature, but their role was soon extended beyond the purely cultural sphere. As Mao grew more and more frustrated with the blocking tactics of the party leadership, he encouraged the clique to examine issues of a more political nature. By the mid-1960s, Jiang and her allies were enjoying a much more active role in political affairs and in November 1965 Yao Wenyuan effectively fired the first shot in the Cultural Revolution by attacking a play written by Wu Han, one of the leading figures of the Beijing party leadership with indirect links to Liu and Deng (as discussed later). By 1966, Jiang and her clique had risen to national prominence and their appointment to the CRG enabled them to form close links with the Red Guards and identify revisionists (often Jiang's enemies) for the Red Guards to attack.

### Red Guards

The final part of Mao's nascent coalition emerged as the Cultural Revolution exploded into action in the summer of 1966 and consisted, at least initially, of university and college students who became known as the Red Guards (Rosen 1982, Chan 1985, Jung Chang 1991). The role played by the Red Guards was to identify and persecute those people who were categorized (often randomly) as revisionists. Assisted by the military, this usually involved dragging victims into an open space, subjecting them to verbal and sometimes physical abuse and publicly parading them wearing dunces caps or placards listing their alleged crimes. In most cases, however, the only crime that they had committed was that of being in a position of authority.

Like the PLA, the student population was divided in its support for Mao. As the Cultural Revolution gained momentum, a clear split emerged between those willing to attack the representatives of the establishment that Mao so opposed and those who sought to defend the status quo. At the risk of over-simplification, the two sides can conveniently be defined as the radical Red Guards (i.e. Mao's allies) and the conservative Red Guards (i.e. Mao's opponents).

The roots of this split stemmed from inequalities within the education system. As places for university admission were reduced during the post-Leap period of economic retrenchment, the criteria for entry changed significantly. Instead of being based on academic ability, admissions were based on a person's class background. Those from a "good" class background (i.e. the offspring of party and military officials) found it much easier to gain places into elite middle schools and universities which in turn meant that they often got the pick of the best jobs after completing their studies. Conversely, those students from a "bad" class background (i.e. the offspring of former bourgeois families such as former industrialists or factory owners) were discriminated against even though they may have achieved better grades. Consequently, those who wanted to uphold the establishment by protecting party bureaucrats (who were often their parents or their parents' friends) were those who had most to gain from maintaining the status quo, whilst those who sought to remove party officials from their positions were those who had lost out under the education system and wanted (or needed) to completely overthrow it. Herein lay the irony. Despite the rhetoric of the period which described the Cultural Revolution as "proletarian", it was the representatives of the former bourgeoisie who were the most radical during the campaign.

As the Cultural Revolution burst into life, urban workers joined the ranks of the Red Guards and they too were divided along pro- and anti-establishment lines on the grounds that they had either benefited from the economic system or had suffered under it. The beneficiaries comprised skilled labourers who worked in large state factories and enjoyed good salaries with benefits. The disadvantaged were unskilled employees from smaller collective factories who suffered acutely from job instability. As Harding (1997: 161) points out, their plight was made even harder by the Worker–Peasant System implemented in 1964 which allowed factory managers to hire workers on a temporary basis, pay them lower wages than those on full-time contracts and be under no obligation to provide medical care or pensions. This disenfranchised sector (comprising about 40 per cent of the urban working class) aligned themselves with their radical counterparts from the education system in an attempt to obliterate the political system, whilst the more privileged workers joined the conservative Red Guards in defending the status quo.

There is little doubt that Mao's success in utilizing the Red Guards during the Cultural Revolution was in large part attributable to the success of the personality cult that was constructed around him in the 1950s and was intensified by Lin Biao during the early 1960s. Scholars frequently point to the strength of Mao's charismatic legitimacy within the student population, a section of society that was drenched in Maoist propaganda from an early age. One essential feature of the Maoist message over the years was the importance of direct political action as a method of making your mark on society and bringing about real change, as Mao himself had shown by masterminding the revolution. Consequently, as Breslin (1998: 129) remarks, when students 'were given the green light to rebel by Mao, they rebelled because Mao could not be wrong, and because rebelling gave them an opportunity to prove their political credentials'.

But is this view entirely accurate? Were students so thoroughly imbued with a Maoist perspective that they believed and acted upon his every last word? If this was the case, then surely the *whole* of the student population would have risen up as one and rebelled against all symbols of authority rather than splintering into factions. Whilst it would take a brave person to refute the influence of Mao's personality cult on the Red Guards, a sense of proportion is required. The very fact that those who supported Mao were those who felt most disenfranchized from society shows that they were influenced as much by a selfish concern for their individual futures as they were by the aggrandizement of Mao via the cult of personality.

## Debate in art and literature

We saw earlier how a split emerged between Mao and his leadership opponents over the direction of rural economic policy and the appropriate method for rectifying corruption within the rural party. Mao's battle with the leadership was not exclusive to these issues. Beyond this (as discussed) Mao was hostile to the application of capitalist methods (i.e. material incentives) in industry and to changes in the education system which emphasized academic ability over commitment to the socialist cause. In these (and other) areas Mao tried to adapt and manipulate party policy such that it would incorporate his radical vision of socialism and in each case he was thwarted by the obdurate resistance of an unwilling party leadership. Undeterred, Mao looked to Chinese cultural policy as a way in and it was through this channel that he finally managed to launch the Cultural Revolution.

The role of art and literature in China goes well beyond the aesthetic pleasure of the general public. Given the closed nature of political debate in China, CCP leaders have often relied on writers and artists to help them espouse a certain viewpoint or criticize a position taken by an opponent. As Cotton (1984) has found, writers, in particular, are invaluable to this end because of their ability to manipulate language in a subtle and esoteric manner with the most common method of making a political point being the use of historical allegory.

Throughout the early 1960s, a number of historical allegories were published that were indirectly critical of Mao's autocratic handling of the Great Leap Forward. As Mao became aware of this trend, he determined to bring about a complete overhaul of cultural policy. The focus of his attention was a play written by the historian Wu Han entitled *Hai Rui Dismissed from Office* (Pusey 1969). In the play, Hai Rui, a Ming Dynasty official, is unfairly removed from his post by Emperor Jiaqing for speaking out against the corrupt activities of his local colleagues. Rightly or wrongly, Mao perceived the play as a metaphor for his dismissal of Peng Dehuai and on this basis alone, he demanded that the article be subjected to comprehensive criticism by the media. In fact, it is far from certain that the play was an attack on Mao's dismissal of Peng Dehuai. Indeed, some scholars suggest that Wu Han wrote the play *before* the infamous Lushan conference (MacFarquhar 1983: 207–12).

Mao's objectives in making this demand were much wider than simply restoring his damaged reputation. First, Mao wanted to use Wu's play to bring about a fundamental change in the direction of Chinese cultural policy. Like Jiang Qing, Mao was alarmed to find that art and literature were no longer serving socialist causes but had reverted back to pre-communist themes, many of which were sharply critical of Mao. For Mao, *Hai Rui* exemplified this deviant trend and by exposing the play for what it really was, Mao hoped to force cultural policy back into line with his Yanan prescriptions. Second, and more importantly, Mao wanted to use Wu's play to get at his opponents in the party establishment. His earlier efforts to attack the leadership through the SEM were eventually sidelined by the American invasion of Vietnam which diverted Chinese attention away from the movement. This left Mao increasingly desperate to find an inroad into the leadership.

Wu Han's position within the Beijing party hierarchy provided Mao with the ideal opportunity. As Deputy Mayor of Beijing, Wu was under the direct authority of Peng Zhen, a long-time opponent of Mao and someone who was closely associated with the moderate market reforms of the post-Leap era and the political network surrounding Liu Shaoqi and Deng Xiaoping. Any criticism of Wu could therefore be directed at Peng for failing to control his wayward subordinate, and if Peng could be implicated the way was then open for an all-out assault on Liu and Deng. If the eventual link to Liu and Deng sounds tenuous, this is probably because it was.

At this juncture, Mao's carefully constructed alliance with the military and the radical intellectual elite came to fruition. Since Wu was part of the Beijing cultural establishment, it was unlikely that Mao would find support from the Beijing media for his proposed attack on Wu's play. Similarly, the centrally appointed Five Man Group which was set up to rectify cultural policy (along much more moderate lines that Mao was proposing) was headed by Peng Zhen and was equally unreceptive to Mao's views. As a result, Mao turned to Shanghai intellectual Yao Wenyuan to assist him, instructing Yao to write a biting critique of *Hai Rui* that established a clear link between the play and Mao's purge of Peng Dehuai and that criticized Wu Han directly for writing the play. Realizing that the Beijing press would simply ignore Yao's paper, Mao then drew on his allies in the military to assist him by ensuring that the article was published in the PLA's very own national newspaper, the *Liberation Army Daily* based in Shanghai. Anecdotal evidence suggests that when Yao's paper appeared in the *Liberation Army Daily*, an outraged Peng Zhen asked Lu Dingyi to telephone Shanghai and demand to know who had given authorization for the publication of the article. On contacting Zhang Chunqiao, Lu was told the answer: Mao Zedong.

The significance of Yao's article cannot be underestimated in that it signalled the start of a new rectification campaign in cultural affairs (specifically against writers and artists) that would quickly open the way to the Cultural Revolution. One of the aims of the article was to show that the publication of *Hai Rui* betrayed an urgent need for a thorough and ongoing reform of cultural policy. According to Yao and Mao, the allegedly anti-Maoist political undertones of the play were evidence of a growing trend towards anti-socialist and counter-revolutionary tendencies in art and literature and this could only be combated by launching a mass rectification movement in art and literature.

Peng Zhen responded to Yao's critique in the same way that Liu and Deng had responded to the SEM; he attempted to control and then modify the movement in order to avoid another damaging mass campaign. The publication of Yao's piece in the *Liberation Army Daily* forced the Beijing-controlled *People's Daily* to follow suit and Peng sought to soften its political impact by writing a carefully scripted editorial in which he stressed the importance of "studying history". As ever, the implication was subtle but significant. Peng was suggesting that *Hai Rui* should only be discussed within a strictly historical context and that any association between the play and the allegedly anti-socialist tendencies of the cultural intelligentsia was a misnomer.

These blocking tactics increased Mao's frustration with the party establishment and only heightened his determination to push for an all-out campaign against intellectuals. On realizing that he was powerless to prevent this from happening following the publication of Yao's paper in Beijing, Peng moved to criticize Wu Han and other liberal writers such as Deng Tuo who had also covertly sniped at Mao. This abrupt change of tack was clearly an attempt by Peng to protect his own position within the party, but it was too late. By April 1966, Peng was under attack from all quarters (including Deng Xiaoping) for his earlier efforts to protect Wu Han, and in May during a landmark Politburo meeting Peng was fired from his post as the First Secretary of the Beijing CCP. Other significant dismissals included Luo Ruiqing as Chief of Staff of the PLA (largely ceremonial at this point), Lu Dingyi as Chairman of the Department of Propaganda and the entire Five Man Group with the exception of Kang Sheng who were replaced by the CRG, heavily staffed with Mao's allies including Chen Boda and Jiang Qing (see Figure 3). Although the main function of the CRG was to continue to expose and criticize bourgeois tendencies in the cultural sphere, the *16 May Circular* released shortly after the May Politburo meeting gave notice of the imminent purge of other high-ranking party-state officials. It stressed the importance of removing:

> Representatives of the bourgeoisie who have sneaked into the Party, the government, and the army. When conditions are ripe, they would seize power and turn the dictatorship of the proletariat into a dictatorship of the bourgeoisie. Some of them we have already seen through, others we have not. *Some we still trust and are training as our successors.* There are, for example, people of the Khrushchev brand still nestling in our midst [my emphasis].

> (Harding 1997: 171)

Within weeks, therefore, a campaign against revisionism in art and literature was broadened to encompass revisionism in all areas of party policy for which certain revisionist party leaders were responsible. By now few people doubted that the "successors" referred to above were Liu Shaoqi and his protege

Deng Xiaoping, subsequently referred to as "the number one and number two persons taking the capitalist road".

Notwithstanding Peng Zhen's closeness to Liu and Deng, neither was prepared to defend Peng against the onslaught from Mao. What was the reason for this acquiescence to Mao? Perhaps the most obvious explanation is that Liu and Deng were simply afraid of Mao. Not only was it clear that the political impetus was firmly with Mao and his radical colleagues, but they would have also remembered what happened to Peng Dehuai when he stood up to Mao in Lushan. Alternatively, the reason might lie in the residual strength of Mao's charismatic legitimacy. Although the failure of the Leap showed that Mao's judgement was flawed, Mao was still admired by his colleagues for his leading role during the revolution and it was perhaps for this reason that they sided with Mao. As Harding (1997: 238) concludes, the compliance of the party leadership over Peng Zhen's dismissal derived from Mao's 'ability to lead the CCP to victory against enormous odds in the late 1930s and 1940s [which] had given him an air of infallibility that had been only slightly tarnished by the disaster of the GLF [Great Leap Forward]'.

## Dissent in the campuses

The epicentre of the Cultural Revolution was the campus of Beijing University. It was here that the CRG built up a network of support for the assault on the party establishment and it was here that the first real attack on authority took place. In keeping with Chinese tradition, the first act of protest came when a large character wall poster was pasted on a campus notice board. Written by Nie Yuanzi, a radical left-wing member of the teaching staff, the poster targeted the university authorities who were accused of stifling open discussion of the Hai Rui issue and siding with Peng Zhen against Mao. In response, the authorities attempted to cover-up news of the wall poster and suppressed any further postings. But by this time Mao had heard about the poster and he quickly ensured that its contents were published throughout China. As intended, this triggered a chain reaction as students from all over the country followed Nie's example by writing their own wall posters. Most of the posters expressed dissatisfaction with the elitist nature of the education system which was heavily prejudiced against students from "bad" class backgrounds. Others focused on overtly political issues by condemning high-ranking university officials for favouring the revisionist ideas of the Chinese leadership.

The manner in which Liu Shaoqi dealt with this wave of critical wall posters ensured that he was top of the "wanted list" when the Cultural Revolution began. Fearing the chaotic consequences of unrestrained student protest, Liu reverted to the familiar tactic of sending in party work teams to control the movement. For example, although students were allowed to write wall posters and hold demonstrations, these activities were to be kept within the strict confines of the university campus. Similarly, whilst criticism of university officials was permitted, legitimate targets were limited to low-ranking bureaucrats carefully selected by the work teams, thus ensuring the protection of higher-ranking officials who had closer links to the party leadership. In some areas, however, *all* forms of student protest were banned and some of the more radical students were subjected to severe criticism and even expulsion to the countryside for a period of "re-education" through manual labour.

Sensing that Liu was attempting to hijack another of Mao's radical initiatives, Mao went on the offensive. After months of seclusion in eastern China, Mao announced his return to Chinese politics in dramatic style by swimming across the Yangtze River in a much-publicized attempt to re-assert his charismatic authority over the masses. Then, on arriving in Beijing, Mao quickly set to work by ordering the dissolution of Liu's party work teams and by convening the Eleventh Plenum of the Eighth Central Committee in August 1966. Packed with Mao's supporters (many of who were not members of the Central Committee), the Plenum sanctioned the removal of Liu Shaoqi from his post as party Vice-Chairman and demoted him from second in the party hierarchy to eighth. Lin Biao replaced Liu as Mao's second-in-command and several other leading Maoists (e.g. Kang Sheng and Chen Boda) were promoted to full membership of the Politburo. The Plenum also gave its backing to Mao's radical theory of class struggle in post-revolutionary society and approved his Sixteen Point Decision on the Cultural Revolution. The document acknowledged the need to fundamentally alter the social and political outlook of the Chinese people by encouraging them to struggle against the omnipresent representatives of capitalism and bourgeois revisionism.

## Unleashing the Red Guards

Within days of approving the Sixteen Points, the first of several mass rallies were held in Beijing during which millions of young Chinese flocked to Tiananmen Square to participate in the Cultural Revolution and catch a glimpse of Mao. The images created by these rallies were dramatic in the extreme. As Mao looked out from above the Gates of Heavenly Peace, he was faced with a seemingly endless sea of youthful Chinese students dressed in makeshift military uniforms decorated in Mao badges, all of them chanting his name, all of them waving his Little Red Book and all of them hysterical in his presence. Decades of carefully constructed Maoist propaganda had finally come to fruition. This was the pinnacle of Mao's cult of personality and the point at which it became clear that Mao as an individual had become more important and more *legitimate* than the party he represented.

Romantic images such as these cannot hide the fact that the Cultural Revolution was beset with problems from the outset. The most striking of these was the Red Guards' obsession with the Four Olds: old ideas, old culture, old customs and old habits. Although Mao had called for the elimination of these "unwanted elements" during the Eleventh Plenum, his main aim was to ensure the dismissal of those party leaders and senior officials who had consistently opposed him throughout the 1960s. Yet, a lack of clear instruction meant that the

Red Guards failed to understand what was expected of them. Although deemed revisionists in the party were attacked and purged as Mao instructed, the Red Guards channelled more of their energy into identifying and destroying the Four Olds.

Almost anything proved to be fair game. Initial targets were any items associated with China's pre-revolutionary past. Valuable antiques such as furniture and ornaments were confiscated or smashed and books and paintings were torn apart or burned in the street. Religious shrines and places of worship were vandalized, especially Buddhist temples. As the movement gathered pace, symbols of the bourgeois West were targeted. Men and women with long hair were shorn on the spot or stripped if they were wearing jeans or mini-skirts. Seemingly decadent music or literature was destroyed and even keeping pets was condemned as an undesirable bourgeois habit (Bennett and Montaperto 1972).

In an effort to appear the most radical and hence the most loyal to Mao, Red Guard groups began to compete with each other. As the competition grew fiercer, so Red Guards activities became more and more extreme. Shopkeepers were coerced into replacing their standard shop names with new revolutionary shop signs. Entire street names were changed, such as the street in Beijing housing the Soviet embassy which became Revisionist Street to reflect the apparent demise of Soviet Marxism. School names were changed to politically correct titles such as the School of Mao Zedong's Doctrine or the School of Anti-Revisionism. Perhaps most infamous of all was the failed attempt by one group of radicals to enforce a new traffic lighting system so that red, the colour of socialism, meant "go" rather than "stop".

But there was also a tragic side to these early stages of the Cultural Revolution involving the persecution of thousands of people accused of epitomizing the Four Olds. Again, targets were random. Former landlords, industrialists and KMT members (and their relatives) were targeted for their previous "transgressions", religious leaders were attacked for their allegedly backward and feudalistic beliefs, and intellectuals were vilified as the "stinking ninth class". Probably the most victimized sector were members of the teaching and administrative staff in schools and universities whose homes were plundered in an attempt to find (often non-existent) evidence of secret "bourgeois tendencies" and who were often subjected to beatings, torture or even execution at the hands of frenzied students (Thurston 1984–5, 1985).

With the Cultural Revolution threatening to go off the rails before it had really begun, Mao re-focused the movement so that it conformed to his original prescriptions. This was achieved in three stages. First, a series of speeches and editorials were published on 1 October 1966 instructing the Red Guards to abandon their obsession with the Four Olds and turn their attention to revisionists within the party. Second, Mao convened a central work conference to assess the progress of the Cultural Revolution. Initially, he tried to encourage party cadres to submit themselves to the movement by assuring them that any sanctions they might face would be mild and that the long-term benefits of rectification would be immeasurable. But when cadres continued to express alarm at this prospect (not surprisingly), Mao took a more aggressive approach, accusing Liu and Deng of leading party resistance to the Cultural Revolution and forcing them to write self-criticisms. Third, the CRG assisted by compiling damaging information about high-ranking officials to be used by sympathetic Red Guards as ammunition for their attacks. Delegations were dispatched to all parts of the country so that Red Guards could hunt down those unfortunate enough to have been identified.

By the end of 1966 several of the party leadership had fallen victim to the Cultural Revolution. Luo Ruiqing, Lu Dingyi and Peng Zhen (amongst others) were each subjected to hours of verbal abuse during a series of mass rallies held in Beijing. As the Cultural Revolution swept through China's provinces, scores of local party and government leaders were singled out for verbal and physical maltreatment. But here again it was apparent that the movement was failing to proceed along the lines that Mao had prescribed. Instead of accomplishing a limited purge of local officials that would sweep away a minority of "bad elements" without disrupting the operations of local government, the Red Guard assault on the provinces quickly brought about the complete collapse of local authority.

## Shanghai under siege

Nowhere was this more true than in Shanghai (Walder 1978). After the redirection of the Cultural Revolution in autumn 1966, the urban work force began to organize itself into groups of Red Guards with the most radical consisting of those people who were the most disadvantaged under the employment system. When Shanghai's Mayor Cao Diqiu refused to acknowledge the concerns of these new groups, they responded by co-ordinating strikes throughout the city, disrupting production and causing panic amongst local residents. The resultant chaos provided an opportunity for radical Red Guards to storm government and party buildings and it was at this point that they met resistance (in some cases armed) from conservative Red Guards, otherwise known as the Scarlet Guards, who had formed to uphold local authority and protect party-state property. Mob rule ensued as street battles broke out between the two rival factions and anyone else who wanted to get involved. Numerous people were killed, shops were looted and burned down and electricity supplies were cut off completely. With the help of sympathetic PLA forces, radical Red Guards quickly succeeded in breaking down Scarlet Guard defences and almost the entire membership of the Shanghai local party-state was attacked, despite Mao's earlier instructions that only high-ranking officials were to be targeted.

As local authority in Shanghai collapsed, radical Red Guards sought to fill the vacuum by establishing their own organs of power. The new model of government, proposed in the main by Zhang Chunqiao and Yao Wenyuan, was based on the 1871 Paris Commune established during the French Revolution. Karl Marx had referred to the Paris Commune favourably in several of his writings and many academics believe it to be the kind of power structure Marx envisaged in the post-revolutionary state (Held 1989: 105–39). Gone was the over-staffed, inefficient and unaccountable bureaucracy that epitomized 1960s China. In its place would be a system of directly elected officials who were paid the same as ordinary workers and were subject to recall and re-election at any time.

Caught up in the spontaneous drama of the Shanghai siege, the Maoist party leadership began to encourage the complete overthrow of local party and government administrations throughout China. On the front page of the *People's Daily*, Red Guard organizations from all over China were implored to 'make up their mind to unite, form a great alliance [and] seize power! seize power!! seize power!!!' (Harding 1997: 193). However, when it became clear that the new power structure in Shanghai did not encompass a leading role for the party, Mao retreated from his radical position, summoning Zhang and Yao to Beijing, criticizing them for confusing revolutionary socialism with anarchy and demanding that they dissolve the Shanghai Commune.

For the radical Red Guards in Shanghai this must have seemed like a betrayal given that Mao had so enthusiastically supported them in their assault on local power. Here at last was an opportunity to establish a truly Marxist political structure and yet Mao was actively opposing it. The reason for Mao's *volte face* was simple. Despite his opposition to the ossification of the party-state, he was ultimately a party man. Mao had devoted his life to the CCP and he was not prepared to see it subside under the weight of disorderly Red Guard activity. Mao never wanted the Cultural Revolution to destroy the party, only to rectify and re-legitimize it by putting it back in touch with the sentiments of the masses. So when Mao realized that the party was in danger of collapsing altogether, he began to climb down from his radical position and dilute the Cultural Revolution.

## The revolutionary committees

The first step towards the de-radicalization of the Cultural Revolution was the establishment of the Revolutionary Committees which began to appear in February 1967. Intended to replace the shattered organs of the local party-state, the membership of the Revolutionary Committees consisted of three groups known as the Three-in-One Combination. These were Red Guards, revolutionary cadres (i.e. those cadres who had not been purged by Red Guards) and the PLA. In theory, the working status of each group was equal in that each would participate equally in running a new, all-inclusive form of government based on the Yanan principles of the mass line. In practice, the Revolutionary Committees were dominated by the PLA who in effect ran the country for the next few years. It was also clear that the Revolutionary Committees were only a temporary arrangement. Mao's long-term objective was to return power to the CCP and rehabilitate purged party officials. Already, it appeared that Mao was moving towards the complete abandonment of the Cultural Revolution.

So why did Mao turn to the PLA at this point? Most likely because it was the only option he had. The destruction inflicted by Red Guards, their lack of coherent organization and their comprehensive failure to understand what Mao wanted from the Cultural Revolution (primarily because of a lack of clear instructions from above) meant that they could no longer be relied upon as an instrument of radical change. Contrast this with the ordered discipline of the PLA who were predominantly loyal to Mao, in most cases eager to wrest control from rioting students and well equipped to restore order to China's towns and cities. More significantly, the PLA was the *only* institution left standing in early 1967 after the Cultural Revolution had swept away the organs of party and state.

But re-establishing law and order was no easy task. The Cultural Revolution had unleashed a number of simmering social tensions between those who felt that their rights had been prejudiced by the education and/or employment system and those who had benefited from the system. Unsurprisingly, therefore, the two groups were not easily reconciled, especially after some of the pitched battles of the previous months and the considerable loss of life. The difficulty in maintaining order was further accentuated by divisions within the military over precisely how far it should go in order to restore peace. Whilst Lin Biao remained steadfast in his support for the radical Red Guards and discouraged the suppression of their political activities, the vast majority of local commanders, who had close ties to purged local officials and were never really in favour the Cultural Revolution, used violent measures to quell the continued radicalism of certain Red Guard factions.

This left Lin Biao in an increasingly precarious situation after 1967. Having aligned himself so closely to Mao in the build up to the Cultural Revolution for which he was duly rewarded with the promise of political succession, Lin's political future was intrinsically tied to the maintenance of the radical movement. A return to the old power structure would mean the return of many of Lin's opponents, making his succession more difficult. Zhou Enlai, who managed to avoid the clutches of the Red Guards, was not an opponent of Lin's at this stage, but Zhou's closeness to Mao was a potential threat to Lin's future inheritance. Consequently, as Mao sought to rein in the excesses of the Cultural Revolution, Lin pushed hard in the other direction with the purge of Zhou Enlai as his ultimate aim. This created a chasm between Mao and Lin that eventually led to Lin's dramatic fall from grace in 1970 (see Chapter 4).

## Abandoning the Cultural Revolution

The events of summer 1967 convinced Mao (under pressure from the military) that the Cultural Revolution should be abandoned altogether if the CCP was ever to regain its grip on political power. In Wuhan (Hubei province) radical Red Guards gained control of a number of government buildings and in an effort to wrest control back from the radicals Chen Zaidao, head of the Wuhan PLA, helped conservative Red Guards to launch an armed counter-attack. Beijing responded by sending two envoys down to Wuhan with strict instructions from Zhou Enlai to put a stop to the siege. However, Chen promptly arrested the two men and then refused to allow Zhou's plane to land when he tried to make a personal visit a few hours later. This led to a state of virtual civil war in which PLA units loyal to Mao and Zhou sent gun boats down the Yangtze to attack the pro-establishment Wuhan PLA and rescue the two arrested officials (Robinson 1971).

Chaotic events such as these forced Mao into issuing a joint directive of party, government and military demanding that Red Guard organizations throughout the country return their arms to the PLA and obey all military orders to cease factional infighting. Mao then took the opportunity of the eighteenth anniversary of the founding of the PRC (1 October 1967) to appear above the Gates of Heavenly Peace in the company of military personnel who had earlier been denounced by radicals. The message was clear: the attacks on authority must stop and the PLA was now in charge. Within days, schools and universities were re-opened and students were told to return to their classrooms and campuses to resume their studies.

The following months were devoted to the consolidation of PLA control and the suppression of further outbreaks of violence between rival Red Guard factions. In July 1968, Mao summoned a number of radical Red Guard leaders to Beijing where he openly criticized them for their violent excesses. Millions of Red Guards were then arrested by the military and sent down to the countryside. Initially, this was meant to be an exercise in rectification. In theory it was thought that a period of manual labour in close contact with the peasantry would bring the wayward students back down to earth by giving them a taste of life in a poor peasant environment. The reality was often far worse. The majority of peasants, though largely unaffected by the Cultural Revolution (Baum 1971), were well aware of what was going on and were contemptuous of the Red Guards. Consequently, when Red Guards arrived in the countryside many were treated with enmity. Perhaps understandably, many from the peasant community were unprepared to share its food and resources with undisciplined and irresponsible youths who had created so much unrest in China. This led to untold suffering on the part of the Red Guards including starvation (Bernstein 1977).

The Ninth National Party Congress in April 1969 is widely acknowledged as symbolizing the end of the violence of the Cultural Revolution (albeit not the radicalism). By this time most Red Guard groups had disbanded and the PLA was functioning as China's *de facto* government. This was reflected in the make-up of the Congress. Of the 1,500 delegates to the Congress, about 65 per cent came from the military and almost half of the elected Central Committee were military men. Another 20 per cent of the Central Committee was drawn from mass organizations, and their representatives were older, more conservative figures from the rural and urban work force who were sympathetic to the PLA (Harding 1997: 229). Perhaps most significantly, Minister of Defence, Lin Biao, was promoted to the position of sole Vice-Chairman of the CCP and the new (1969) party constitution formally declared Lin as Mao's designated successor.

But if the Cultural Revolution was officially over (or at least under military control), the way ahead was far from certain. Although both Liu and Deng had dropped out of sight altogether, the composition of the newly elected Politburo did not represent an outright victory for Mao. To be sure, Mao and Lin were in a much stronger position than they had been before the Cultural Revolution, but within the Politburo there were several different factions each with their own interests. To counter-balance the five central military officials close to Lin, there were three regional military commanders and a PLA marshal, none of whom were close to Lin. In addition, there were three mid-level party officials who had been promoted as a result of the Cultural Revolution and two senior officials who had been persecuted during the campaign. The Politburo also comprised six members of the CRG who were committed to continuing the policies of the Cultural Revolution. All of this, combined with the uncertainty over the future direction of policy and the continued fragility of the party-state apparatus led to a period of instability and infighting that characterized the last few years of Mao's life.

## The collapse of party legitimacy

The destructive course of the Cultural Revolution makes it difficult to remember precisely what Mao had in mind when he began planning the campaign back in 1962. It is easy, for example, to concentrate on the chaotic events in Shanghai and Wuhan and for this to detract from a clear understanding of Mao's rationale for launching the movement. Whilst Mao cannot escape responsibility for the cata-strophic consequences of the period, focusing exclusively on what the campaign *became* creates an unbalanced picture. Mao never intended the Cultural Revolution to wreak such havoc on the country but once the movement developed a momentum of its own he found it impossible to control the forces he had unleashed without abandoning the campaign altogether. Instead, Mao's rationale was ideological, or at least it was *initially*. In his mind, as we have discussed, the party and Chinese socialism in general were undergoing a crisis of legitimacy. With revisionism endemic in just about every area of government policy, Mao saw the PRC drifting further and further away from its revolutionary socialist foundations. This was compounded by an increasingly bureaucratic party and an increasingly apathetic population. China, Mao believed, was following its Soviet neighbours down the path towards capitalist restoration. The very future of Chinese socialism was at stake.

For Mao, therefore, the Cultural Revolution was a means of restoring the legit-imacy of the party and of Chinese socialism, and instinctively Mao looked to the Yanan model of mass mobilization to effect this change. So, for example, when it became apparent that the rural party apparatus was corrupt, Mao called on local non-party people to lead the rectification process, not least because it was they who had been prejudiced by such corruption. Rejecting the sole reliance on cen-tral party work teams proposed by Liu and Deng, Mao argued that the only way the party and the socialist system would regain its credibility was if those who had suffered most were directly involved in the rectification process. Through direct political action, the masses would come to feel once again (as they did during land reform) that they shared a common cause with the party and that they were still an intrinsic and essential feature of the political process. This, in turn, would resurrect popular sentiments that the CCP was the only worthy and legitimate ruler of China.

Mao applied the same rationale to the Red Guard movement. Although China's youth had been exposed to political propaganda from an early age and were familiar with the principles of revolutionary socialism, this was not enough. For young people to *genuinely* believe in the legitimacy of socialism and for the revolution itself to survive indefinitely in China, the young needed to *participate* in their very own revolution. As heirs to Mao's legacy and the next generation of revolutionary leaders, the young needed to experience what it was like to be involved in a revolution. For Mao, that revolution was the Cultural Revolution.

But Liu and Deng refused to contemplate the prospect of another mass movement, especially at a time when they were trying to repair the damage inflicted by Mao's last radical initiative, the Great Leap Forward. The Leap cast a huge cloud over Mao's mobilization mode of legitimacy and led Liu and Deng to conclude that the only way to restore party legitimacy was to stabilize the economy through limited market reforms (a form of performance based legitimacy) and to create a more predictable political environment free of mass campaigns. Only this approach would enable the CCP to achieve the levels of popularity that it enjoyed in the early post-revolutionary period. In an attempt to prevent Mao from mobilizing the people *en masse*, Liu and Deng repeatedly stifled Mao's radical proposals by using the full force of the central party apparatus.

These blocking tactics infuriated Mao to such an extent that he determined to remove Liu and Deng from power altogether by insinuating that *they* were responsible for corruption in the party and revisionism throughout society. When Yao Wenyuan launched his literary attack on *Hai Rui Dismissed from Office* in November 1965, it was no longer clear whether Mao was still genuine about the *need* for a cultural revolution or whether he was simply using the idea as an excuse to topple his opponents.

It is ironic, of course, that in seeking to restore party and socialist legitimacy through the Cultural Revolution, Mao resorted to *illegitimate* measures. When Mao found himself in a minority in the early 1960s over key issues such as the appropriate method for rectifying rural party corruption, he refused to adhere to the principles of democratic centralism by accepting the majority party line. Instead, he carefully crafted a powerful coalition of allies from outside the central party apparatus which he used to *force* his views on the recalcitrant party leadership. Then, once Mao had regained his position at the helm of the party, he dispatched his opponents in the leadership with the same scant concern for legal rational procedures. We saw earlier how the Eleventh Plenum of the Eighth Central Committee was packed out with Mao supporters, many of whom were not members of the Central Committee, in order to ensure there were enough people to be able to dismiss Liu Shaoqi as party Vice-Chairman and demote him down the party hierarchy. Liu's removal as state Chairman (in October 1968) was also carried out via a conveniently "enlarged" session, and even then not by the NPC which was the only organ legally entitled to do so, but by a plenary session of the Central Committee, a party (not a government) organ. Likewise, outside Beijing, local party and state officials were invariably removed without any adherence to the correct legal rational procedures. Indeed, in many cases they were *physically* removed.

The collapse of legal rational authority during the Cultural Revolution had much to do with the strength of Mao's charismatic legitimacy at the time. As noted in earlier chapters, a rise in the charismatic authority of a single leader often coincides with a decline in the legal rational legitimacy of the system because the former is invariably made at the *expense* of the latter. This was certainly the case during the Cultural Revolution. In building the tri-party coalition that he used to topple the CCP leadership, Mao drew on an almost unlimited reserve of charismatic authority (particularly amongst students and soldiers) that derived from his reputation as China's great revolutionary helmsman. Whilst coalition members had their own personal reasons for aligning themselves with Mao, it was the draw of "Mao the man" that pulled them towards him in the first place.

But if Mao's objective in launching the Cultural Revolution was to re-legitimize socialism and the party, he failed abjectly. If anything, Mao achieved the exact reverse effect. For many people, the suffering they endured during the Cultural Revolution destroyed their faith in the CCP altogether. Whilst almost every member of urban society was affected by the movement, one of the worst affected groups was academics and intellectuals who were ruthlessly maltreated by Red Guard organizations. According to figures released during the trial of the Gang of Four in 1980, 142,000 teachers, 53,000 scientists and technicians and 2,600 artists and writers were victimized by Red Guards, although it is not known how many of these people died (Harding 1997: 242). The suffering inflicted on party and government leaders at all levels was also marked. According to Scalapino (1972), of the 6 regional party First Secretaries incumbent at the outbreak of the Cultural Revolution, only 2 remained in their posts afterwards whilst only 6 of the 29 provincial party First Secretaries survived with their jobs in tact. The pattern was repeated at the centre with 9 of the 23 Politburo members, 4 of the 13 Secretariat members and 54 of 167 Central Committee members remaining in their posts after the movement was curtailed. Notable fatalities at the very top of the party included Peng Dehuai, Deng Tuo, and Wu Han. Liu Shaoqi, who was arrested in 1967 and repeatedly beaten by Red Guards, died in 1969, deprived of the medical treatment he needed to keep him alive. Luo Ruiqing, after a long period in solitary confinement, repeatedly attempted suicide. Interestingly, Thurston (1984–5: 606) notes that suicide was not necessarily a way out during the Cultural Revolution. Often, if someone killed himself he was not remembered fondly during a conventional Chinese memorial service but was criticized for his counter-revolutionary sentiments, as confirmed by his suicide.

Ironically, those who were probably the most disaffected by the Cultural Revolution were the very people who spearheaded the movement in the initial stages: China's youth, the Red Guards. Called upon to carry out the campaign in 1966, the Red Guards must have experienced an unbelievable sense of importance and honour as they were given almost unlimited authority to change the face of Chinese socialism by overthrowing leading members of an apparently corrupt and revisionist party. But within a few months, the Red Guards turned from heroes to villains. Once Mao (under pressure from the PLA) decided to abandon the Cultural Revolution, the Red Guards were suddenly dropped, blamed for the excesses of campaign and then ultimately punished for their over-exuberance. In 1968–9, over four million students from Chinese universities and high schools were sent down to the countryside for a period of re-education through manual labour. In a political system already prone to political scapegoating, the young and naive participants of the Cultural Revolution were probably the biggest scapegoats of them all. Indeed, many former Red Guards were not able to return home until the late 1970s by which time they had lost out on their education to the detriment of their careers. For this reason, they are often referred to as China's "lost generation" (Luo Ziping 1990).

Fundamental to the ideological legitimacy of any communist regime is a perception amongst the populace that the regime is upright and moral and leads by example. Moreover, in keeping with its role as the Dictatorship of the Proletariat, the ruling party must rule exclusively in the interests of the people and without any separate interests of its own. The turmoil of the Cultural Revolution exposed a party that was more concerned with political differences and factional infighting than the welfare of the masses, had failed to prevent one man from issuing directives seemingly at will and had allowed the country to deteriorate into chaos. Amongst the young in particular, these factors, and the fact that many of them lost years of their lives in rural exile, precipitated a huge loss of faith in the CCP and must have led many to question whether the party was still fit to run the country at all. As Harding concludes:

> The fact that so calamitous an event was launched in the name of Marxism served to undermine their faith in ideology, and the inability of the Party to prevent the Cultural Revolution served to weaken their confidence in the existing political system.
>
> (1997: 245)

# 4   Redefining party legitimacy

## The succession to Mao and the rise of Deng

The Cultural Revolution was an unmitigated disaster for the CCP. A campaign which began as a bid by Mao to roll back the tide of revisionism and resurrect party legitimacy succeeded only in decimating the institutions of party and state and damaging the party's credibility almost irreparably, especially amongst the young. As a first step towards repairing the harm inflicted on the party, the leadership needed to reunite and oversee a new era of political and socio-economic stability. But this did not happen. In the years leading up to Mao's death in 1976, China underwent yet another period of political upheaval characterized by bitter infighting amongst rival factions of the party elite. In the meantime, any concern for the legitimation of party rule was forgotten.

That the leadership was afflicted in this way was not altogether surprising. Although Mao was firmly at the helm when the Cultural Revolution was formally abandoned in 1969, the struggle for succession was already well under way. Initially, it was expected that Lin Biao would succeed Mao as paramount leader following his anointment at the Ninth National Party Congress in April 1969. Yet just two years later, having marginalized himself completely from Mao, Lin was dead under highly suspicious circumstances. The most prominent of the remaining contenders were the "radicals" led by Jiang Qing and her Shanghai clique (see Figure 4) who wielded enormous and often arbitrary power during the Cultural Revolution as part of the CRG and who appeared well placed to force home their advantage. Known as the Gang of Four (a term coined disparagingly by Mao) and also including Yao Wenyuan, Zhang Chunqiao and the relatively unknown Wang Hongwen, the Gang represented a radical form of Maoism and pledged to continue with the extremist policies of the Cultural Revolution after Mao's death.

At the other end of the political spectrum were the "survivors" (see Figure 4), comprising Zhou Enlai and a handful of veteran military officials who survived the Cultural Revolution unscathed. Although loyal to Mao, Zhou and his allies stood for a much more moderate alternative founded on economic reconstruction under the new banner of the Four Modernizations (in agriculture, industry, defence and science and technology) and the rehabilitation of senior cadres who were purged during the Cultural Revolution. As we shall see, however, Mao surprised everyone by opting for a virtual unknown as his successor in the form of Hua Guofeng, one of several "beneficiaries" of the Cultural Revolution

**Paramount Leader: Mao Zedong**

| Radicals | Beneficiaries | Survivors |
|---|---|---|
| Jiang Qing | Hua Guofeng | Zhou Enlai |
| Yao Wenyuan | Wang Dongxing | Zhu De |
| Zhang Chunqiao | Chen Xilian | Ye Jianying |
| Wang Hongwen | Wu De | Dong Biwu |
| Kang Sheng | Ji Dengkui | Li Xiannian |

*Figure 4*  The post-Lin Biao CCP leadership.

(see Figure 4) and a man who Mao felt could be relied upon to pursue a Maoist agenda without resorting to the dangerous extremism of the Gang of Four.

Yet, the emergence of Hua did not bring an end to the succession crisis. Another contender was Zhou Enlai's protege Deng Xiaoping who, after being purged from office in 1968, was reinstated in 1973 only to be purged again in 1976. In 1977, Deng returned to the leadership and within 18 months he eclipsed Hua as paramount leader. Although Deng's defeat of Hua was testament to his superior qualities as a political tactician and the superior strength of his charismatic legitimacy, Deng's popularity derived primarily from his far reaching proposals to reform the economy in an effort to raise individual income and improve living standards. Sensing the time was right, Deng moved to re-invent party legitimacy along economic lines by appealing directly to the socio-economic aspirations of the much maligned Chinese masses.

## The fall of Lin Biao: the 'uncharismatic' leader

The fate of Liu Shaoqi during the Cultural Revolution showed how the promise of political succession to Mao was something of a poisoned chalice. In 1959, Liu replaced Mao as state Chairman and it was widely assumed that Liu would succeed Mao as paramount leader when the time came. Within a few years, however, Liu was out of favour following his refusal to adhere to Mao's radical policy initiatives and by 1969 the venomous forces that Mao unleashed brought about Liu's ignominious death. Lin Biao, Mao's second chosen successor, experienced much the same fate only more quickly. Anointed as Mao's heir in 1969, Lin soon found himself frozen out of the central political arena and by September 1971 he too was dead.

The cause of Lin's rapid fall from grace was due mainly to acute disagreements with Mao over the reconstruction of the state and the direction of Chinese foreign policy. This is dealt with adequately in other texts and it is not my intention to analyse the issues here (Bridgham 1973, MacFarquhar 1997, Jin Qiu 1999). Of more relevance to our discussion of legitimacy is the clear relationship between

Lin's failure to succeed Mao as paramount leader and his lack of charismatic legitimacy, most notably amongst his colleagues. Although Lin, like Mao, was acknowledged as one of the principal military strategists of the civil war, Lin's standing amongst his contemporaries paled in comparison to that enjoyed by Mao. We saw in Chapter 1 how Mao's charismatic authority within the leadership stemmed mainly from his ability to excel at times of crisis, as demonstrated, for example, by his stubborn resistance of Soviet control at the 1935 Zunyi conference. Lin was not able to draw on the "crisis factor" (perhaps unfairly given his central role in the victory civil war) and whilst attempts were made during the Cultural Revolution to promote a cult of Lin (for example, the Little Red Book contained a picture of Lin on the page immediately after the page with Mao's picture on it), Lin was a deeply unpopular figure within the leadership. Anecdotal evidence suggests that an authentic Little Red Book can be identified as such if it has the second page, the one featuring Lin, ripped out. This is because after Lin was accused of plotting to kill Mao (see shortly) every owner of a Little Red Book was encouraged to tear out Lin's page in outrage.

Why was Lin so unpopular? The Gang of Four disliked Lin because he was too close to Mao and constituted a threat to their own political ambitions. Zhou Enlai and the "survivors" disliked Lin (for same reason that they disliked the Gang) because of his unbridled radicalism and the implications this would have for a post-Mao era led by Lin. Deng Xiaoping and other purged returnees disliked Lin for the role he played in their downfall. Given this absence of legitimacy amongst his leadership colleagues, Lin realized (quite rightly) that without the full support of Mao his political career was doomed. Once Lin lost that patronage, he quickly disappeared out of sight.

The circumstances surrounding Lin's death in September 1971 are far from clear. According to the official line, when Lin realized that he had lost Mao's backing he and his military allies (e.g. Wu Faxian and Huang Yongsheng) plotted to assassinate Mao and set up a rival regime at Lin's stronghold in Guangdong province. When the plan was allegedly foiled by Mao and Zhou Enlai, Lin and his family attempted to escape by air to the Soviet Union only for the plane to crash in the Mongolian mountains after running out of fuel.

The official story leaves several questions unanswered. Why would Lin flee to the Soviet Union, a country whose political system he had denounced for years, especially when he already had a power base in Guangdong? How can we explain the Soviet medical reports which show that the remains of all those on board Lin's plane were female? Finally, is it really conceivable that a plane carrying China's Minister of Defence would not have enough fuel in it before it took off? We may never discover the real cause of Lin's death, but the official line seems highly implausible. An alternative theory is that Lin's considerable power base in the military and the party represented an increasing threat to Mao's own position. As Mao and Lin pulled in opposite policy directions, Mao feared that after his death Lin would steer China back towards the chaos of the Cultural Revolution. Consequently, Lin and his family members were secretly arrested by the security forces and executed. This might explain why the news of Lin's death was not officially disclosed until 1972. It took the leadership this long to think up such an elaborate cover story! Yao Ming-le (1983) probably goes a bit too far, however, suggesting that Lin was murdered (on Mao's direct instruction) by a rocket which was launched when Lin was driving home in his car!

## Legitimacy suspended: the post-Lin succession crisis

With Lin gone, the battle to succeed Mao now appeared to involve a head-to-head between Jiang Qing's "radicals" and Zhou Enlai's "survivors". In an effort to eclipse Jiang, Zhou succeeded in securing the rehabilitation of several high-ranking party officials (e.g. Tan Zhenlin and Li Jingquan) who had been purged during the Cultural Revolution and who were staunchly opposed to Jiang's policies. The most senior of these returnees was Deng Xiaoping who survived the Cultural Revolution (with the help of certain military allies) during which time he was made to work as a part-time fitter in a Jiangxi tractor factory. Deng was restored as Vice-Premier in April 1973. Less than five years after being purged as "the number two person in authority taking the capitalist road", Deng was back, if only for a while.

If the rehabilitation of Deng Xiaoping was a boost to the "survivors" then this was more than countered by the rapid ascendancy of the radical Wang Hongwen who was promoted to Vice-Chairman of the CCP in August 1973. Like several others, Wang rose to national prominence during the Cultural Revolution. In 1966, Wang was employed in a modest capacity as a Shanghai factory worker but after catching Mao's eye as an adept labour activist in the Shanghai Commune, Wang was catapulted into the central party apparatus within six years. Youthful (37 years old in 1973) and genuinely proletarian, Mao saw Wang as a viable alternative to the other radical members of the party leadership. Furthermore, Wang was untainted by the destruction of the Cultural Revolution and, for the moment at least, he was independent of any leadership faction, although he was soon to become labelled as a member of the Gang of Four (MacFarquhar 1997: 281).

The simultaneous elevation of political rivals such as Wang Hongwen and Deng Xiaoping shows just how polarized the party leadership was in the early 1970s. This was further exemplified by the fact that several of Deng's leadership colleagues in 1973 had only a few years earlier driven him from office. Although Wang himself was not involved in Deng's purge in 1968, Jiang Qing, Yao Wenyuan and Zhang Chunqiao had all played a part in the demise of a man with whom they were now obliged to work. Unsurprisingly, the atmosphere within the leadership was highly charged to say the least and co-operation between rival factions proved to be entirely unattainable.

The political uncertainty of this period was further accentuated by the new official line on Lin Biao. Given Lin's dishonourable demise, the party could no longer portray him as a great socialist as it had done during the Cultural Revolution. Instead, Lin was depicted as a rightist who had opposed socialism and opposed the party. But how could the party explain such a radical turnaround? How could Lin move from one side of the political spectrum to the other almost overnight? The answer was simple: Lin had only *pretended* to be a socialist when in fact all along he was a rightist. As the new party line insisted, Lin was "left in form but right in essence" and during the Cultural Revolution he had "waved the red flag to oppose the red flag".

The rationale behind this incredulous claim was twofold. First, the party needed to devise a way of avoiding any further embarrassment to Mao. Whatever the truth was behind Lin's death, the amended official line on Lin as "anti-party" implied that Mao had committed a gross error of judgement in allying himself to the former Minister of Defence. By portraying Lin as someone who deceived Mao by faking his socialist credentials, Mao could justifiably be excused for making such a mistake. In other words, Lin was such an adept trickster that *anyone* would have been taken in by him. Second, Lin's fall had serious implications for Jiang Qing and the Gang of Four. Since both Lin and Jiang occupied the radical left of Chinese politics, Lin's fall meant that he had seriously tainted Jiang's own political credentials as a fellow leftist (and a former ally). Once again, by depicting Lin as "right" rather than "left", the official line put clear water between Lin and Jiang. Ironically (and confusingly), after their arrest in October 1976, the Gang of Four were also officially depicted as erstwhile rightists. This enabled new paramount leader Hua Guofeng to pursue a left-wing policy agenda without being tarred with the same radical brush as the disgraced Gang.

Exactly what political benefit could be gained by this remarkable *volte face* is difficult to decipher. Whilst the revised position on Lin was specifically designed for public consumption, in reality it must have left the public feeling both confused and disillusioned. After years of being told that Lin was the deserved successor to Mao they were subsequently told that he was in fact a traitor who had been out all along to betray the Chinese revolution once he got to power. In this context, the masses must have wondered whether they could trust *any* party leader anymore. Would it later be revealed that Zhou Enlai was a traitor or even Mao himself? Moreover, if Mao and the party leadership could be so easily fooled by Lin Biao's alleged deception then what did that ultimately say about the party's ability and indeed *right* to rule? Many people in China were already alienated from politics and the party following the calamity of the Cultural Revolution. The ludicrous reinvention of the official line on Lin Biao must have augmented this process.

The main battleground in the struggle to succeed Mao was the Chinese media. In keeping with the Chinese communist tradition of elite point-scoring through historical analogy, a series of esoteric academic articles were published in the national press in which the radical left attempted to discredit their reformist opponents and initiate a political campaign against them. The most renowned of these attempts culminated in the Criticize Lin Biao Criticize Confucius Campaign launched in January 1974. Although the relationship between Lin and Confucius was less than obvious, Mao decreed in 1973 that they could be criticized together and this provided Jiang Qing with an opportunity to attempt to purge Zhou Enlai. Without naming him directly, the new campaign portrayed Zhou as a Confucian restorationist by drawing an analogy with his namesake the Duke of Zhou, a

Confucian statesman. Duke Zhou was famed for his efforts to reunite China during the tumultuous Warring States period (475–221 BC) and for his calls to rehabilitate those who had been driven from office so that China could ultimately return to the golden age of feudalism. Criticizing a famous Confucianist for his restorationism meant that Zhou Enlai could be criticized as someone who was likewise attempting to restore revisionists (i.e. purged colleagues) to the party apparatus and return China to the feudalism of the pre-revolutionary era (Goldman 1981: 166–76). The implication was arcane to say the least, and combined with the growing reluctance of the population to embark on yet another political campaign, the Criticize Lin Biao Criticize Confucius Campaign failed to gather any real momentum.

Soon after the campaign subsided, Zhou succumbed to the reality of his impending death (he was dying of cancer) and in June 1974 he gave up his duties as Premier in order to undergo major surgery. This left Mao with the difficult decision of who would replace him. The obvious candidate from the radical left was Wang Hongwen but within months of his promotion to the centre, Mao realized that Wang not only lacked the aptitude for high political office but was also too easily manipulated by the other members of the Gang of Four, none of whom could be trusted with the mantle of the leadership because of their factional activities during the succession crisis. As such, in a move that exemplified the paucity of viable candidates to lead the party, Mao was forced to opt for his erstwhile nemesis Deng Xiaoping who he made First Vice-Premier and Vice-Chairman of the CCP in January 1975 (MacFarquhar 1997: 288–96).

Deng's incumbency was fraught with difficulties from the very outset. Surrounded by hostile political opponents and without his key ally Zhou Enlai, Deng was stymied at every instance. For example, when Deng suggested that economic output could be increased by importing foreign technology, introducing material incentives for workers and focusing on expertise at the managerial level rather than class background, Jiang publicly dismissed the idea as a manifestation of Deng's bourgeois restorationism. Deng was further thwarted by Mao himself who, whilst publicly supporting Deng's economic measures, actively encouraged Zhang Chunqiao and Yao Wenyuan to develop a standpoint that was critical of Deng's proposals. This allowed them to begin a campaign against right deviationism that quickly led to Deng's second purge in eight years.

The succession crisis came to a head in 1976, the year in which both Zhou and Mao died. Zhou was admired throughout the country as Mao's urbane understudy who had enhanced China's reputation abroad and (arguably) did much at home to soften the impact of radical activities during the Cultural Revolution. (Later research suggests that Zhou was actually quite radical during the Cultural Revolution. It is thought, for example, that he facilitated the national publication of *Hai Rui Dismissed From Office* and that he defended the activities of the CRG until early 1967.) Zhou's death precipitated a spontaneous outbreak of national mourning. During the annual Sweeping of the Graves Festival in April 1976, millions of admirers poured into Tiananmen Square to lay wreaths in Zhou's memory at the Revolutionary Heroes Monument, a symbolic act of respect reserved only for revered individuals (Garside 1981). When the public were banned from any further expressions of grief, a mass demonstration broke out in protest at the radicalism of the Gang of Four which by implication supported the moderate stance of Deng Xiaoping. The unknown Hua Guofeng, as acting state Chairman, gave the order for the military to disperse the demonstrators and at Mao's behest Deng was blamed for encouraging the allegedly counter-revolutionary Tiananmen demonstrations. Removed from all his official posts, Deng retreated to military safety in the south, albeit temporarily.

The fall of the Gang of Four came less than one month after Mao's death in September 1976. According to MacFarquhar (1997: 307), the Gang's best course of action was probably to retreat to their power base in Shanghai where they could have re-grouped to consider their options. But the Gang were accustomed to the free rein they had enjoyed during the Cultural Revolution and were not prepared to bow to a relative novice in the form of Hua Guofeng, the new incumbent head of the party, government and military (as discussed shortly). Instead, they committed the tactical error of going all out for power almost from the second that Mao died (It is thought, for example, that during a Politburo meeting held just a few hours after Mao's death, Jiang was already agitating for the expulsion of Deng Xiaoping from the party, notwithstanding that Mao's funeral arrangement had not been finalized!). With Mao out of the way, the Gang hurriedly published a series of press articles in which they asserted their right to succeed Mao and cast doubt over Hua's credentials as the future paramount leader of China. They also sought to undermine Hua's authority by setting up independent decision making committees and trying to dominate proceedings during party meetings. Finally, when rumours surfaced that the Gang were arming a militia in Shanghai (allegedly comprising 100,000 people) Hua acted decisively. On 6 October, he ordered the arrest of the Gang of Four on charges of conspiracy to ferment civil war and on planning a coup d'etat. This signalled the end of the Cultural Revolution (Onate 1978).

## Hua who and why Hua?

At this juncture, it is not unreasonable to ask who was Hua Guofeng and how did he manage to succeed Mao as paramount leader where others more senior and more experienced than him had failed? Mao had known Hua for some years. Posted to Xiangtan in 1949 (Mao's native district in Hunan province) Hua endeared himself to Mao by personally overseeing a number of infrastructure projects, including an irrigation works in Mao's native village of Shaoshan. In 1970, Hua was promoted to First Secretary of the Hunan provincial party committee and three years later at the Tenth National Party Congress, he became a member of the Politburo. In 1975, Hua was appointed Minister of Public Security and it was from this position that he climbed to the very apex of political power (Oksenberg and Sai-cheung Yeung 1977).

To some degree, Hua's political ascendancy was attributable to luck; he was invariably in the right place at the right time, or perhaps more accurately not in the wrong place at the wrong time. So, for example, at the height of the

Cultural Revolution in early 1967, Hua was too junior in provincial party status to be the focus of Red Guard hostility. Several of his seniors, however, were not so fortunate and Hua found this to his advantage as their demise left an opening for him to become head of the Hunan party apparatus. This new-found seniority left Hua well placed for further promotion after the death of Lin Biao since the removal of Lin's allies created a number of vacancies within the central party hierarchy. As Mao cast around for a viable successor in the mid-1970s, Hua appeared to him to be the least of high risk of all the candidates.

Following Zhou's death, the most obvious candidate to succeed Mao as paramount leader was Deng Xiaoping. But Mao had grave doubts about Deng's commitment to the radical Maoist cause and feared (quite rightly) that if Deng was at the helm in the post-Mao era he would seek to unravel Mao's radical legacy. Wang Hongwen was an inappropriate choice for the reasons already discussed and the other three members of the Gang of Four were despised by the public for their extremism during the Cultural Revolution. Handing over power to one of the Gang would in all probability have sparked a national outcry well beyond that seen in April 1976 which could jeopardize Mao's political agenda and the incumbency of the CCP. In the end, therefore, Mao went for the compromise candidate, a man who stood somewhere in between the two extremes of the Gang of Four and Deng Xiaoping and someone who Mao hoped would feel duty-bound to repay Mao for his patronage by continuing indefinitely with the Maoist tradition.

Hua was only too happy to oblige and following his assumption of Mao's posts as Chairman of the party and the CMC and Zhou's post as Premier, Hua appeared to be in an insurmountable position of power. One man who had other ideas, however, was Deng Xiaoping and within months of Hua's trio of appointments, Deng emerged to challenge this position of apparent supremacy. It is to this period that we must now turn our attention in order to analyse how Deng's legitimacy and Hua's lack thereof was central to the outcome of the power struggle between the two men.

## Hua versus Deng: the battle for traditional legitimacy

We saw in Chapter 1 how the Weberian notion of traditional legitimacy was especially pertinent to the early post-revolutionary period when the party attempted to enhance its popularity by borrowing heavily from certain time-honoured Confucian customs. During the Hua–Deng leadership struggle, traditional legitimacy took a slightly different form as both men promised to continue with certain Maoist rather than Confucian traditions into the post-Mao era. Although the failure of the Cultural Revolution cast a huge shadow over the methods and wisdom of Maoism, Mao remained extremely popular amongst many sections of the population. In this context, both Hua and Deng realized that in order to fortify their own individual legitimacy in the battle to succeed Mao, they would need to draw on Mao's political legacy. The difficult question was finding aspects of this legacy that were still considered credible.

## Hua's strategy

Hua was intrinsically bound to the more radical form of Maoism and as a "beneficiary" of the Cultural Revolution he was obliged to remain loyal to this most radical of Maoist campaigns. What else could he do? As MacFarquhar explains:

> To disavow the Cultural Revolution would be to undermine the position of the man who had chosen him as his successor, and indeed to negate the whole period whose upheavals had permitted Hua to rise from relative obscurity to his current eminence.
>
> (1997: 312)

As a result, whilst Hua appealed for calm and political unity in the new post-Mao era, he vowed to continue with the radicalism that epitomized the Cultural Revolution. As he explained at the Eleventh National Party Congress in August 1977:

> Smashing the 'Gang of Four' is yet another signal victory in the Great Proletarian Cultural Revolution. The victorious conclusion of the first Great Proletarian Cultural Revolution certainly does not mean the end of class struggle or of the continued revolution under the dictatorship of the proletariat. Political revolutions in the nature of the Cultural Revolution will take place many times in the future. *We must follow Chairman Mao's teachings and continue the revolution under the dictatorship of the proletariat to the end.* [my emphasis].
>
> (Saich 2001: 43)

Hua's economic pronouncements were equally Maoist. Recalling the formula used during the Great Leap Forward, Hua proposed a strategy of reliance on communal farming and mass mobilization to achieve ambitious production targets such as a 40 per cent increase in grain output. In industry Hua adopted a new Ten Year Plan (1976–85) aimed at increasing steel output by 150 per cent and oil output by over 200 per cent. This would include establishing 120 major industrial projects and 14 new heavy industry plants. However, in contrast to Mao's favoured model of economic self-reliance, Hua preferred to look abroad for investment by encouraging imports of modern technology (Saich 2001: 49–50).

Hua undertook a number of other measures in an effort to enhance his legitimacy as the true standard-bearer of Maoism. Just two days after the arrest of the Gang of Four, Hua announced that he would personally edit a fifth volume of the *Selected Works of Mao Zedong* and that he was arranging for Mao's memory to be honoured by housing the late Chairman in a giant mausoleum at the south end of Tiananmen Square (which is still standing today). In so doing, Hua contradicted a decision made by the Central Committee in March 1949 prohibiting the public glorification of CCP leaders by entombing them in mausolea, celebrating their birthdays or using their names for places or streets. Working closely with his main ally Wang Dongxing (Mao's former bodyguard), Hua adopted a slogan which he hoped would bind him permanently to Mao's legacy: "whatever policy Chairman Mao decided upon, we shall resolutely defend; whatever directives Chairman Mao issued, we shall steadfastly obey". Finally, just in case anyone secretly doubted Mao's faith in the new paramount leader, Hua declared that during a private meeting between the two men, Mao had handed Hua a note on which he had written the legitimizing words: "with you in charge, I am at ease". Although news of the note was widely propagated by the national press, there is much doubt as to its authenticity.

### Deng's strategy

Just as Hua associated himself with the radical form of Maoism, so Deng embraced an altogether more moderate version. Following his reinstatement to all leadership posts in July 1977 (MacFarquhar 1997: 312–16), Deng emerged as a fervent exponent of Seek Truth from Facts, a slogan drawn from an essay that Mao wrote as a young man. In it, Mao emphasized the importance of linking theory (i.e. ideology) with practice so that if a particular theory did not prove consonant with the practical realities of the day it was necessary to take a more flexible and pragmatic approach to the application of that theory and possibly even to revise it. In this way, policy issues were to be governed less by rigid adherence to dogma and more by practical considerations.

Tactically, the adoption of the young Mao's Seek Truth principle was a stroke of genius since it allowed Deng to challenge Hua's authority as Mao's chosen successor without appearing to be anti-Mao. Quite the contrary. As Deng looked for support in his quest to oust Hua he argued that Seek Truth from Facts was a return to the *best* traditions of Maoism and the only genuine way of understanding and applying Mao's ideas to Chinese conditions. Remarkably, Deng was trying to play Hua at his own game by presenting *himself* as the true inheritor of the Maoist legacy. This was an audacious claim by someone who Mao disliked intensely and who had been purged by Mao on two occasions.

## Deng ascendant

On his return to the leadership in 1977 Deng found that his central support base was tenuous given that Hua had surrounded himself with political allies. For the time being, therefore, Deng was forced to compromise by promising to support Hua's leadership and by endorsing, albeit tepidly, certain radical Maoist concepts such as continuous revolution and class struggle. Behind the scenes, however, Deng searched for a way to undermine Hua's authority from outside the established boundaries of the party leadership and he eventually found a vehicle for his views in the national media. On 11 May 1978, the *Guangming Daily* published an article entitled Practice is the Sole Criterion of Truth which applauded the common sense approach of Seek Truth from Facts and impliedly criticized Hua's stance that the truth derived from whatever Mao decreed. As Deng and his allies had anticipated, the article was subsequently published throughout China, causing considerable embarrassment to Hua and ensuring that Deng's reformist ideas were placed firmly on the national agenda. Deng then exploited this publicity by organizing a series of regional work conferences where he derided Hua's slavish adherence to radical Maoism and reiterated his own pragmatic application of Mao's ideas.

Within a few months Deng secured the support of almost all of China's regional leaders, both from the party and the military. Although the PLA had relinquished much of the power it enjoyed during the Cultural Revolution, it remained a powerful force in Chinese politics which meant that acquiring the support of the military was essential for any aspiring leader. Central military leaders also began to support Deng's campaign, most significantly Li Xiannian and Ye Jianying, both of whom were senior members of the PSC. During Hua's battle with the Gang of Four immediately after Mao's death, Li and Ye had thrown their weight behind Hua's leadership and acted decisively in supporting the arrest of the Gang. However, as regional military leaders began to move towards the Deng camp, so Li and Ye followed suit. Given their seniority and the strength of their political support, this was a serious blow to Hua's future as China's paramount leader.

The watershed came at the Third Plenum of the Eleventh Central Committee in December 1978 which saw the promotion (and in some cases reinstatement) of a number of Deng's supporters. Chen Yun, Deng's most loyal ally, returned to his post as a PSC member and Vice-Chairman of the party whilst Deng Yingchao (Zhou Enlai's widow), Wang Zhen and the pro-reform Hu Yaobang were all appointed to the Politburo. Combined with the appointment of nine Dengists to the Central Committee and the removal of Wang Dongxing as head of the Central Committee General Office (the equivalent of the Secretariat), the Third Plenum tipped the scales of power decisively in Deng's favour. With Deng's allies in the majority, delegates to the Plenum abruptly turned on Hua, voting to abandon his neo-Maoist position on continuous revolution and class struggle and denigrating his "whateverist" approach to Mao's political legacy. The Plenum also abandoned Hua's proposed Ten-Year Plan and from here it was just a matter of time before Hua was removed from power altogether. As Saich (2001: 50) notes, China had neither the money to pay for these projects nor the skills base to manage them and as a result of Hua's policy suffered a massive growth in its trade deficit with developed countries from US$ 1.2 billion in 1977 to US$ 4.5 billion in 1979.

## Utilizing popular legitimacy: Democracy Wall

Although Deng's ascendancy was principally attributable to the depth of support that he enjoyed amongst provincial leaders and senior officials, he also benefited from the support of China's literary intellectuals. Vilified at regular intervals under Mao, writers were invariably prohibited from expressing themselves freely and were restricted instead to the publication of socialist realist material which focused exclusively on the virtues of Chinese socialism. The brief lapse in political control during the Hua–Deng struggle gave writers a rare opportunity to escape from these narrow confines and for the first time since the Hundred Flowers scores of books and articles were published which moved away from the rigid Yanan prescriptions that literature and art should "serve politics and the people". Instead, attention focused on the traumas of China's recent past as writers described the personal suffering endured during the Maoist heyday of political campaigns and mass purges, especially during the Cultural Revolution. This signalled the beginning of a new genre in Chinese literature appropriately referred to as "scar literature" or the "literature of the wounded" (Barme 1997).

By articulating the misery that characterized the Cultural Revolution, Chinese literary intellectuals legitimized Deng's cause in two interrelated ways. First, without mentioning his name directly, they besmirched the political reputation of Hua Guofeng who was intrinsically associated with the ill-fated movement. As we saw earlier, not only did Hua's political career benefit from the Cultural Revolution, but he also continued to espouse the principles underlying the campaign after Mao's death by which time most of the country had turned its back on the whole harrowing period. Second, this bolstered Deng's image as someone who could bring economic growth and political stability to China after decades of turmoil and uncertainty.

Deng also benefited from the support of China's urban work force who formed part of a new movement that became known as Democracy Wall. With party members gathering for the landmark Third Plenum in December 1978, posters began appearing on walls in central Beijing expressing candid opinions on a number of sensitive issues. As scholars such as Goodman (1981) and Brodsgaard (1981) have shown, the Cultural Revolution was again the focal point and Mao was criticized in name for masterminding the campaign and for lending his support to the Gang of Four. Other posters concentrated on the redundant policies of Hua's "whateverist" faction, depicting Hua as a puppet controlled by Mao from beyond the grave. Another popular theme was the optimism symbolized by the theory of the Four Modernizations developed by Zhou Enlai, and several posters endorsed Deng Xiaoping as Zhou's natural successor as Premier.

Yet, in a manner reminiscent of the Hundred Flowers over 20 years earlier, some Democracy Wall activists went beyond the boundaries of permissible expression. Having dealt with the injustices of the past, they began to explore contemporary injustices such as the absence of multi-party democracy and a system of human rights. This precipitated the formation of a number of unofficial political discussion groups and human rights journals. A leading figure in these new developments was Wei Jingsheng, an electrician who worked at Beijing Zoo. Wei was editor of a journal called *Exploration* and in it he published an article which implored China to embrace democracy as a "fifth modernization". Wei also launched a personal attack on Deng Xiaoping, rebuking him for his lack of genuine commitment to the principles of democracy and rights:

> After the arrest of the Gang of Four, the people eagerly hoped that Vice-Chairman Deng Xiaoping, who might possibly 'restore capitalism', would rise up again like a magnificent banner. Finally he did regain his position in

the central leadership. How excited the people felt! How inspired they were! But alas, the old political system so despised by the people remains unchanged.

(Wei Jingsheng 1997: 199–212).

It was at this point that Deng turned against the Democracy Wall activists. Emerging triumphant after the events of the Third Plenum, Deng judged that the movement had served its purpose in promoting his policies against Hua Guofeng. On Deng's orders, the posters on Democracy Wall were taken down and the movement was hastily suppressed. Wei Jingsheng was arrested and sentenced to a 15 year jail term. Like Mao before him, Deng showed that he could be ruthless in the face of dissent.

## Hua defeated

The Third Plenum was the beginning of the end for Hua Guofeng (Fontana 1982). Outnumbered in the leadership by Deng's supporters and with no backing at all for his ill-conceived economic policies, Hua's political career was in a process of inexorable decline. Deng moved to consolidate his advantage by appointing more of his allies to senior party and government posts. At the Fourth Plenum of the Eleventh Central Committee in September 1979, a number of former Central Committee members who had been purged during the Cultural Revolution were restored to their posts, replacing those who had benefited from the movement. Of further significance were two appointments to the Politburo: Peng Zhen, the former Mayor of Beijing, and Zhao Ziyang, head of the Sichuan provincial party. Peng's appointment marked the return of one of the first high-profile casualties of the Cultural Revolution whilst Zhao was promoted on the strength of his reputation as an economic reformer. Along with Hu Yaobang, Zhao came to characterize the dynamism of economic reform in the 1980s, pushing the reforms well beyond the limited parameters set by Peng Zhen and Chen Yun. Hu and Zhao were also anointed (on different occasions) as Deng's chosen successors, only to be subsequently fired from their posts for dissenting from the party line (Hu in 1987 and Zhao in 1989). As we shall see in Chapter 5, the poisoned chalice in Chinese politics known as political succession duly passed from the Mao era to the Deng era.

Deng's ascendancy continued into 1980. At the Fifth Plenum of the Eleventh Central Committee in February, Hua's main allies Wang Dongxing, Chen Xilian, Wu De and Ji Dengkui, (referred to as the "little gang of four"), were all fired from their party and government positions and Hu Yaobang and Zhao Ziyang were both appointed to the PSC. Hu also became General Secretary of the CCP, a post vacated by Deng when he was purged during the Cultural Revolution but subsequently resurrected so that Hu could directly rival Hua as Chairman of the party. The Secretariat was reconstituted (led by Hu in his capacity as General Secretary) and almost its entire membership was staffed with Deng supporters. In April, the State Council was cleansed of "whateverists" following the dismissal of Chen Xilian and Ji Dengkui (both Vice-Premiers) and in August Zhao Ziyang formally replaced Hua Guofeng as Premier.

The way was now open for Deng to launch his final assault on Hua. At a Politburo meeting in December 1980 Hua's political record was mercilessly dissected. Although Hua was commended for authorizing the arrest of the Gang of Four, he was criticized for persisting with the inflammatory language of the Cultural Revolution after Mao's death, for obstructing the rehabilitation of its victims, for purging Deng Xiaoping in 1976 and for stubbornly adhering to the indictment of the Tiananmen incident as "counter-revolutionary". Hua was also criticized for the rash decision to construct the Mao mausoleum and for his flawed economic policies. In the light of these damning conclusions, Hua attempted to resign his remaining posts as party and CMC Chairman but in an effort to demonstrate a new commitment to legal rational procedures, Hua was made to wait to be formally removed from these posts. In the meantime, Hu Yaobang took over Hua's duties as party Chairman until the post was abolished in 1982 whilst Deng assumed Hua's responsibilities as Chairman of the CMC.

So why did Hua lose so much power so quickly? If we examine this question within the context of legitimacy it is apparent that Hua never really enjoyed the right *type* of power. Although Hua appeared to be in an unassailable position as leader of China's three main institutions, in practice he found that institutional power did not automatically confer legitimacy. In particular, Hua lacked a vital legitimizing attribute that his predecessor had enjoyed so much of, namely charisma. This was not for want of trying. In the months after Mao's death, Hua went to great lengths to develop his very own cult of personality. So, for example, a plethora of pamphlets and books were published which greatly embellished Hua's revolutionary activities in the 1930s and 1940s, exaggerated his personal and political relationship with Mao and endowed him with many qualities that he simply did not possess. In addition, scores of pictures and wall posters appeared featuring Chairman Hua as China's new paramount leader. In some of these posters Hua stood side-by-side with Mao in the hope that some of Mao's charismatic authority might rub-off on him. In those posters in which Hua stood alone, he often adopted the same pose as Mao and sometimes even the same hairstyle!

We have seen in previous chapters just how useful Mao's cult of personality was for enhancing his charismatic legitimacy amongst the people, and given time Hua too might have benefited in the same way. Maybe with enough propaganda, Hua could have "persuaded" the public that he was the rightful new leader of China. Within the party leadership, however, Hua, like Lin Biao, lacked the personal charisma enjoyed by Mao. In contrast to Mao, Hua cut a rather ordinary figure as a man with few revolutionary credentials who had abruptly risen to national attention after an unexceptional political career in Hunan province. In this context, Hua was incapable of inspiring the respect and admiration required to convince his contemporaries that he was the natural successor to Mao. Ironically, it was the very reputation of the man who had handed Hua power that contributed to Hua's failure to establish himself amongst his leadership colleagues.

But the demise of Hua Guofeng was not just about his lack of charismatic authority. It was also caused by his attempt to pursue a radical Maoist agenda that in truth than no-one really wanted anymore. Whilst it made sense for Hua to utilize Mao's legacy in his power struggle with Deng, Hua associated himself with the wrong type of Maoism. The 1976 Tiananmen demonstrations showed just how unpopular radical Maoism had become and subsequent reports of industrial sabotage and rural unrest suggested that many people remained deeply unhappy with the immediate post-Mao situation. The popular feeling was that China needed a decisive break from its recent radical past not a continuation of it. The only person who could bring this about was Deng Xiaoping.

## The charismatic legitimacy of Deng Xiaoping

Deng's emergence as China's new paramount leader began a process of steady decline for Maoism. Although Deng paid lip-service to the "greatness" of the late Chairman, he quickly distanced himself both from Mao's turbulent political legacy and from his failed economic policies. Yet, the manner in which Deng secured his succession to Mao showed that he and Mao had at least one thing in common; they were both expert political tacticians. Indeed, in outwitting the luckless Hua Guofeng, Deng employed a degree of cunning and political guile that would have had Mao applauding from his mausoleum. As already discussed, in launching his political comeback Deng shrewdly associated himself with one of Mao's more pragmatic and credible ideas in the form of Seek Truth from Facts and this put Deng in the dual position of being both a Mao supporter *and* an advocate of reform and change. Likewise, when Deng's power base in the party leadership was too weak to launch a direct attack on Hua, Deng used the classic Maoist technique of building a support base *outside* the central party apparatus in order to put pressure on the centre. Finally, just as Mao had done with the Red Guards in the 1960s, Deng formed a convenient coalition with the Democracy Wall movement only to break this coalition once the movement had served its purpose.

We shall see shortly how the legitimacy of the new Deng regime was based primarily on a performance based platform of economic reform which brought with it the prospect of material incentives and an improvement in personal wealth and living standards. Before we turn to this discussion it is important to identify another key source of Deng's legitimacy, his charisma. The extent of Deng's charismatic authority was much more apparent in his relationship with his leadership colleagues (and other party members) than with the masses, mainly because of his determination not to cultivate a cult of Deng. The source of this charisma derived from his unquestionable resilience and strength of character. Using Teiwes' "crisis" theory, Deng showed that when the odds were stacked against him he would invariably come out fighting. Captured and beaten by Red Guards during the Cultural Revolution, Deng lived to tell the tale where others (e.g. Liu Shaoqi) had perished. After six years labouring in a tractor factory (albeit only in a part-time capacity), Deng returned to the leadership in 1973 where he managed to hold his own in an intensely hostile political environment. Purged again in 1976 as a right-deviationist, Deng again disappeared from public view but a year later he was back at the centre, plotting the eventual downfall of Hua Guofeng. Deng's ability to endure the wrath of the Red Guards, the Gang of Four and Mao Zedong and still come out victorious revealed a formidable inner strength and resolve and it was this that marked Deng out amongst his colleagues as a man of exceptional quality.

But like Mao, Deng was also prepared to exploit his charismatic authority to get what he wanted. As Mao had done on several occasions during his political career, Deng used his prestige within the party as a way of building up support for his ideas from outside the central party apparatus in order to then force the centre into line. Mao used this technique during the mid-1950s debate over rural collectivization and then again during the Cultural Revolution. Deng used the same technique in his bid to overthrow Hua Guofeng. As we saw earlier, in order to compensate for his minority position in the leadership, Deng looked to the provinces to build a support base, giving a series of high-profile speeches in order to get his message across. Although Deng's promise of a wealthier and stronger China was no doubt appealing to his audience, it was also the sheer presence of Deng Xiaoping in person that helped win the support of provincial leaders.

In circumventing the party centre in this way, Deng displayed another characteristic that he shared with Mao – a contempt for legal rational procedures. As a minority member of the leadership back in 1977, Deng was obliged, in accordance with the collective principles of democratic centralism, to adhere to the majority party line without dissent. But like Mao, Deng was impatient for change and he deliberately violated these principles in order to secure his succession to Mao. As we shall see in Chapter 5, during the early stages of the post-Mao era Deng placed great emphasis on the need for institutional reform and a new commitment to legal rational procedures. Yet, he continued to abrogate such procedures whenever it suited him.

## Defusing the past: deconstructing Mao

In order to create the right social environment for his economic reform programme, Deng quickly set about diffusing the political legacy of the Cultural Revolution by ordering the trial of the Gang of Four in late 1980 amidst much public fanfare. According to official findings, the Gang persecuted over 700,000 people of which over 30,000 died (Bonavia 1984). Whilst these figures are not necessarily reliable (the Gang, much like Lin Biao, were made political scapegoats for many of Mao's own misdemeanours) the purpose of the exercise was not to give the Gang a fair trial but to show the masses that justice was at last being done. In an effort to add weight to the process, some of those who had been terrorized by the Gang were given an opportunity to criticize their oppressors during the trial. In this way, the trial was a cathartic experience allowing the harrowing legacy of the Gang of Four to be brought finally to a close.

Rightly or wrongly, the Gang were found guilty of planning a coup d'etat from Shanghai and attempting to ferment civil war. Jiang Qing and Zhang Chunqiao were sentenced to death with 2 years' reprieve (both ended up serving life sentences), Yao Wenyuan was sentenced to 20 years and Wang Hongwen received a life sentence. Chen Boda, who had not been seen since the Lin Biao affair, was also prosecuted at the trial and he received an 18 year sentence for being a member of the Lin Biao and Gang of Four cliques. This was a little odd. Although Chen and Lin were close allies, his subsequent ten year absence from political life made it impossible for him to have ever worked with the Gang.

In keeping with her fearsome reputation, Jiang Qing defended herself vigorously throughout the trial, resolute in her insistence that all the crimes she had carried out were at Mao's behest, portraying herself as "Chairman Mao's dog" (i.e. whoever he told her to bite, she bit). Unpopular as she was, there was no avoiding the fact that Mao was indeed answerable for many of the excesses of the Cultural Revolution and this served to highlight just how important it was for the party to critique Mao's record as quickly as possible. In so doing, however, Deng faced an intriguing quandary. Whilst it was necessary to hold Mao chiefly responsible for many of the radical excesses of the period, an outright condemnation of the deceased leader could prove counter-productive. Mao was the man most closely associated with the revolution. If the party denounced him as a ruthless tyrant, this might destroy the very origins of the party's legitimacy leaving Deng with no platform upon which to build his plans for the future. It is perhaps remarkable that even after his death, Mao's unlimited reservoir of charismatic authority ensured that he still commanded the respect of many ordinary people. This meant that a careful balance had to be found between apportioning blame to Mao and preserving his status as the founding-father of the Chinese revolution. As Nathan concludes:

> The challenge facing the Deng group was to repudiate all that had been done in Mao's name during the Cultural Revolution without discrediting the monopolistic structure of power that had enabled him to do these things. They had to separate the party from twenty years' deeds of the man who had led it, while leaving the party dictatorship intact.
>
> (1986: 7)

A similar point is made by Kluver (1996: 53): 'the leaders of the nation were caught in a dilemma; they needed to "demystify" Mao and move forward with reforms, and yet in so doing they risked undermining their own base of authority'.

After pouring over numerous versions of Mao's official assessment, Deng finally achieved the balance he required in a document entitled the *Resolution on Certain Questions in the History of our Party* which was published in July 1981. In order that justice was seen to be done, Mao was held culpable for the failed mass campaigns of the Great Leap Forward and in particular the Cultural Revolution:

> The 'Cultural Revolution', which lasted from May 1966 to October 1976 was responsible for the most severe setback and the heaviest losses suffered by the Party, the state, and the people since the founding of the People's Republic. It was initiated and led by Comrade Mao Zedong.
>
> (MacFarquhar 1997: 330)

References were also made to Mao's arrogance in his later years, the destructive nature of his cult of personality and his inability to see right from wrong when pursuing the Cultural Revolution, although this was deliberately qualified by the claim that his colleagues did not do enough to control his actions.

But in an effort to retain the party's revolutionary legitimacy, Mao was commended as a great proletarian revolutionary and someone who was sincere about his vision of a socialist society, even if he was at times misguided. In the end, therefore, it was concluded that Mao's mistakes paled in comparison to the contributions and sacrifices he made in the cause of Chinese socialism. This was measured on a ratio of 70 per cent "good", 30 per cent "bad" (Saich 1995, Kluver 1996: 51–61).

In terms of dominant modes of legitimacy, the *Resolution on Party History* represented an important turning point for the party. In denouncing the megalomania of the Mao era as well as Mao's leading role in the Great Leap Forward and the Cultural Revolution, the party in effect turned its back on two key Maoist modes of legitimacy: the cult of personality and mass mobilization, both of which had proved to be disastrous during Mao's incumbency. Zheng Shiping (2003: 54) notes that at this point, the party changed from being a 'revolutionary party' based on class struggle and mass mobilization to a "ruling party" based on stability and order'. More important, however, was the party's embrace of economic reform as part of a new emphasis on performance based economic legitimacy.

## Defining the future: economic legitimacy

We have already seen how key changes in personnel during the Third Plenum of the Eleventh Central Committee represented a decisive shift in power from Hua to Deng. In addition to this, the Plenum is acknowledged as the beginning of the new era of economic reform in China. Invoking Zhou Enlai's theory of the Four Modernizations, it was at the Third Plenum that Deng pledged to rebuild China in the areas of agriculture, industry, defence and science and technology. Whilst he also referred to the need for political and institutional reform (in light of the destructive impact of the Cultural Revolution) the focus of CCP work was placed squarely on economics.

In terms of "selling" the whole concept of economic reform to the masses, it is interesting to note that Deng drew on a form of traditional legitimacy to reinforce his message. In Chapter 1 we saw how the new communist regime drew on specific Confucian traditions to remind people of the "good old days" and to reassure them that there was a certain degree of continuity between the old and the new. Similarly, as part of the propaganda effort to legitimize the new era of economic reform, numerous analogies were drawn with the early post-revolutionary period, widely thought of as a halcyon era before the calamity of the Leap and the Cultural Revolution.

### Economic factors

On the face of it, the urgency for economic reform was not immediately obvious. Indeed, statistics in some sectors suggested that the economy had been quite successful during Mao's reign, especially in the context of severe political disruption. Industrial output grew by approximately 11 per cent per annum between 1952 and 1978 whilst agriculture rose at a (seemingly) respectable 3 per cent per annum during this period (White 1993: 32). GNP grew at an annual rate of more than 2 per cent during this period (compared with an average growth rate of only 1.6 per cent for other low-income countries) and combined with the implementation of a comprehensive social welfare system as well as greater income equality, the Mao regime went some way towards alleviating poverty in China (Gittings 2005). Even the Cultural Revolution had only a limited impact on the economy with both agricultural and industrial input recovering quickly after 1969 (Harding 1997: 240–1), leaving the World Bank to cite 'China's most remarkable achievement over three decades as making its low-income groups far better off in terms of basic needs compared with their counterparts in most other poor countries' (Gittings 2005).

Beneath the surface, however was a raft of chronic economic ailments. As with most communist states, the CCP ploughed a disproportionate amount of money into industry (e.g. 60 per cent of GNP in 1977) at the expense of other sectors, most notably agriculture. Notwithstanding the 3 per cent increase noted earlier, a lack of proper state investment in the agricultural sector meant that growth rates barely exceeded population growth raising obvious concerns over China's ability to feed its people. Economic efficiency was also a problem, especially during the 1960–70s as productivity rates in both agriculture and industry remained largely static.

Perhaps of most concern to Chinese leaders was the dire situation regarding individual income. As Saich (2001: 219) notes, from 1957–77, average wage rates for government bureaucrats were stagnant whilst earnings for urban state workers and industrial employees actually fell by 5.5 per cent and 8.4 per cent respectively. Living standards also stagnated, especially in relation to the consumption of food and light industrial products and the availability of housing (Nolan and Dong Fureng 1990: 11). This created a vicious circle whereby apathetic workers under-performed thus impeding levels of productivity which, in turn, restricted growth in personal income. As White (1993: 35) suggests, 'since the legitimacy of the CCP regime, even in the Maoist period, rested heavily on its ability to improve the living standards of the population, such disappointing performance posed a serious political challenge to the Party leadership'.

The dismal economic situation at home looked even worse in the context of much of the rest of East Asia with several of China's neighbours achieving phenomenal growth rates. Japan led the way with an economy that grew by over 10 per cent per annum during the 1960–70s. Not far behind were the Newly Industrialized Communities of Singapore, South Korea, Hong Kong and Taiwan (known colloquially as the "four tigers"), geographically much smaller than China but economically much bigger. All of this was humiliating for the CCP. Japan, China's arch-enemy during the 1930–40s, had become a leading economic power, respected throughout the developed world for its economic achievements. Worse still was the economic progress of Taiwan under the rule of another arch-enemy, the KMT. As China under the CCP lurched from one political calamity to another, Taiwan quietly focused on economic matters and by the late 1970s had built a strong and reputable economy.

### Political factors

The need for economic reform was therefore palpable. With wages in decline, living standards stagnant and barely enough food to go round, urgent measures were required to lift China out of the economic doldrums. Yet, it was not only economic factors that pushed Deng towards economic reform. The party's fragile political predicament was just as significant. Under normal circumstances, the CCP, like its Brezhnevian counterpart in the Soviet Union, could probably have struggled on for years with an under-performing economy, maintaining control over the population through a mix of political propaganda and coercion (White 1993: 35–6). But the events of the previous decade were far from normal. China had endured the Cultural Revolution and the party was still reeling from the after-effects.

In the years before the split in the party leadership which precipitated the Cultural Revolution, the party had benefited from a number of legitimizing factors including a consensual party leadership, a coherent structure of party and state institutions and a comprehensive and widely disseminated political ideology. The Cultural Revolution changed all this. The institutions of party and state were destroyed by the Red Guards, especially at the local level where they collapsed in a matter of weeks. The previously united party leadership splintered into rival factions which declared a bitter and public war on each other. Perhaps, most importantly, the party's Marxist ideology which had been so effective in unifying the country under a common cause was thoroughly discredited. Far from being a vanguard of the people, the only political body capable of representing the interests of the proletariat, the party had shown itself to be incapable of understanding what the people wanted. In the context of this political crisis Deng was left with little option but to re-invent the party along economic lines. As White concludes:

> The political appeal of market reform was a recipe, in the eyes of significant sections of the Party elite at least, for recouping the Party's political credibility by demonstrating its capacity to raise living standards and achieve China's national aspirations.
>
> (1993: 36–7)

## Rural reform

The most radical aspect of the reforms was initially in the agricultural sector (Byrd and Lin 1990). For years the rural economy had been the victim of inconsistent and often unpredictable policies reflecting deep ideological divisions in the party leadership over the extent to which the countryside should be organized collectively. This led to periods of boom and slump in production, culminating in the catastrophic Great Leap Forward when grain production fell to its lowest level in a decade contributing to the starvation of millions of people. Agriculture also suffered from a lack of proper state investment which meant, amongst other things, that machinery and farming equipment were outdated and not fit for purpose.

To help the sector recover Deng implemented a number of urgent policy initiatives. State investment as a proportion of GNP was immediately increased and more credit was made available by state banks and other credit organizations. Material incentives were introduced as the state reduced the amount of grain and cotton under compulsory purchase, increased its procurement prices and allowed rural workers to sell any excess produce on the local market. In addition, the production of specialized "cash crops" (e.g. tomatoes or bananas) was encouraged to be sold exclusively in the market place. Under the old Maoist system, the state procured a high proportion of grain from farmers and invariably forbade the use of markets, leaving farmers uninterested in growing anything other than what they needed for their own subsistence purposes. By reducing state procurement amounts and introducing rural markets the new Deng regime encouraged farmers to intensify crop production and diversify what they grew.

Another major innovation was the introduction of the household responsibility system (Putterman 1985). During the Mao era, the production team was the basic unit for the production of goods and the distribution of income (comprising around 50 households after 1962). Although Deng continued with this collective model, albeit at the smaller production team level (see later), some farmers simply ignored central government policy and began organizing themselves into single households. According Qian Yingyi (1999: 5–6), the first recorded instance of this occurred in Anhui province in December 1978. The Xiaogang Production Brigade (comprising 20 households) drafted an unofficial contract which allocated each household with a separate plot of land. With the support of provincial Governor (and future Vice-Premier) Wan Li, other regions in the province and then other provinces (e.g. Sichuan) quickly followed suit leaving the centre increasingly out of step with events at the ground level. Central policy finally fell into line in 1983 by which time almost 98 per cent of production teams had been disbanded. Under the new system, households entered into a contract with the local authorities allocating a plot of land for each household for up to three years. This contract included the supply of all raw materials, although access to resources such as water remained under the control of the collective as did the right to dispose of the land.

Those farmers who did not join the household responsibility system instead joined the Town and Village Enterprises (TVEs) which were established as part of the non-state sector (Wietzman and Xu Chengguang 1994, Fu Xiaolan and Balasubramanyam 2003). Originating from the commune and brigade-run industries established during the Leap, the objective of the TVEs was to bolster the agricultural sector through the production of rural industrial materials such as chemical fertilizers, farming tools and hydro-electric power. Initially, the role of the TVEs was quite limited (in 1978 rural areas accounted for only 9 per cent of total industrial input). But once the state relaxed its purchasing monopoly on agricultural goods in the early 1980s, the TVEs became the most vibrant feature of the rural economy, soaking up excess rural labour and diversifying production to encompass consumer and export goods.

The material benefits of agricultural reform were immediate, particularly as a result of the increase in procurement prices paid by the state (an average of 20 per cent more for quota grain, 50 per cent more for above-quota grain and 30 per cent more for cotton). According to Saich (2001: 222) 'this single act did more than anything else to lift large numbers of peasants out of poverty'. The introduction of rural markets had a similarly beneficial effect, transforming rural towns and villages into centres of vibrant economic activity where traders sold produce that was more varied and of better quality (although, of course, more expensive). The resultant rise in production figures was marked. Between 1978 and 1984, grain output increased by more than 5 per cent per annum and by 1985 China had become a net exporter of grain. Production figures for "cash crops" grew even faster and by 1984 per capital income for rural households had increased by more than 50 per cent over a 6 year period (Lee Travers 1985). Finally, the expansion of the TVEs saw rural industrial output grow by 21 per cent per annum from 1978 until the early 1990s.

### Urban reform

A second feature of the early reforms was the restructuring of the urban economy, particularly of China's state-owned enterprises (SOEs) (Lee 1987, Naughton 1995). Under the Mao regime SOEs were controlled entirely by the state. The state set production quotas, provided all necessary equipment and materials, took charge of distribution matters, appointed and paid all employees and fixed sale and purchase prices. Employees enjoyed considerable job security (otherwise known as the "iron rice bowl"). Not only did they receive a fixed (although not always constant) wage, they also enjoyed generous state subsidies in, amongst other things, housing, health, education, transportation and food. Moreover, it was almost impossible to be sacked. Once in employment workers literally had a "job for life".

But SOEs were beset with a myriad of interrelated problems. Whilst production quotas were usually met, the quality of the goods produced was often poor. One of the main reasons for this was due to the fixed wage structure. With salaries set in stone, there was no tangible incentive for working hard or with any care and even the most slothful worker was unlikely to be fired. Managers were also under-motivated. Like their work force, they were paid a fixed sum regardless of individual performance whilst their responsibilities as managers were limited because financial and distribution issues were decided by the central state plan.

In an effort to remedy these problems the Deng leadership moved towards the introduction of material incentives and increases in managerial autonomy. Like the reforms in agriculture, a number of local level experiments were initially undertaken, although with much greater central control. As Qian Yingyi (1999: 7–8) has shown, the first tentative steps were made in Sichuan in October 1978. Under the auspices of the provincial head (and later General Secretary) Zhao Ziyang, new powers were introduced to six SOEs. These gave managers limited rights to produce and sell products on the market place once all central quotas were fulfilled and to promote lower level staff without prior government approval. Any profit was put into separate funds, including a workers' bonus fund which managers distributed according to individual performance.

The popularity of this new system convinced the party to implement it more widely throughout China, although still on an experimental basis (e.g. about 100 enterprises in Sichuan joined the experiment). By April 1981, the economic responsibility system had been introduced along similar lines to the household responsibility system in agriculture (Qian Yingyi 1999: 8). However, for reasons noted in Chapter 5, successfully reforming SOEs proved much more difficult than reforming the agricultural sector.

Early reforms to the urban (and to a certain extent rural) sector also saw the emergence of individual entrepreneurs in China (Guthrie 2001). Under the Mao era, this kind of individual was vilified as capitalist, but in keeping with the market-based principles of economic reform, the Deng regime sought to breathe life and entrepreneurial vitality back into China's cities and suburbs by offering an opportunity for resourceful individuals to make some money. The main area of activity was the provision of consumer services. Small outdoor stalls began to line Chinese streets selling anything from cigarettes to basic household appliances. A number of "open-air" bicycle repair shops appeared and some people tried their hands as restaurateurs, hairdressers or beauticians. Not everyone embraced these new opportunities. Many were concerned about the prospect of a sudden party backlash against the reforms akin to what happened after the post-Leap reform programme. Others had grown accustomed to the security provided by their state jobs and were not prepared to take a gamble on the open market. By the end of 1983, however, at least 17 million people had moved over to the private sector and as the reforms intensified this number increased.

### Foreign trade and investment

Another central tenet of the Deng reform programme was the opening of Chinese markets to foreign trade and investment, known as the open door policy. In contrast to the Mao period when the emphasis was placed firmly on economic autarky, the Deng regime realized that a modern economy was only achievable if China opened up to the outside world. Imports of advanced foreign technology were a first priority and these could only be paid for if China created an export-based market primarily from its light industrial sector. There was also a pressing need for financial assistance from international organizations such as the World Bank and the International Monetary Fund. This could only be obtained if China demonstrated a readiness to participate in the international economy after decades of self-imposed isolation.

Like the reforms in the rural and urban sectors, the open door policy was initially implemented on an experimental local basis. This saw the establishment of four Special Economic Zones (SEZs) along China's south eastern coast, three in Guangdong province (Shenzhen, Zhuhai and Shantou) and one in Fujian (Xiamen). Each SEZ was granted subsidies to help encourage exports and allowed to retain 70 per cent of all foreign exchange income (the other 30 per cent was remitted to the state). The SEZs were accorded greater autonomy over their own economic development, including the freedom to approve foreign investment projects of up to US$ 30 million without prior authorization from the state (Qian Yingyi 1999: 6). In a simultaneous effort to attract foreign investors into China, the government offered free access to land and building equipment and special emphasis was placed on the opportunities to employ cheap Chinese labour. Customs duties on imported raw materials and equipment were abolished and a tax exemption was granted for the first four years of any foreign operation, rising to a discounted rate of 15 per cent thereafter.

By 1984 another 14 coastal cities and Hainan island were granted SEZ status, but overall progress was mixed. Overseas concerns that China might return to the Cultural Revolution era made it difficult to convince foreign companies to commit themselves. This led to a disappointing foreign investment figures (less than US$ 4.6 billion from 1979 to 1985), much which was made up of the capital from Hong Kong businessmen who had relocated their operations across the border into southern China. Indeed, of all the SEZs, only Shenzhen managed to attract a significant amount of capital outside Hong Kong (although most of this was used to repay the central government for the money it had spent on developing Shenzhen's infrastructure). Domestic discontent also stemmed from the selective nature of the open door policy with representatives from the poorer central and western provinces complaining that they were being deprived of the chance to trade with the West. Moreover, as we shall see in Chapter 5, many traditionalists in the party leadership were unhappy about the ideological implications of the open door policy failing to see how a policy which embraced foreign capital and encouraged foreign investors to take advantage of (i.e. exploit) cheap Chinese labour could be considered in any way socialist.

## The end of an era

The 1970s was yet another tumultuous decade in the history of the CCP. Plagued by political extremism and acrimonious leadership infighting, the decade saw the demise of Lin Biao within two years of his ordainment as Mao's chosen successor, the rise and fall of the radical Gang of Four (including another potential successor Wang Hongwen), the death of Mao and Zhou Enlai in 1976, the emergence of a complete outsider as leader in the shape of Hua Guofeng and the subsequent (and rapid) eclipse of Hua by Deng Xiaoping, returning from his second period in political exile.

The emergence of Deng Xiaoping was of huge significance in that it marked the end of radical Maoism and the beginning of a new era of economic reform. After decades of political instability characterized by a succession of militant mass campaigns, the party in effect turned its back on the discredited Maoist paradigms of mass mobilization and charismatic legitimacy and re-invented itself as the party of economic performance. But this shift in emphasis brought with it new and pressing problems for the CCP and it is to this period that we must now turn our attention.

# 5 New era new crisis

## Problems of legitimacy in the 1980s

The introduction of economic reform in the late 1970s was part of a desperate attempt by Deng Xiaoping to resurrect the legitimacy of the CCP. The devastation of the Cultural Revolution brought the party to the brink of collapse, forcing it to re-invent itself as a force for economic prosperity rather than revolutionary change. After Mao's death in 1976 the Maoist legitimation techniques of mass mobilization and charismatic authority were abandoned and replaced with a new performance oriented paradigm under which the party's legitimacy was measured by reference to its ability to achieve ambitious economic goals. Based on the crude logic that improvements in the economic welfare of the individual would revive the popular fortunes of an ailing party, the 1980s saw the intensification of the economic reform process which by the end of the decade had gone well beyond the scope originally intended.

The economic achievements of the 1980s are well documented (Nolan and Dong Fureng 1990, Lardy 1994). Average annual growth rates of 10 per cent in agriculture meant that China became self-sufficient in grain production for the first time since 1949. This facilitated the doubling of rural per capita income. Growth rate increases likewise occurred in the industrial sector, especially in the coastal provinces of Guangdong, Fujian and Hainan where per capita income rose more than three fold. Shops began to stock an increasing number of light industrial products and luxury consumer items such as colour televisions, fridges and automatic washing machines. Reforms were also implemented in the fiscal and banking sectors, and perhaps most controversially, attempts were made to lift state controls over pricing.

To some extent Deng was able to honour his original promise of increases in personal wealth and improved living standards and on the face of it this success probably helped to restore a degree of credibility to CCP rule that was absent at the start of the reform era. Paradoxically, however, as the pace of economic reform accelerated throughout the decade, a number of reform-related issues emerged that served to detract from the legitimacy of the party. How, for example, could the party continue to rely on Marxist ideology as a source of its authority to rule in light of the clear contradiction between Marxism and market economics? To what extent would the party be willing to reform the political system without threatening its monopoly on power? How would the party cope with some of the socio-economic side-effects of economic reform such as official corruption, growing inflation and high unemployment? By the end of the decade, it was clear that none of these issues had been dealt with effectively and as tensions rose amongst the urban population millions took to the streets as part of the ill-fated mass demonstrations of spring 1989.

Much of the dissatisfaction expressed by China's urban populace stemmed from the absence of a clear and unified vision within the party leadership over economic reform (see Figure 5). Whilst the leadership did initially unite behind the new policy line, fundamental differences of opinion soon emerged (Hamrin 1984, Bachman 1986). For the ideological left (the "conservatives") led by Deng Liqun (head of the Propaganda Department) the reforms progressed too quickly, creating a nation of avaricious and selfish individuals with no concern for social-ist principles. Rather than enhancing the party's legitimacy, it was argued, eco-nomic reform risked destroying the Marxist principles upon which the party's legitimacy was based. For this reason Deng Liqun and his colleagues attempted to derail the reform process at every opportunity. Conversely, for "reformers" such as Hu Yaobang (General Secretary after 1982) and Zhao Ziyang (Premier after 1980) the reforms did not progress quickly enough. Determined not to shy away from the unsettling socio-economic transition to a full market economy, Hu and particularly Zhao advocated, amongst other things, the decentralization of decision making to SOE managers and the lifting of price controls. Both men were also keen exponents of political reform. However, in pledging their support

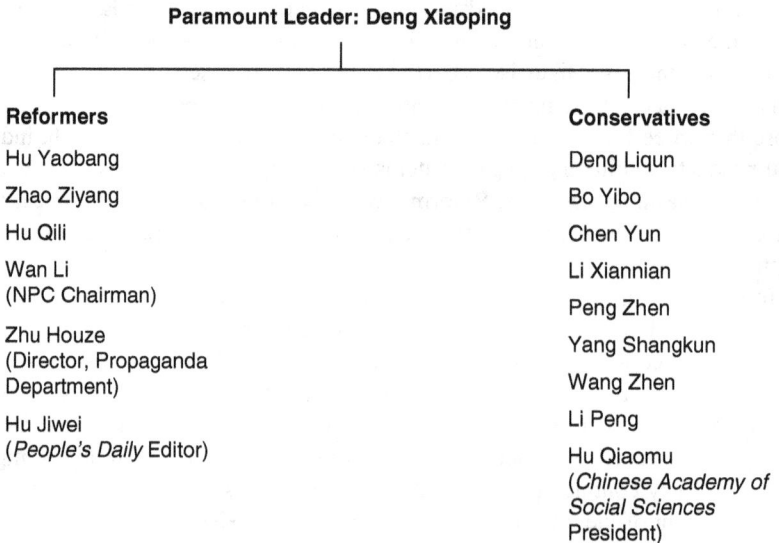

**Paramount Leader: Deng Xiaoping**

| **Reformers** | **Conservatives** |
|---|---|
| Hu Yaobang | Deng Liqun |
| Zhao Ziyang | Bo Yibo |
| Hu Qili | Chen Yun |
| Wan Li (NPC Chairman) | Li Xiannian |
| | Peng Zhen |
| Zhu Houze (Director, Propaganda Department) | Yang Shangkun |
| | Wang Zhen |
| Hu Jiwei (*People's Daily* Editor) | Li Peng |
| | Hu Qiaomu (*Chinese Academy of Social Sciences* President) |

*Figure 5* The 1980s CCP leadership.

for like-minded students and intellectuals, both came into conflict with Deng Xiaoping.

## Problems of ideology

One of the most pressing issues for the CCP was how to revise its Marxist ideology such that it was somehow compatible with the market-based economic realities of the day (Ding Xueliang 1994, Feng Chen 1995, Misra 1998). Given the party's authority to rule as the People's Democratic Dictatorship derived theoretically from its unique and detailed knowledge of Marxism, it was essential for party theorists to present a coherently Marxist explanation for economic reform. This was no easy task given that Marx saw no role for markets in a socialist society. Indeed, socialism, Marx believed, would ultimately replace the capitalist market place.

During the first few years of the reforms the party was able to avoid facing up to this problem by relying on the theory of Seek Truth from Facts as reinterpreted by Deng in the late 1970s. As discussed in Chapter 4, the principles of Seek Truth encouraged greater flexibility in the application of ideological principles to specific issues and this provided Deng with the political space he required to experiment with market reforms to the economy (White 1993: 151–2). Also, simply not being the old Maoist party or the Gang of Four gave Deng some room to manoeuvre. But as the reforms gathered pace and the use of markets became more and more entrenched, the pressure increased on Deng to authorize an official reformulation of Chinese Marxism.

### *Socialist Commodity Economy*

The first reformulation came in 1984 following the implementation of a document known as the October Directive. The October Directive signalled a significant intensification of the economic reform process by, amongst other things, restructuring small-and medium-sized SOEs so that the enterprise (rather than the state) had control over certain aspects of decision making (e.g. in relation to marketing and procurement), removing restrictions on the number of workers (previously eight) that could be employed by China's growing number of entrepreneurs. The Directive also expanded the categories of products or commodities that could be produced for sale on the open market rather than for distribution under the central state plan (Wong 1985).

In an effort to reconcile Marxism with this economic initiative, the party declared that China was entering a new phase of development known as the Socialist Commodity Economy. Put simply this was an economy in which those SOEs enjoying greater independence than before were allowed to sell an increasing number of commodities in the market place. Notwithstanding the conventional Marxist antipathy towards markets, party theorists argued that a limited role for market forces was not only beneficial to China's socialist development but *essential*. Although the state plan remained a key part of the socialist economy (especially in relation to large industry where the state continued to set production targets and allocate funds and resources), a commodity economy based on supply and demand was an ideal means of stimulating production at the medium and lower levels of the economy. As Liu Guoguang and Wu Jinglian (1979: 15) explained, 'the state plan can only reflect the needs of society in totality, but cannot reflect correctly and flexibly the kaleidoscopic needs of our economic life'.

Such rationalization demonstrated a commendable degree of conceptual innovation on behalf of the party, but the end product did little to reunite China's changing economic situation with its Marxist ideology. In effect what the party appeared to be suggesting was this: if an economic model is good for the development of production and the productive forces then it can be usefully defined as socialist. As we shall see, this kind of open-ended, "anything goes" approach came to characterize subsequent attempts to revise Chinese Marxism.

The failure to present a convincing Marxist explication of the Socialist Commodity Economy ignited a mini-debate in the Chinese media over the continuing relevance of Marxism to post-Mao China. Leading the debate was none other than the party's official mouthpiece, the *People's Daily*. On 7 December 1984 a front page commentary entitled *Theory and Practice* announced that:

> [Marx's] works were written more than 100 years ago. Some were his tentative ideas at that time, and things have changed greatly since then. Some of his ideas were not necessarily very appropriate. We cannot expect the writings of Marx and Lenin of that time to provide solutions to our current problems.
>
> (Goldman 1994: 136–7)

On the following day the *People's Daily* partially retracted this statement by announcing (conveniently) that a typing omission had been made so that the last sentence should have read 'we cannot expect the writings of Marx and Lenin of that time to provide solutions to *all* our current problems' [emphasis added] (Goldman 1994: 137). However, two weeks later the same paper published another front page article (*More on Theory and Practice*) this time claiming that Marxism may not only be irrelevant to the reforms, but could even be *detrimental* to them. In particular the author challenged Marx's assertion that socialist society did not need money or commodities, arguing on the contrary that 'the practice of China's socialist construction has proved that commodities and money are necessary for socialist society and that we must develop commodity production'. In a thinly veiled attack on Marxism, the author called for the elimination of 'outdated ideas, customs and conventions' that 'hinder' China's development (Goldman 1994: 137).

Any further contributions to this debate were hurriedly circumvented and this was followed by a campaign against intellectual and press freedom organized by Deng Liqun with the backing of Deng Xiaoping (albeit temporarily) (Goldman 1994: 150–65). Yet, this could not disguise the fact that Chinese Marxism was rapidly losing touch with the realities of economic reform and was increasingly irrelevant to the needs and aspirations of the Chinese people. Following a brief period of economic slowdown in 1985 (primarily as a result of the afore-mentioned campaign), the reforms intensified and it was only a matter of time before official theorists were called upon again to try and reconcile the seemingly irreconcilable.

### Primary Stage of Socialism

The next attempt to revise China's Marxist ideology came in 1987 in the form of the Primary Stage of Socialism, expounded by Zhao Ziyang (then General Secretary). In a considerable departure from the conventional Marxist understanding of the socio-economic transition towards communism, Zhao insisted that, notwithstanding China's claims to be a communist state, China was still an underdeveloped nation and remained in the initial (or primary) stage of socialism. During this inter-mediary phase before the inexorable shift into communism, the priority of the day was the rapid development of the means of production and in order to realize this objective, Zhao argued, it was permissible to introduce an eclectic range of economic policies, including overtly capitalist measures. Zhao acknowledged that the more orthodox members of the party leadership were uncomfortable with the pace of economic reform. However, if China was ever to lift itself out its protracted state of economic backwardness and finally advance towards the higher phase of socialism as envisaged by Marx (i.e. communism), it was necessary to adopt a more flexible and pragmatic approach to economic policy.

Essentially, Zhao was arguing that after 1949 China tried to "jump" the capitalist stage of development straight into communism only to find that its economic conditions were not sufficiently developed to accommodate this final phase. Marx himself prophesied that capitalism was the necessary penultimate stage of development because it created the material abundance necessary for the realization of communist principles of distribution ("from each according to his work to each according to his need"). But Chinese conditions were not ready for communism, Zhao insisted, and it was thus necessary for the CCP to *create* the right conditions by implementing, amongst other things, economic policies of a capitalist nature (although Zhao deliberately avoided using the word "capitalism").

Reformers in the leadership were delighted with Zhao's novel concept for several reasons. First, it helped explain why China remained poor despite almost 40 years of CCP rule. This was not the fault of the party but was due instead to objective historical circumstances. As Kluver (1996: 88) explains, theorists argued that the party 'could not be expected to change historical progression itself, it could only guide the nation through historical stages that in themselves are immutable'. Second, it accounted for the party's embrace of economic reform using the required Marxist terminology. Despite appearances, China had *not* become a capitalist country but was only *utilizing* capitalist mechanisms in order to arrive at communism. In other words, capitalism was simply a means to communist ends. Third, it gave the reformist wing of the leadership *carte blanche* to continue implementing economic reform for the foreseeable future. According to Zhao, it would take at least 100 years from the date of the revolution for China to reach an advanced state of socialism, a process that would therefore be achieved sometime around 2050.

Although Zhao's theory was an ambitious attempt to bring Marxist ideology into line with economic policy, it fell short on a number of counts. It failed, for example, to provide a realistic prognosis of any kind of communist future in China since the crucial question of when communism would be realized was conveniently deferred for 100 years or so. Nor did it provide committed party members with the degree of inspiration required from Marxist theory. In contrast to the predictive and utopian nature of orthodox Marxism, the Primary Stage of Socialism (like the theory of the Socialist Commodity Economy) seemed to imply that anything could be called socialist as long as it boosted Chinese economic growth. White (1993: 162) point outs that this led some party theorists to dub it 'the theory a hundred treasure bag', 'a ragbag into which anything can be stuffed'. Ultimately, the Primary Stage theory exposed the increasing irrelevance of Marxist ideology in the modern era of Chinese economic reform and underlined the increasing failure of ideology to act as a legitimizing force for CCP rule. As Dirlik and Meisner conclude:

> The distinctive features of Ideology – its ability to motivate and guide the political elite; its claim to provide a framework for a long-term strategy leading towards a credible future; its aim to establish a coherent and credible set of moral principles to provide a new social identity for the members of a 'socialist' society – seem to have atrophied. In the political world of Chinese reformism, Ideology has increasingly become residual.
>
> (1989: 365)

## Institutional and political reform

Just as economic reform forced the party to revise its Marxist ideology so it also put pressure on the party to reform the political system. As economic reform intensified throughout the decade, much of this pressure was exerted from outside the party. One of the main grievances expressed by those who took part in the public demonstrations of 1986 and 1989 (see later) was that political reform had been left behind by economic reform; in other words, the party had focused too much on the latter and neglected the former. At the same time, the party itself recognized the need for political reform, partly in an effort to keep up with a rapidly modernizing economy but also because of the grave experiences of the Mao era which inflicted untold damage on the CCP's legal rational legitimacy. As we have seen in previous chapters, in an effort to overhaul central party policy or isolate rival leaders with whom he disagreed, Mao frequently undermined the principles of collective decision making and adherence to the majority view by forming powerful coalitions outside the party centre and sometimes even outside the party itself. During the Cultural Revolution, in particular, any notion of established democratic procedure was completely abandoned as decisions were taken either by Mao alone or by *ad hoc* political groups such as the CRG who dismissed party leaders arbitrarily with the coercive assistance of the Red Guards and the PLA.

### Changes to party and state

In light of the experiences of the Mao era, a strong consensus formed around the need to institutionalize a more regulated and predictable system of decision making. Particular emphasis was placed on re-establishing the principles of democratic centralism at all levels of the party hierarchy through an intensive programme of in-house training. Here the stress was on the importance of freedom of expression and adherence to the party line once it was democratically agreed upon. The correct procedures for party meetings and for appointing and dismissing party members were re-affirmed and to a certain extent updated through the implementation of new guidelines (e.g. Certain Guiding Principles for Inner-Party Political Life published in 1980). Measures were taken to ensure tighter control of local level party secretaries so as to prevent a reoccurrence of the personal abuses of power that took place during the Cultural Revolution. More generally, proposals were made via a new body called the Central Discipline Inspection Commission (CDIC) to rectify the party's work-style by cleansing it of "unhealthy tendencies" such as nepotism, authoritarianism, and particularly corruption (more of which is discussed later) and by restoring the old "Yanan link" between the party and the masses (Stavis 1988, White 1993: 170–97).

At the highest level of the party, Deng took the largely symbolic step of abolishing the post of CCP Chairman, a position that had become synonymous with Mao's cult of personality and his domination of the party apparatus. Instead, the party was to be led by a General Secretary (Hu Yaobang in 1982) whose authority was restricted by a provision in the 1982 party constitution which made him "first amongst equals" rather than in sole command. The Vice-Chair of the party (a position usually held by more than one person) was abolished to avoid an over-concentration of power in the PSC and the Secretariat, a body which was dissolved during the Cultural Revolution, was resurrected in order to dilute the previously unrivalled power of the Politburo. In addition, measures were implemented to increase the powers of the National Party Congress and the Central Committee in relation to the Politburo and PSC respectively.

Reforms were also made to the state apparatus as enshrined in the 1982 state constitution. In order to increase its powers *vis-à-vis* the State Council, the Standing Committee was authorized to supervise the enforcement of the state constitution, examine and approve any recommended changes to the state budget and national plan and exercise greater controls over lower level state organs. The NPC, so long considered as a rubber-stamp rather than a fully functioning legislature, was given greater powers of debate and decision making (O'Brien 1990). Other significant changes included a limit of two consecutive five year terms for government posts such as President and Premier and restrictions on officials serving concurrently in more than one leadership post. In general, the objective was to improve the legal rational legitimacy of both party and state by ensuring that decisions and decision makers were controlled by a transparent legal process and by introducing checks and balances on the authority of certain higher bodies (e.g. the Politburo and the State Council).

The question of checks and balances was similarly relevant to the inter-relationship *between* party and state (not just within the separate institutions). During a well documented speech on political reform in August 1980, Deng (1984: 302–25) identified the need for a clear demarcation of powers between the two institutions. As discussed in Chapter 1, an over-abundance of party personnel in leading government positions allowed the party to dominate government deci-sions. Moreover, by over-extending itself in this way, Deng argued, the party was less well equipped to perform its proper duties whilst the role of government was rendered practically redundant. In an effort to separate party from state, Deng authorized the removal of all party groups from government and administrative bodies and ordered that party secretaries would no longer be empowered to take charge of government work. Certain government bodies (mainly at the lower level) were also accorded new powers to appoint their own officials without interference from the party.

Another important measure was the establishment of the Central Advisory Committee (CAC), a body designed to gradually phase out elderly cadres from the highest levels of the party (i.e. those over 70 years old with more than 40 years service to the party) who could then be replaced by younger personnel. Throughout the Mao era, as Oksenberg (1976) points out, there was no effective retirement device and party leaders usually remained in charge until they were either purged or died. Mao was paramount leader until he died at the age of 83 and when Deng looked around him at the Twelfth National Party Congress in September 1982, he found that he was surrounded by octogenarians and septua-genarians (of which he was one). Of the five other members of the PSC, for example, Ye Jianying was 86, Chen Yun was 77 and Li Xiannian was 73. This left only Hu Yaobang (67) and Zhao Ziyang (63) under the age of 70 years old. In light of this, the CAC was set up as a "half-way house" to retirement for super-annuated cadres. Although its members would no longer enjoy voting rights, Vice-Chairmen of the new body would still be allowed to attend plenary sessions of the Politburo whilst ordinary members could continue attending Central Committee plenary meetings if they so wished. In this way, CAC members would still be part of the consultation process even if they no longer had a direct role in decision making.

### Electoral reform

Significant changes were also made to the electoral system, specifically the method of electing deputies to people's congresses. During the Mao period, direct elections were only permitted at the township level. These were invariably dull and predictable affairs since the number of candidates always equalled the number of available positions, diminishing the whole concept of choice which is so fundamental to the electoral mode of legitimacy. The candidate nomination process was dominated by the party with non-party members discouraged from standing. Election campaigning was non-existent and voting usually consisted of a show of hands in a public meeting place raising issues of voter privacy and voter intimidation. Indirect elections (used for the election of deputies to county level and above) were no more inspiring, notwithstanding the greater use of secret ballots.

In an effort to legitimize the electoral process and as part of the post-Mao emphasis on socialist democracy, a revised Election Law came into practice in 1979 (updating the 1953 version) and was further amended in 1982 and then again in 1986 (Womack 1982, Nathan 1986, Jacobs 1991). This new legislation contained several key changes. The scope of direct elections was expanded to include the county as well as the township level and it became compulsory to have more candidates than available positions. The nomination process was altered to allow a greater role for popular associations or ten or more members of the electorate jointly to nominate candidates (although for indirect elections this process was still dominated by the party). A new "fifty per cent rule" was introduced and applied in two different ways. First, in order for an election to be valid over 50 per cent of the electorate were required to vote. This provided voters with an opportunity to force a re-ballot by simply not turning up if they did not like any of the candidates on offer (known as "negative democracy"). Second, in order for a candidate to be elected he or she was required to receive over 50 per cent of the votes cast. As an alternative, voters could vote to oppose a candidate or vote to abstain. Other changes included the introduction of campaigning in an effort to provide voters with more information about candidates and the replacement of public election meetings with polling stations in order to improve voter secrecy.

### Assessing the reforms

The success of political reform in the 1980s was mixed. Despite increases in the power accorded to the NPC and its Standing Committee, the ultimate authority of the State Council remained pretty much untouched. The same can be said for the PSC which maintained its grip over all key decisions made by the party. The all important separation of party from state was largely confined to lower level institutions, suggesting a lack of commitment on the part of the leadership to implement a genuine division of powers throughout the entire system. There were also certain practical difficulties involved in untangling the complicated network of interlocking institutions which had become so entrenched over the years as well as instances of obstructionism by officials who were unhappy with the dilution of their authority resulting from the new initiatives.

Attempts to retire party elders from the upper echelons of the party also met with internal resistance. Whilst 65 septuagenarians moved from the Central Committee to the CAC in 1982, no-one from the PSC was prepared to make the transition. Deng neatly side-stepped the question of his own retirement by appointing himself Chairman of the CAC, a position under which he was constitutionally (and conveniently) entitled to remain as a PSC member. The other three PSC members over the age of 70, namely Li Xiannian and Chen Yun and Ye Jianying simply refused to move in the strongly held belief that there was no-one else better qualified to run the country (Baum 1997: 346). In sum, therefore, although the CAC proved useful in relieving the Central Committee of many of its elders, it had no impact at all on the key decision making body in China, namely the PSC. Moreover, as we shall see, those PSC members who did finally join the CAC later on in the decade were able to use the body as an effective institutional base from which to undermine the reforms. This caused Deng to abolish the CAC in 1992.

Reforms to the electoral system were more successful and are thought to have introduced a much needed democratic edge to elections. The "fifty per cent rule", in particular, yielded some interesting results. A significant number of direct and indirect elections saw candidates defeated for failing to secure the requisite 50 per cent of the votes cast as well as re-ballots when less than 50 per cent of the electorate turned out. In one of the most high-profile cases, during 1988 indirect elections to the Guangdong Provincial People's Congress, neither of the two candidates for President of the People's High Court received more than half of the votes cast. This proved to be particularly embarrassing for the Guangdong authorities who were forced to organize a new round of voting with completely new candidates (Goldman 1994: 252). The introduction of secret ballots was also significant in that it reduced the pressure to vote in accordance with the party's wishes, stretching all the way up to the very top. When the Standing Committee of the NPC elected Li Peng as acting Premier in November 1987, two people voted against Li and another abstained. This was the first ever instance of the Standing Committee dissenting from the party's nominee for Premier (Jacobs 1991: 192).

Despite these (and other) notable successes, a number of problems remained inherent in the electoral system. One of the most fundamental was continued party interference in the selection of candidates. Although the candidate nomination process was much more open and inclusive in the ways noted earlier, the process of reducing the number of nominees to the final number of candidates to stand for election invariably remained under tight party control. According to Jacobs (1991: 183), this process, known (ironically) as "consultation," 'generates the most dissatisfaction with the electoral process' and is thought to have caused a considerable degree of voter apathy at the polls. Another shortcoming was the continued absence of genuine election campaigning despite efforts to the contrary. In his study of the 1987 elections in Nanjing (Jiangsu province), Jacobs (1991: 186) observes that whilst (in an unprecedented move) information about the candidates was posted in prominent outdoor cases (including their photographs), there were very few public meetings where candidates could address voters and no instances of door-to-door campaigning. As such, voters rarely met candidates.

Yet, perhaps the most fundamental flaw with the Chinese political system remained the party leadership's inability (or unwillingness) to break free from its clandestine straight-jacket and adhere more rigidly to a transparent and legal rational process of decision making. Whilst Deng was far less domineering as a political figure than Mao and refused to develop his own personality cult, elite decision making in China continued to be characterized by the whims of the individual, namely Deng, rather than by legal procedure. This was apparent throughout the entire decade as Deng played the role of final arbiter in each of the key disputes that arose between economic reformers and their more conservative counterparts. Indeed, this was even the case *after* Deng relinquished all of his leadership posts in 1987.

One example of Deng's pivotal role in the decision making process came during the prelude to the Anti-Spiritual Pollution Campaign which was launched in October 1983 (Mackerras 1984, Saich 1984, Goldman 1994: 113–32). Following the publication of a series of academic articles that critiqued, amongst other things, Marx's theory on alienation (Kelly 1987), Deng Liqun, together with other orthodox figures in the leadership such as Chen Yun, Wang Zhen and Peng Zhen, instigated a media campaign against allegedly liberal and anti-Marxist trends amongst intellectuals. Deng Liqun's objective was to convert this mini-campaign into a fully blown political campaign. However, in order to do so it was necessary to secure the backing of Deng Xiaoping (no relation) who remained the party's paramount figure even though Hu Yaobang as General Secretary occupied the most senior post in the party.

Initially, Deng charted a middle course between those who wanted to intensify the campaign and those who were opposed to it because of the consequences on economic reform (e.g. Hu Yaobang and Zhao Ziyang). During the Second Plenum of the Twelfth Central Committee in October 1983 Deng supported *both* sides of the argument by authorizing an internal party rectification campaign against remnant leftists on the one hand (thereby placating Hu and Zhao) and Marxist revisionists on the other (thereby placating Deng Liqun *et al.*). Reading between the lines, however, Deng appeared, albeit subtly, to be in favour of the Anti-Spiritual Pollution Campaign. Warning of the potentially dire consequences of ignoring deviant views from within the party, Deng insisted that it was necessary to 'immediately curb this phenomena'. This was taken as an oblique signal for Deng Liqun to launch his campaign.

Just as Deng's political blessing was required to initiate the campaign, so it was required to call it off. Within a week or so of the commencement of the campaign things began to get out of hand. Modern Western youth culture (as perceived) such as wearing high heeled shoes, earrings or tight fitting trousers was attacked both by the media and by specially organized vigilante groups who confronted "offenders" in the street. As concerns increased that China was heading towards another Cultural Revolution, rumours surfaced that some foreign companies were stalling over plans to enter into joint venture contracts with their Chinese counterparts. Fearing the collapse of the entire economic reform programme, Hu and Zhao implored Deng to abandon the campaign and by early December 1983, under Deng's instruction, the campaign subsided.

The lack of transparency surrounding the Anti-Spiritual Pollution Campaign did nothing to enhance the party's legal rational legitimacy. In the absence of any official policy statement on the issues, few people outside the party leadership knew what was going on. Instead, the public was left to examine the tone of articles published in official party journals such as *Red Flag* or look for clues in the state-controlled media. Perhaps the best example of this enforced guessing game is provided by Baum. According to Baum (1997: 360), an indication that Hu and Zhao were in the ascendancy by December 1983 came when they were both photographed wearing suits and ties during separate overseas visits to Japan and America. Ordinarily, Chinese leaders were expected to wear the traditional Chinese Mao jacket on such occasions. However, by dispensing with this protocol and wearing Western style clothing, a subtle message was being relayed to the public that those who supported closer links with the West were back in favour with Deng Xiaoping.

### The first wave of student protests

The inadequacy of those political reforms that were implemented in the first half of the 1980s was one of the key reasons behind the wave of student demonstrations that took place during late 1986 (Dittmer 1988, Kwong 1988, Goldman 1994: 191–203). The protests began at the Chinese University of Science and Technology (CUST) in Hefei (Anhui province), the work place of the astrophysicist Fang Lizhi who was renowned for his openly critical stance on issues such as political reform and official corruption. Encouraged by Fang to stand up for their democratic rights and freedoms, the students of CUST directed their anger at the university authorities for hand picking the head of the Students' Union without first canvassing student opinion. The students were also aggrieved by the absence of any consultation in the candidate nomination process for the forthcoming elections to the Anhui township people's congress, which instead had been controlled entirely by local party leaders. Following relentless student pressure for the right to nominate their own candidates, the Anhui authorities finally yielded and Fang along with several student candidates were nominated and then comfortably elected.

Inspired by the success of their colleagues in Anhui, students from neighbouring Shanghai organized their own demonstrations encompassing participants from all of the city's major universities such as Fudan, Jiaotong and Tongji. After marching to the Bund (waterfront) and the People's Square (Shanghai's symbolic political centre), separate rallies were held and demands were made for greater student union autonomy and more student control over their own newspapers (although grievances over certain non-political issues were also voiced with regard, for example, to squalid dormitory conditions and the poor quality of food served in student canteens). In the wake of the Shanghai demonstrations, similar demonstrations took place at university campuses in Nanjing, Tianjin, Xian and Beijing and by late December student protests spread to at least 150 campuses spanning 17 different cities.

In contrast to the ill-fated protests of spring 1989 (see later), the 1986 demonstrations were not marked by bloodshed. Whilst a moderate degree of force was applied in some areas and arrests were made (mainly of the handful of urban workers that participated), the authorities acted with restraint compared with what was to come in 1989. Consequently, in the absence of any obvious provocation, the demonstrations gradually dissipated and by early January 1987 almost all the students had returned to their campuses.

With the exception of the victory scored by CUST students during the elections to Anhui township people's congresses, the 1986 demonstrations failed to bring about any significant political change in China. This was partly because the demonstrators' objectives were vague. Demands for political rights and democratic freedoms were often expressed in a generalized and unspecific manner, reflecting a political naiveté that was perhaps understandable in a nation that had been ruled autocratically for millennia. At the same time, the strength of feeling encompassed by the demonstrations should not be underestimated. Whilst the students may have been unable to articulate precisely what they wanted in terms of political reform, they were clearly dissatisfied with the perceived inability of the party to implement change in this area, not least because change had been promised but not delivered. This dissatisfaction gradually intensified and culminated ultimately in the 1989 demonstrations, a far more potent manifestation of public discontent with the party.

One thing the 1986 demonstrations did bring about (completely unintentionally) was the dismissal of Hu Yaobang as General Secretary. Ignoring Deng's demands that force (or the threat thereof) should be used to coerce the students back to their classrooms, Hu advocated peaceful dialogue. As a result, Deng lost patience with his former protege and during a Politburo meeting in January 1987 Hu was forced to resign his post. Ironically, given the context of the student demonstrations, the method by which Hu was removed was entirely unconstitutional. First, the decision was taken by the Politburo despite the provision in the 1982 party constitution that the General Secretary can only be appointed or removed by a plenary session of the Central Committee. Not only this, but the Politburo meeting was conveniently enlarged to include opponents of Hu from the CAC, the CDIC and other outsiders, all of whom were granted the right to vote (Goldman 1994: 207). Notwithstanding Deng's pledge to reform China's political and decision making process, little had changed in this respect since the Mao era.

Hu was replaced as General Secretary by Zhao Ziyang in 1987. It is often assumed that Zhao and Hu were close allies during the 1980s, but as Goldman (1994: 208) notes Zhao increasingly resented Hu's efforts to involve himself directly in matters relating to the economy, perhaps understandably given that Zhao's role as Premier was to take charge of the economy. Indeed, as early as 1984 Zhao is reported to have written to Deng Xiaoping and Chen Yun requesting that Hu be dismissed. Consequently, Zhao declined to support Hu during the January Politburo meeting and may even have opposed him. In time, however, Zhao probably came to miss having Hu around. As Zhao moved over to head up the party, he was replaced as Premier by the fiscally conservative Li Peng who also took over from Zhao as head of the State Council, thereby causing Zhao to relinquish considerable economic power. By the late 1980s Zhao and Li were locked in a heated debate over the very future of economic reform, a debate which Zhao was to lose (see later).

## Side-effects of economic reform

Although the importance of issues such as political and ideological reform should not be under-stated, the principal focus of party work during the 1980s was on the modernization of the economy. Whilst students and intellectuals may have been dissatisfied with the lack of progress made in reforming the political system or adequately reformulating Chinese Marxism, party leaders clearly felt that if they could significantly increase individual income and improve living standards, these "other issues" could be safely pushed to the periphery. Yet, by relying so heavily on economic performance as the basis for its legitimacy the party was taking a considerable punt on its own political future. Not only was there little else to fall back on should things go wrong, but things, at some stage, were *likely* to go wrong. The task of over-hauling an entrenched state-controlled economy by introducing market-based reforms was always going to be fraught with uncertainties. As these uncertainties began to emerge (particularly during the second half of the 1980s), so the party began to experience a noticeable downturn in its economic legitimacy.

### *Official corruption*

One of the most pronounced side-effects of economic reform was the rise in official corruption. Although corruption was not unprecedented during the Mao era (cases often involved securing "favours" rather than embezzling money (Meany 1991)), the post-Mao emphasis on increased personal income made the growth of corruption almost inevitable. As the early cases of corruption came to light, it soon became apparent that one of the underlying reasons for this rising phenomenon was the piecemeal nature of the reform programme itself, particularly in the industrial sector. Whilst the majority of SOEs at the small and intermediate level were required to operate on the open market following the implementation of the October Directive (see earlier discussion), large scale SOEs remained firmly under the control of the central plan. This meant that when it came to the central allocation of scarce energy and mineral resources (e.g. coal, iron ore and oil), the latter were prioritized at the expense of the former. The acute demand that this created amongst small and intermediate SOEs led to situations in which bribes were offered in order to gain access to these resources. Almost all large SOEs were run by senior party cadres, and given the modest salaries they received (especially in comparison to the earnings of managers of smaller SOEs), the temptation to supplement their modest income by accepting (and sometimes demanding) bribes often proved irresistible.

It was not just high-level cadres who became immersed in corruption. So too did many of their children and relatives, often referred to colloquially as "princelings". The political contacts enjoyed by this privileged group enabled many of them to make money through legitimate means by, for example, securing bank loans with which to set up small businesses or establish lucrative networks for marketing or supply purposes. By the mid-1980s, reports began to surface that the "princelings" were also making money illegally, especially those located in the SEZs and open coastal cities where economic activity was particularly frenetic. One of the main profiteering activities involved the smuggling into China of luxury foreign items which could then be sold on the black market at inflated prices. The most high-profile case took place on the duty-free island of Hainan in August 1985 where military cadres and their offspring spent over US$ 1 billion on illegally importing cars, television sets and video recorders which were then sold on the black market for two or three times the purchase price (Chang 1985).

During its formative years in Yanan, the party established an almost impeccable image of honesty and integrity in its dealings with local people. One of the defining characteristics of a party member was a willingness to subordinate one's personal interests to the good of the party and society (Munro 1977, Gong Wenxiang 1989). In his work on moral guidelines for party members, Liu Shaoqi (1980: 56) wrote that 'every Party member should completely submit himself to the interests of the Party and self-sacrificingly devote himself to the public duty'. But by the 1980s this image had evaporated almost completely as reflected in a wave of officially sponsored opinion polls, the first to be held in the PRC (Rosen 1990). In a nationwide poll conducted in 1988, 1,700 people were presented with a list of over 20 occupations and asked to rank them in order of desirability and public image. On average, government, local party and national party cadres all came in the bottom third of the list, below manual workers and only just above the universally despised tax collector! In another poll conducted in 1988, over 600,000 workers were asked whether they thought the party was winning the fight against corruption within its own ranks. Only 7 per cent of interviewees answered in the affirmative.

Rosen (1990: 83–4) suggests that the results of these polls reflected a deep dissatisfaction with official measures to combat corruption. During 1982–7 as part of a highly publicized CDIC clampdown on corruption almost 800,000 party members were disciplined. Yet, the vast majority of these people were at the lower end of the party hierarchy (almost 92 per cent) with those higher up the party hierarchy appearing to be somehow immune from punishment (only 97 individuals to be disciplined were at or above the provincial level). To make matters worse, those at the top end who were found to be corrupt were often dealt with quite moderately. For example, the former Governor of Jiangxi province who was found, amongst other things, to have embezzled US$ 60,000 in scarce foreign exchange was given a two year jail sentence and released early.

Perhaps of most concern to the party leadership was the decline in the party's image amongst young people as a result of corruption scandals. Throughout his reign, Mao consistently looked to China's youth as the obvious successors of the Chinese revolution. During the Cultural Revolution, in particular, Mao encouraged the young to take part in their very own "revolution from below" in order to prepare them for the time when they would assume the mantle of the revolution.

During the post-Mao era, however, young people seemed uninterested in China's revolutionary legacy and were increasingly disinclined to join a party which they perceived as inherently corrupt. In a poll carried out in Gansu province in 1988, 2,000 educated rural youths were asked whether they were interested in joining the CCP. Barely 6 per cent said they were. In another survey involving Chinese university students conducted just after the 1986 demonstrations, 92 per cent of graduates and 62 per cent of undergraduates felt that the protests arose as a result of official corruption and less than 10 per cent expressed any optimism that corruption would decrease in the future (Rosen 1990: 82–3). Despite official efforts to root out corruption, this negative impression of the party continued to escalate and as millions gathered in protest during 1989, official corruption was at the top of their list of grievances.

### Social and economic dislocations

If corruption was not damaging enough to the legitimacy of the party, a number of economic shortcomings emerged that served to deepen the party's woes. Rising inflation was especially problematic (Naughton 1989). Unprecedented during the Mao era, by 1987 inflation spiralled to around 35 per cent in some urban areas (despite official estimates which put the figure at 21 per cent). One contributory factor was the increased purchasing power (at least *theoretically*) of the urban work force. Enjoying greater autonomy as a result of the October Directive and the regional decentralization policy in general (Goodman 1989, Breslin 1996), SOE managers granted large salary increases to employees without obtaining prior authorization from the central authorities. Flush with money, employees began to spend increasing amounts on consumer goods, causing a sudden influx of money to flood an economy that was already overheating. Inevitably as consumer demand increased so too did retail prices despite attempts by the state to retain control over such prices. Initially, only luxury household items were affected such as colour televisions, fridges and automatic washing machines. However when the price of essential items such as meat, fresh fruit and vegetables began to spiral (in some areas by a reported 50 per cent) the leadership was confronted with a genuine economic crisis as people throughout the country complained that despite having more money than ever before, their purchasing power was actually *falling*. For example, in a 1987 survey of residents from 33 Chinese cities, more than 65 per cent of those sampled stated that their real income was in decline, whilst over 70 per cent identified rising prices as their principal source of concern (Baum 1997: 416–17).

This dire economic situation was accentuated by the (arguably ill-timed) implementation of price reform by Zhao Ziyang. In April 1988 controls were officially lifted on 14 kinds of foodstuffs and when the Politburo announced shortly afterwards that price controls were to be relaxed on all consumer goods, a spate of panic buying swept the country in a manner reminiscent of the last days of the KMT. In anticipation of further price rises (which duly came), the urban population purchased anything they could get their hands on ranging from basic foodstuffs to expensive electronic household goods. As shop shelves emptied so too did bank accounts, causing unprecedented problems for the banking system as the national money supply began to dry up. The problem was particularly acute in Fujian province where savings plummeted by RMB 57.8 million (£4.1 million) in seven days during July 1988. Similarly, the Shenyang (Liaoning province) branch of the Industrial and Commercial Bank saw an RMB 52 million (£3.7 million) fall in reserves between 25 July and 5 August (Breslin 1996: 70–1). In an effort to lure investors back, many banks put up their interest rates on long-term deposits, but with inflation already eating away at savings, the public concluded that it was wiser to spend than to save.

Other reform-related ailments served to heighten the anxieties of China's urban population. After decades of state subsidized accommodation (as part of the "iron rice bowl"), rents began to go up as part of the party's plans to gradually remove housing price controls and eventually sell off state owned accommodation (which it did ten years later) (Saich 1991). The timing could not have been worse. Already faced with rises in food prices, urban dwellers were now being asked to pay a larger share of their household income on rent.

Unemployment was also fast becoming an issue. Following the implementation of the 1987 Enterprise Reform Law which placed greater emphasis on cost cutting and profit margins, nervous employers began to lay off large numbers of employees, primarily those on temporary contracts who could be made redundant immediately and without the expense of redundancy pay. By mid-1988, party officials claimed that over four million people from urban areas were out of work, although the real figure was thought to be much higher (somewhere between 20 and 30 million). Many of those still in work found that their salaries were frozen and in some areas even reduced, and confronted with the very real prospect of redundancy, this lead to a sharp rise in walk-outs and other forms of labour unrest.

Ultimately, it was a combination of these and other socio-economic hardships that forced people on to the streets during spring 1989, most infamously in Beijing's Tiananmen Square (Naughton 1990). Whilst the international media focused on the political demands of the student protestors and the image of the Goddess of Democracy erected opposite the portrait of Mao that hangs below the Gates of Heavenly Peace, many of the demonstrators were ordinary urban dwellers protesting about the decline in living and working standards and rises in prices. Having directed its efforts almost exclusively towards economic reform and having re-moulded the basis of its legitimacy accordingly, the party discovered just how fragile its support base could be if the reforms were not perceived to be working all the time. As White concludes, the rise in popular expectations induced by the reforms put the leadership on a kind of treadmill:

> To the extent that their own popularity and the credibility of the political system they represent depends on their ability to deliver ever higher amounts of welfare, even temporary reverses, often prompted by the dictates of sound economic policy (such as the austerity programme beginning in 1988), bring

popular discontent which is translated by opposition activists into a challenge to the regime itself (as in early 1989).

(1993: 205–6)

This is not to under-estimate the strength of feeling of those who campaigned for political reform. It was the perceived failure of political reform that caused the students to demonstrate in the first place beginning during April 1989 after which they were joined by an increasingly disillusioned urban population. Yet, whilst some of the demonstrators (including influential figures such as Fang Lizhi) demanded the complete overthrow of the CCP and the immediate implementation of a multi-party system of free and democratic elections, a significant number of the student protestors called for democratic changes from *within* the existing political structure. Although the "fifty per cent rule" (discussed earlier) was seen as a step in the right direction, many students wanted this provision extended up to the NPC level and also for non-party candidates to be allowed to stand for a place on the NPC, a measure that Hu Yaobang favoured during his time as General Secretary. Another popular demand was for greater autonomy to be granted to township and county people's congresses in the same way that many SOE managers enjoyed greater freedoms. Other demands included proper legal guarantees for the rights of free speech and assembly, a comprehensive system of checks and balances on the powers of the party and the state and greater independence for China's fledgling interest groups, including the establishment of their own newspapers.

## Conflict at the centre

The public unease created by economic reform during the late 1980s precipitated a fierce debate within the leadership over the future direction of the economy (Hsu 1988: 1225–8, You Ji 1991: 75–91). Generally speaking, two sides emerged, one led by Zhao Ziyang and the other by the increasingly ascendant Premier Li Peng with the support of Yao Yilin (Chairman of the powerful Central Finance and Economics Leadership Group). For Zhao, the solution to China's economic difficulties was to maintain the rapid pace of economic reform. If China was ever to complete the difficult transition from Stalinist central plan to a fully liberalized market economy, the populace would have to endure certain short-term socio-economic hardships but would ultimately reap the long-term benefits. So, for example, in advocating the further restructuring of SOEs, Zhao acknowledged the likelihood of an increase in unemployment at least until those out of work could find meaningful employment in the growing entrepreneurial sector (in theory). But in the long term, Zhao insisted, a radically "downsized" system of SOEs would perform more productively and have a less burdensome effect on central spending.

Zhao also espoused what You Ji (1991: 78) describes as the "coastal strategy." This was a new economic system to be established initially in the coastal regions of southern China and then gradually spread to the rest of the country. Under this system, manufacturers would have clear and emphatic property rights, workers would have freedom of movement within an increasingly fluid job market and most importantly production would move away from the demands of the domestic market and be geared more towards meeting the export needs of the international community: 'as the practice of "what we have, we export" gave way to "what they need, we make and export," central planning over these provincial economies would gradually lose much of its relevance' (You Ji 1991: 78).

Most controversially (and perhaps unfairly), Zhao was closely associated with the reform of China's pricing system. Under the two-tier system introduced in 1983, prices were fixed by the state for essentials such as basic foodstuffs and scarce mineral and natural resources required under the state plan, whilst the prices of other goods were subject to market forces. In some circumstances, however, the retention of price controls led to hoarding and speculation as some people (mainly officials) with access to goods at fixed state prices (especially natural resources) bought up as much as they could and then held them until they could sell them at higher negotiated prices. The elimination of fixed prices, it was claimed, would eliminate this problem.

Li Peng, by contrast, championed a much more cautious approach to the economy. In an effort to slow down economic growth, reduce inflationary pressures and reverse the process of decentralizing economic decision making, Li proposed to restrict state investment in private and rural enterprises, tighten credit ceilings for domestic banks and raise interest rates on bank loans in order to discourage entrepreneurs and private businesses from borrowing more money. Li also sought to re-assert central control over foreign trade and investment by restricting the number of foreign companies authorized to import into China and by expanding the number of imported products that were subject to export licences and quotas. In addition, Li insisted that the SEZs should be required to reduce the amount of foreign exchange retained from foreign exports with the remainder going straight to the central treasury.

As ever, Deng Xiaoping's political blessing was imperative in determining who would win this crucial policy debate. By mid-1988 it appeared that Deng was firmly in the Zhao Ziyang camp. Indeed, if anything, Deng was *more* economically radical than Zhao, especially on the question of price reform and it was reportedly Deng who instructed Zhao to prepare a proposal for the rapid acceleration of price deregulation (Baum 1997: 425). Despite his reservations on this key issue (Zhao had apparently gone off the idea of price reform following early signs of inflation in 1984–5), Zhao was indebted to Deng for his promotion through the ranks of the party and as such he had little choice but to accede to Deng's wishes. However, word of the new proposals quickly became public and this led to the spate of panic buying and the run on banks described earlier.

In light of this impending economic crisis Deng abruptly abandoned his support for price reform (Wilson and You Ji 1990: 35). This left Zhao to take sole responsibility for a policy that he never really favoured and a declining economic situation for which he was not entirely culpable. As conservative opponents in the leadership closed in on Zhao during a tumultuous party summit at Beidaihe,

Deng, with the full support of the CAC, whose support was instrumental in defeating Zhao (Wilson and You Ji 1990: 37), shifted his weight firmly behind Li Peng and within weeks austerity measures were introduced to freeze retail prices, bring money supplies under control and curb inflation. From this point on, Zhao's authority quickly receded and it was not long before Zhao disappeared from sight altogether.

One final point to note of significance to the question of legal rational legitimacy (although of no consolation to Zhao!) was the greater transparency surrounding the leadership tussle over economic policy, particularly in relation to the 1988 meeting at Beidaihe. Whereas previous such meetings were known to be highly secretive affairs, the 1988 gathering was characterized by an unprecedented degree of openness, including interviews and policy briefings with the Chinese media and receptions for foreign guests. Ironically, it was this very openness that created the subsequent wave of panic buying which in turn caused Deng to back-track on the question of price reform. As Baum concludes:

> Such unprecedented elite openness and accessibility – reflections of a new Chinese commitment to *glasnost* – provided much of the grist for the PRC's hyperexcitable rumour mill. In this respect it was the Party's own top leadership, including Deng Xiaoping himself, who arguably bear much of the responsibility for precipitating the consumer panic of 1988.
>
> (1997: 427)

## The death of Hu Yaobang

Just as the death of Zhou Enlai was the impetus for the 1976 Tiananmen demonstrations, so the death of Hu Yaobang in April 1989 (following a heart attack) was the spark that ignited the 1989 protests. Like Zhou, Hu was seen as a moderate force in the face of an intransigent party leadership, particularly amongst the student population who admired Hu's refusal to authorize military force during the 1986 demonstrations (for which he was subsequently fired). As such, it was the students who began the spontaneous outburst of national mourning for Hu which then led to nationwide demonstrations.

Feelings on university campuses throughout Beijing were already running high. Like ordinary urban residents, students were adversely affected by runaway inflation and rising prices and throughout 1988 a series of minor protests took place in reaction to the growing disparity between low student grants and the increasingly high cost of living. There were also reports of open hostilities between Chinese students and their African counterparts; the latter were randomly accused of harassing Chinese women and spreading the AIDs virus. Although such incidents were overtly racist in nature, they were ultimately a reaction to the socio-economic pressures brought to bear on the student population by the reforms (Baum 1997: 433–4).

As news of Hu's death filtered out, hundreds of students marched from Beijing's university district in the north west to Tiananmen Square to lay wreaths at the foot of the Revolutionary Heroes Monument (drawing parallels again to Zhou Enlai's death). Although this was a symbolic act of respect, the student demonstrators had another agenda and within days, as their numbers rose to more than 10,000, this agenda became apparent. As part of a list of demands sent to the NPC Standing Committee, students requested the implementation of genuine legal rights of freedom of speech and expression, an increase in student grants and academic salaries and the full publication of all income received by leading officials and their relatives, a demand designed to flush out corruption within the party. The list also included demands for a more objective official verdict on Hu's role in the 1986 demonstrations. Students clearly used the occasion of Hu's death to voice their overall dissatisfaction with the party. This was also evident on the day of Hu's memorial service on 22 April. Over 100,000 mourners (of which 30,000 were non-students) flocked to Tiananmen to pay their respects, but once the service was over, some students attempted to intercept party leaders as they left the memorial hall. Most notably, demands were made for Li Peng, increasingly portrayed as a demonic figure within student circles, to make himself available for dialogue with (unofficially declared) student leaders of the incipient student movement.

The leadership's response was unyielding. They refused to meet with student leaders (at least initially), reverse the official verdict on Hu Yaobang or recognize any of the other student demands noted in the previous paragraph. Moreover, in an attempt to intimidate students into calling off the demonstrations, the *People's Daily* published an editorial on 26 April which denigrated the demonstrations as 'turmoil' and 'an act of hooliganism' initiated by a group of individuals with 'evil motives'. The editorial had the reverse effect. Outraged by the apparent injustice of these accusations, students now claimed that they were part of a patriotic movement and within days the number of students marching into Tiananmen Square multiplied.

## The military crackdown

The events leading up to the military crackdown are well documented (Dittmer 1989, Landsberger 1989, Salisbury 1989, Saich 1990). Hundreds of thousands of protestors carrying placards demanding improvements to socio-economic conditions, reforms to the political system and an end to party corruption; the erection of the Goddess of Democracy directly opposite the large portrait of Mao Zedong; a visibly ruffled Deng Xiaoping dining with the visiting Soviet President Mikhail Gorbachev (Deng committed the ultimate *faux pas* of dropping food from his chop-sticks in full view of the international media); over 3,000 student hunger strikers lying by the steps of the Great Hall of the People in symbolic protest at an unresponsive regime; the televised meeting between Li Peng and the student leaders Wan Dan and Wu'er Kaixi which turned into a verbal confrontation; the image of a broken Zhao Ziyang apologizing to demonstrators in the square through a hand-held amplifier; the chaotic events of 4 June when the PLA killed more than 1,000 unarmed civilians.

The orthodox wing of the party leadership contemplated military action from the very outset of the demonstrations. Of the five members of the PSC, the hardliners Li Peng, Qiao Shi and Yao Yilin all expressed support for a military solution during an emergency session of the PSC in April 1989 which was deliberately called when Zhao Ziyang (another PSC member) was on an official visit to North Korea. Only Hu Qili expressed misgivings over the use of military force for which he was later dismissed from the PSC. Yang Shangkun, President and a PLA marshal, but significantly (for the purposes of legal rational legitimacy) *not* a member of the PSC, also attended the session and he too expressed his support for military action. Deng Xiaoping, however, was less certain and when Zhao returned from North Korea in early May he persuaded Deng (temporarily) to adopt a more conciliatory attitude towards the demonstrators. Moreover, in an attempt to diffuse the increasingly tense atmosphere on the streets of Beijing, Zhao publicly acknowledged during a meeting with overseas officials that most of the demonstrators were loyal supporters of the party whose demands for political reform and an end to party corruption were perfectly legitimate.

Initially, it seemed that Zhao's softer approach may have worked. In contrast to the inflammatory *People's Daily* editorial of 26 April, Zhao's candid recognition of student demands served to disarm student leaders and led to a gradual decrease in the volume of demonstrators. But Zhao was ultimately undone by events. On 15 May, Mikhail Gorbachev touched down in Beijing for a landmark three day visit and with him arrived the international media. Suddenly, the eyes of the world were on Beijing and this provided student leaders with a perfect opportunity to revive the demonstrations by launching a series of high-profile hunger strikes. Although the hunger strikes succeeded in drawing thousands of deserting protestors back to the square, they also caused acute embarrassment to the leadership, especially during the aforementioned televised confrontation between Li Peng, Wan Dan and Wu'er Kaixi (Baum 1997: 448–9). This ultimately persuaded Deng that force rather than dialogue was the only way to resolve the situation.

Of particular concern to the party leadership was the meticulous way in which the demonstrations were orchestrated. In contrast to the 1986 demonstrations which came together more randomly and were less focused in their objectives, the 1989 protest comprised a series of carefully organized groups with precise and often wide ranging agendas. As we have seen, the principal organizers were university students. It was they who co-ordinated the early marches from north west Beijing into Tiananmen Square, setting up their own cordons and employing student monitors to keep things under control, and it was they who were the first to issue specific demands to Li Peng and the rest of the leadership. As the demonstrations became more firmly entrenched in the square, organizational methods became even more sophisticated. For example, in response to the official propaganda broadcasts which excoriated the cause of the hunger strikers and dismissed the demonstrations as "anti-party," the students set up their own electronic loudspeaker equipment to counter the party's message. Hand bills explaining student demands poured out of specially installed mimeograph machines and were disseminated to anyone who was interested. In addition, motorcycle brigades such as the Flying Tigers were established to deliver messages to other student groups participating in the demonstrations.

Initially, student demonstrators were grouped into universities and within them academic departments. But it was not long before more autonomous student groups began to appear declaring their full independence from the existing state-controlled students union (the National Students' Union of China) and demanding that the government recognize their independent status. The first and most active of these groups was the Beijing Students' Autonomous Federation (BSAF), led by Wu'er Kaixi who played a highly prominent role in the demonstrations before fleeing to America after the crackdown. Once the BSAF was established, other autonomous student unions sprang up throughout the country. Given the party's claim to be the only legitimate political organization in China, these groups were perceived as a direct threat to CCP authority.

Intellectuals also began to organize themselves more coherently. In the past, intellectuals were renowned for remaining aloof from public demonstrations, perceiving their correct role in society as a conduit between the people and their rulers. But throughout the 1980s, intellectuals became increasingly outspoken, especially in their demands for political reform, and for the first time in modern history many of them joined the students in demonstrating for improvements to the political system. Furthermore, a hardcore of radical intellectuals' broke out from the state-controlled organization (All-China Federation of Literary and Art Circles) and established the Beijing Intellectuals' Autonomous Federation, which like the BSAF, declared its full independence from party control.

Yet, of most concern to the CCP was the large number of ordinary urban workers that participated in the demonstrations, especially those who organized themselves into independent workers' unions. The urban workforce was one of the largest and most important sectors in Chinese society and for this reason the party maintained a tight grip on its activities through the state-controlled All-China Federation of Trade Unions. The establishment of a handful of independent unions suggested that this control was waning and that some workers believed that their interests were no longer represented by the party. This was certainly apparent in a manifesto released by the Beijing Workers' Federation (BWF) which criticized the party for rising inflation and declining urban living standards, encouraged Beijing's urban workforce to stand up to a corrupt and dictatorial party and pledged its support for the cause of China's students. Notwithstanding that only a small number of independent trade unions formed during 1989, this was enough to confirm Deng's worst fear that a Chinese version of the Polish workers' Solidarity movement was emerging and might attempt to launch a direct challenge to the authority of the CCP. On many occasions throughout the 1980s, Deng had warned that the lesson to be learned from Solidarity was that workers' movements were dangerous and should not be allowed to operate in China. It was no coincidence that when the troops finally broke into Tiananmen Square in the early hours of 4 June, the first place they went was to the BWF's temporary headquarters.

## The legacy of Tiananmen

The economic achievements of the 1980s cannot be over-stated. After years of economic under-performance under Mao when the CCP seemed more concerned with class struggle and political infighting than with economic and social development, Deng Xiaoping presided over a decade of phenomenal economic growth. This not only improved the living standards of much of China's population but it also put China in a position where it began to be acknowledged as an important economic player in the international community.

But by the end of the decade it was difficult to gauge whether the CCP was in better shape in terms of its legitimacy than it had been at the start of the decade. Although the CCP had re-invented itself as the party of economic performance, the reforms had thrown up a number of new issues which served to damage the party's legitimacy. Despite best (and imaginative) efforts to the contrary, the party's long-standing Marxist legitimacy was in terminal decline with Marxism no longer serving as a credible guiding force for the masses. Nor had the party successfully confronted the thorny issue of political reform, a failure which ultimately brought it into direct conflict with the student and intellectual population. Most importantly, the growth of official corruption, together with dramatic increases in inflation and unemployment raised fundamental questions about the party's ability to manage the economic reform process to which it was so closely bound.

As the party commemorated the fortieth anniversary of the founding of the PRC in October 1989 there seemed little cause for celebration. The armed military assault on unarmed students had damaged (albeit temporarily) China's hard-earned reputation amongst Western powers as a reforming communist state. Beijing was under martial law, its population subdued and disillusioned. An aging orthodox clique, including members of the CAC, had taken control of the party leadership. Even economic reform, the very lifeblood of the party throughout the 1980s, appeared to have run out of steam. As China stumbled into the 1990s, the CCP's legitimacy had reached a new nadir and it was far from clear whether the regime could remain in power without further resort to force.

# 6  In search of new paradigms of legitimacy

## China since Tiananmen

The experience of the 1980s taught the CCP that it was politically dangerous to rely too heavily on economic performance as a basis for legitimacy. Unable to reconcile its Marxist ideology with the increasingly active role of the market and unwilling to wholeheartedly embrace institutional and other political reforms, the party looked more and more to the economy as a means of shoring up its popular appeal. Notwithstanding the economic achievements of this period and the financial benefits enjoyed by many people, the reforms also brought with them some undesirable, if inevitable, socio-economic side-effects as discussed previously. In the absence of any other credible form of legitimacy to deflect public attention away from these problems, many people in China began to resent the CCP, culminating ultimately in the national demonstrations of spring 1989.

Since then, the party has sought out other potential sources of popular support to supplement its economic legitimacy. We will see in this chapter, for example, how greater attention has been paid to legal rational legitimacy, particularly in the post-Deng era of Jiang Zemin and the post-Jiang era of Hu Jintao and how efforts have been made to develop an electoral mode of legitimacy with far reaching reforms to village elections. We will also examine the very recent phenomenon of stability as a basis of legitimacy; the assertion that continued CCP rule is the only way of guaranteeing the political stability and personal safety that disappeared after the collapse of communist states in Eastern Europe. Finally, we will assess developments in the CCP's ideological legitimacy, not only with regard to Marxism and the continued revision thereof, but also in relation to anti-foreign nationalism, an area in which the party has expended most energy in attempting to broaden its popularity.

But things have not gone particularly smoothly for the CCP since Tiananmen. Whilst the economy has continued to grow at near double digit rates, thus enhancing the party's economic legitimacy amongst those who have benefited from this growth, the social and economic disruptions that were evident in the 1980s have, if anything, become even more pronounced. Instances of official corruption have increased innumerably and become much more high profile, unemployment has risen sharply in both urban and rural areas and the PRC is now acknowledged as one of the most unequal societies in the world (an irony in itself given the country is run by a nominally communist party). These and other factors have led to almost daily instances of social unrest in places worst affected by reform-related hardships. Nor have attempts to diversify the party's legitimacy been especially successful. Most notably, the increased emphasis on nationalism appears to have backfired on the CCP. After whipping up an anti-foreign fervour in the early 1990s, the party has since been confronted by an increasing number of unofficial nationalist groups which are highly critical of China's foreign policy, especially with regard to America and Japan. Ironically, nationalism in China is now threatening to detract from rather than bolster party legitimacy.

## Developing legal rational legitimacy

One of the most recurrent themes of this book has been the fragility of the CCP's legal rational legitimacy. Although this was especially marked during the Mao era which was characterized by a complete disdain for decision making procedures (most notably, during the Cultural Revolution), Deng Xiaoping did little to improve the party's credibility in this respect after coming to power in the late 1970s. Indeed, in a manner not dissimilar to the Mao era, elite politics in China during the 1980s, whilst free of Maoist political purges, continued to be run by individuals rather than in accordance with legal procedure, with Deng, like Mao, invariably acting as the final arbiter on key decisions of party and state.

### Zhao's dismissal and Jiang's appointment

The post-Tiananmen era started off badly in legal rational terms, as evidenced by the manner in which Zhao Ziyang was dismissed as General Secretary in June 1989 and Jiang Zemin was appointed to that post. The increasingly orthodox party leadership held Zhao almost entirely responsible for the economic tensions that led to the 1989 demonstrations, despite the fact that in some cases (e.g. price deregulation) Zhao was simply following Deng's directives. Zhao also stood accused of supporting the demonstrators through his espousal of dialogue rather than military action and his impromptu visit to Tiananmen Square where he publicly apologized to the demonstrators. The pressure brought to bear on Zhao in the weeks before the crackdown pushed him into tendering his resignation on at least two occasions. But even though Deng had already decided that Zhao was no longer fit for office, he refused to let Zhao simply walk away from the job, claiming that this would expose divisions in the leadership which might intensify the demonstrations. Whilst Deng's logic was probably accurate in this regard, he had another reason for holding out on Zhao. Deng wanted to sack Zhao publicly. Just as Mao used Lin Biao as a scapegoat for the Cultural Revolution, so Deng needed to use Zhao as a scapegoat for the Tiananmen demonstrations.

Zhao was formally dismissed as General Secretary during a plenary session (the Fourth) of the Central Committee (the Thirteenth). On the face of it, this was in accordance with constitutional practice. Crucially, however, the Plenum was enlarged so as to accommodate, amongst others, almost 200 CAC elders, most of whom were hostile to Zhao (Shambaugh 1989). As with Hu Yaobang's dismissal as General Secretary in 1987, the provision forbidding CAC members from voting at Central Committee plenary meetings was conveniently ignored in order to ensure that Zhao was comprehensively voted off as General Secretary and that Jiang was elected to that post.

Elite manoeuvrings before the Fourth Plenum also betrayed a disregard for legal rational procedure. According to Nathan and Link (2001: 260–1, 308–14), the decision to remove Zhao and appoint Jiang was reached during a series of informal meetings held between Deng, Chen Yun and Li Xiannian some weeks before the Fourth Plenum. News of this decision was then transmitted to prospective attendees who were "advised" on how to vote. During a meeting with PSC members Li Peng and Yao Yilin not long before the Fourth Plenum, Deng was almost contemptuous in informing them of his decision on Zhao (Baum 1997: 474). This episode showed that even members of the highest decision making body in the party were not properly consulted about this key change of personnel. Instead, the decision appears to have been reached by three non-PSC members, each of whom had in theory retired from active political life!

By way of background, it is important to note why Jiang Zemin, a relative outsider as Mayor of Shanghai until 1987 (when he was promoted to the Politburo), was catapulted into the limelight as General Secretary of the CCP. Deng Xiaoping was again a key player in this promotion and he backed Jiang for at least four reasons (Baum 1997: 465). First, Jiang occupied the centre of the political spectrum, favouring economic reform but without the emphasis on political reform (in contrast to his predecessors Hu Yaobang and to a lesser extent Zhao Ziyang). Second, Jiang was an import from Shanghai and as such was untainted by the political factionalism that was rife within the party leadership. In this respect, Deng probably thought that Jiang would be able to strike out on his own without being dragged down by party infighting. Third, Jiang had consistently taken a firm stance against bourgeois liberalism in Shanghai and in this sense was seen to be tougher than Zhao and Hu had been. Finally, Jiang was able to defuse the student protests in Shanghai during 1986–7 without resorting to military action or martial law (Maier 1990). In this respect, he had acted skilfully and moreover his hands were "clean".

### The battle for control of the economy

Irrespective of the leading role that Deng played in removing Zhao and appointing Jiang, for some time after the Tiananmen crackdown Deng found himself frozen out of the economic decision making process. To be sure, Deng was never directly involved in the specifics of formulating economic policy, choosing instead to set overall agendas (Bachman 1988), but by 1990 he was largely ignored by his leadership colleagues on a number of key economic matters. Deng's subsequent success in re-imposing himself on the centre was testament to his skilful political manipulation. At the same time, it also exposed his continued contempt for legal rational procedures.

The demise of Zhao Ziyang was a considerable blow to Deng's political credibility. Despite Deng's efforts to distance himself from Zhao's economic radicalism in favour of Li Peng's more moderate retrenchment programme, there was no avoiding the fact that much of the responsibility for the economic crisis of the late 1980s lay ultimately with Deng. After all, Zhao was Deng's man. Deng had hand picked Zhao as a future successor and the person best equipped to accelerate the reform process. As such, when Zhao lost control of the economy it reflected badly on Deng. Add to this the embarrassment of Hu Yaobang's dismissal in 1987 (another of Deng's chosen successors) and Deng was beginning to look like a poor judge of character. Consequently, as the party sought to move on from Tiananmen, the resurgent conservative faction in the leadership led by Li Peng and his mentor Chen Yun, attempted to sideline Deng from key decisions affecting the economy and turn him into a national figurehead with no real power. Ironically, as Fewsmith (1997: 498) points out, the objective of Li Peng and his allies 'was to turn Deng into the titular leader of the Party, much as Liu Shaoqi and Deng himself might have hoped to do to Mao in the early 1960s'.

Deng's isolation from the decision making process was manifested by a shift towards the restoration of central economic control in direct contradiction to his decentralization policy of the 1980s. One aspect of this change in direction was the establishment of the State Council Production Commission, a new central planning body heavily staffed with allies of Li Peng. In accordance with Li's instructions, the new body implemented a policy known as the Double Guarantee System. The first guarantee was that SOEs would be re-prioritized when it came to the allocation of raw material and state money, another key concern of the central planners. The second guarantee, on the other hand, was that such enterprises would deliver a greater proportion of their income (mainly in the form of taxes) and output to the state (Fewsmith 1997: 481).

In seeking to reverse what appeared to be the abandonment of his reforms (many of the fiscal austerity measures imposed just before Tiananmen remained in place), Deng employed the classically Maoist technique of utilizing his support network outside the party leadership. Just as Mao had done during the mid-1950s leadership dispute over the pace of agricultural collectivization, Deng turned to his allies in the provincial party apparatus in an effort to generate enough support to overwhelm his opponents at the centre.

Deng's first, albeit unsuccessful, assault on the centre was made via his support base in Shanghai where he had formed a close relationship with Mayor (and soon to be Vice-Premier) Zhu Rongji. With Zhu's blessing, Deng gave a series of speeches in late 1990 and early 1991 in which he championed the need for further economic reform and espoused a theory known as the Criterion of Productive Forces (ironically, touted some years earlier by the now disgraced Zhao Ziyang). This held that any method which contributed towards the reforms, whether it be the central plan or the open market, could accurately be defined as socialist (see later discussion). In an effort to force the centre into line, the content of Deng's speeches was published in the influential Shanghai newspaper *Liberation Army Daily*. But opposition in Beijing remained firm and Deng's views were dismissed (albeit carefully) by Chen Yun and his son Chen Yuan (Deputy Governor of the People's Bank of China) (Fewsmith 1997: 486–7).

The second (this time successful) attempt at a breakthrough came in January 1992 when Deng made a symbolic visit to the southern cities of Shenzhen and Zhuhai, the SEZs most closely associated with the achievements of economic reform (Zhao Suisheng 1993, Wong and Zheng Yongnian 2001). Adopting a more aggressive posture than in Shanghai, Deng publicly dismissed his rivals' assertion that the acceleration of the reforms caused the Tiananmen crisis and would eventually destroy the CCP. For Deng, the exact opposite was true. Economic reform *saved* the CCP after the turmoil of the Cultural Revolution and helped the party overcome the crisis that it faced in 1989. The real threat to China's future came from the conservatives in the leadership who sought to sabotage the reforms and return China to an era of uncertainty, dominated by ideological campaigns and class struggle. In concluding, Deng reiterated his Criterion of Productive Forces theory and called on Guangdong (which encompasses Shenzhen and Zhuhai) to catch up economically with the wealthy "dragons" of South East Asia (i.e. Taiwan, South Korea, Singapore and Hong Kong) in 20 years.

As provincial leaders from the south gathered in support of Deng, the Politburo was forced to disseminate the content of Deng's speeches to cadres at and above the ministerial, provincial and army ranks. Pressure from local media sources then forced the national media to break its silence on Deng's southern tour with a *People's Daily* editorial on 22 February 1992. This in turn forced conservative leaders at the centre to yield. Although Yao Yilin and Song Ping (PSC member since 1989) remained hostile to the acceleration of the reforms, Jiang Zemin endorsed Deng's position, and with key figures such as Yang Shangkun, Qiao Shi, Zhu Rongji and Li Ruihuan also firmly in the Deng camp, Li Peng found that he had little alternative but to fall into line. With the Politburo rallying behind Deng (albeit with the help of yet another enlarged plenary session), the way was set for the resurrection of economic reform and on 31 March 1992 Deng's victory was finally acknowledged by the *People's Daily* with a laudatory front page publication of his southern tour.

Deng's victory over the conservatives said much about the continued importance of the individual in Chinese elite politics. Only in a country like China could the public appearance of one man have such an impact on the direction of government policy. In a manner not dissimilar to Mao's notorious swim across the Yangtze in 1966, Deng scotched rumours of his ill-health by turning up in person in Shenzhen and Zhuhai with dramatic effect. Underlying Deng's success in this regard was the residual strength of his charismatic authority. To be sure, provincial leaders probably supported Deng in part for pragmatic reasons. They were no doubt keen, for example, to retain the considerable autonomy they now enjoyed as a result of Deng's decentralization policy and many simply ignored Li Peng's attempts to claw back power at the centre (which unquestionably contributed to Li's defeat). But they also backed Deng because of *who* he was, namely the man who survived the violence of the Cultural Revolution to become the founding-father of post-Mao modern China.

At the same time, however, in exploiting his charismatic authority amongst local leaders, Deng simultaneously violated the legal rational norms of democratic centralism which assert that the party line must be adhered to once a majority decision is reached. After Tiananmen, Deng's desire to intensify reform was very much a minority view amongst the orthodox leadership. His refusal to accept this situation showed that he was still committed to using any method possible to get what he wanted. Here again we can see the incompatibility between legal rational legitimacy and charismatic legitimacy as noted throughout this book.

### The question of leadership succession

Notwithstanding his neglect of legal rational procedures in the example provided in the previous section, Deng consistently espoused his commitment to a more institutionalized political process, first made during his landmark 1980 speech on political reform. One aspect of this relates to the transition of power from one generation of party leaders to the next. In light of his own experience of political purges during the Mao era and the power struggle with Hua Guofeng, Deng was determined to ensure that an orderly transfer of power took place after he died (which he finally did in February 1997) such that Jiang Zemin, officially acknowledged as the "core" of the party after 1989, would retain his grip on Chinese politics. Although Jiang concurrently held the top posts in each of the party (General Secretary from 1989), the government (President from 1993) and the military (Chair of the CMC from 1993), the experience of Hua Guofeng (the last man to concurrently hold these three posts) showed that high office alone would not guarantee Jiang's succession. As such, with Deng's political backing, Jiang moved to fortify his position within these three institutions before Deng died such that when Deng did finally die Jiang was able to hold on to power.

What was noticeable about the consolidation of Jiang's power base (and indeed Jiang's leadership career in general) was the absence of resort to political purge and a reliance instead on institutional procedure. As a member of the post-Long March generation of Chinese leaders, Jiang was not really able to draw on a vast reservoir of charismatic legitimacy and as a university educated technocrat with no military record to speak of, Jiang also lacked personal authority over the PLA, still a key institution in Chinese politics. In this sense Jiang had little alternative but to utilize legal rational methods to build himself up (Hamrin 2001, Shambaugh 2001, Shirk 2001).

One example of this was the ousting of political opponents such as Chen Xitong, Secretary of the Beijing party and member of the Politburo. Chen was exposed during a high-profile corruption investigation in 1995 personally orchestrated by Jiang. In formally removing Chen from office during the Fifth Plenum of the Fourteenth Central Committee in September 1995, Jiang drew specifically on a resolution (passed at the Fourth Plenum in September 1994) that no party member was above being punished following a breach of party discipline and that any violation was to be dealt with severely (Fewsmith 2001: 166). Similarly, in securing the removal of another opponent, Qiao Shi, from the Central Committee in 1997, Jiang applied the provision requiring that all those over the age of 70 years old should step down from political office, although, conveniently, party elder Bo Yibo insisted the rule should not apply to Jiang himself (Fewsmith 2001: 193).

Arguably, an even greater test of the party's commitment to legal rational procedures came at the Sixteenth National Party Congress in October 2002, the point at which power was scheduled to be formally transferred from the third generation of CCP leaders represented by Jiang Zemin to the fourth generation represented by Hu Jintao (Lyman Miller 2002, Fewsmith 2003a). In contrast to the transition from Jiang to Deng in 1997 which effectively involved Jiang *retaining* his positions of power in the face of possible opposition after Deng's death, the Sixteenth National Party Congress required that one generation of leaders actually *give up* power, as most clearly symbolized by the transfer of the post of General Secretary from Jiang to Hu.

In the context of PRC history, the Sixteenth National Party Congress was successful in legal rational terms in that the transition of power from Jiang to Hu as the new General Secretary proceeded in accordance with constitutional law and without a fight. The key issue, however, was the extent to which Jiang would continue to wield influence in the new Hu era from behind the scenes. Despite pressure from some of his colleagues, Jiang retained his position as Chair of the CMC beyond 2003 (when he was constitutionally obliged to give it up) in an apparent attempt to ensure continuity in foreign policy, particularly with regard to the United States (Jiang finally relinquished the post to Hu in September 2004). Jiang was also allowed to continue receiving minutes of PSC meetings (apparently with Hu's blessing) even after he relinquished the Presidency to Hu at the Tenth National People's Congress in March 2003 (again, in accordance with constitutional practice). In addition, Jiang retained a considerable say in PSC appointments, enabling him to continue influencing party policy. As such, whilst giving up most of his official positions of power in 2003, Jiang, like Deng before him, remained a pivotal figure in the decision making process.

As Jiang himself once was, Hu Jintao is currently head of party, state and military, suggesting a continued unwillingness on behalf of the CCP to implement a genuine separation of powers and a continued belief in the importance of the paramount leader. Despite this, Hu's incumbency has represented something of a breakthrough in legal rational terms, specifically in relation to the transparency of his regime. Examples of this include Hu's openness over the true extent of the HIV epidemic in China, and in particular over the SARS (Severe Acute Respiratory Syndrome) crisis which first emerged in Guangdong in November 2002. Hu and his new Premier Wen Jiabao inherited a cover-up on SARS. Initially, the official line held that SARS had been successfully contained. However, once the scale of the problem became clear during 2003 Hu was swift to move, firing the Mayor of Beijing (Meng Xuenong) and the Minister of Public Health (Zhang Wenkang) for their role in the deceit and allowing unprecedented access to inspectors from the World Health Organization. In addition, Hu quickly lifted the ban on publicity that was imposed the year before by inviting China's media to report openly on the crisis. He also authorized a team of high-profile political leaders to tour the country urging people to rally behind the party in defeating the epidemic. At the same time, it should be noted that Hu was careful not to invest the media with *too* much autonomy on this subject for fear of precipitating calls for greater press freedom. In addition, editors of those publications which took a particularly bold stance on the epidemic were censured and, just for good measure, a ban was imposed on reporting on the outbreak of Encephalitis B in China.

Hu's relative candidness on such a thorny issue as SARS is unheard of in the PRC and left Jiang Zemin and his colleagues, who were largely responsible for the cover-up, looking embarrassed. This embarrassment was enhanced by the delay in announcing the deaths of 70 Chinese sailors in a submarine accident in February 2003. Jiang, as Chair of the CMC, would have known, and may well have been responsible, for such delay. By contrast, Hu's dramatic *volte face* on SARS has allowed the new Hu–Wen team to emerge as a much more open and accessible alternative to the old Jiang leadership, as reflected in opinion polls which show a rising confidence in the regime (Hays Gries and Rosen 2004: 17–18).

## Towards the electoral mode?

Another important development since Tiananmen has been the expansion of grass roots electoral democracy in China as part of an effort by the party to boost its electoral legitimacy. We examined in Chapter 5, some of the key reforms made to the election of deputies to people's congresses (e.g. the extension of direct elections to the county level) but noted that a number of problems remained. Voters were still largely uninformed about candidates and the candidate selection process remained broadly under the control of the party, leading to voter apathy at the polls. The situation since the 1980s has improved. Voters are much better informed about who they can vote for and what the candidates stand for, party control of the candidate selection process has reduced and voter participation has increased (O'Brien 2001: 415–16).

Of perhaps greater significance is the increasing sophistication of elections (and the electorate) at the Villagers' Committee (VC) level (the level immediately below the township people's congress) following the enactment of the Organic Law of Villagers' Committees (OLVC) in 1987 (revised in 1998). Like the people's congress elections, and perhaps because of their experience of such elections, voters were initially sceptical of VC elections and in many places turnout was poor (O'Brien 1994: 51–3). Since the early 1990s the quality of VC elections has improved, increasing voter interest and participation and attracting attention from both within China and abroad.

One of the main factors that distinguishes VCs from township people's congresses is the greater autonomy that the former are granted. Whilst VCs (each of which comprise between three and seven members elected for a three year term) are empowered to assist in township work, the townships by contrast are forbidden by Article 4 of the OLVC from participating in VC affairs. VCs also enjoy more control over local resources than township people's congresses. In a study of eight Fujian villages (Fujian is widely recognized as a pacesetter in VC electoral developments) carried out by O'Brien (2001: 416) VCs controlled an average of 15 per cent of the annual income earned by village residents. Moreover, as Oi and Rozelle (2000) point out, although the local party secretary usually controls enterprise management in wealthy regions, even those VCs that might be described as weak own the village land and usually enjoy a veto over decisions relating to the application of village resources.

In terms of empowering citizens' with rights, the VC system allows all adults registered in a particular village to vote and stand for election (Article 12), although in some areas the mentally handicapped are still excluded (Elklit 1997: 6). Women's rights have become increasingly robust. During the initial period after the OLVC was first promulgated, "family balloting" was commonplace, allowing a "representative" of the family (usually the male head) to cast a vote on his family's behalf. This practice has since been banned in Fujian and many other provinces (Shi Tianjian 1999: 394). Women are also guaranteed "appropriate" representation on VCs (Article 9).

Amendments to the OLVC have increased voter privacy and freedom of choice. In contrast to the 1987 draft, secret voting (previously many voters filled out their ballots in public) and open counts are now compulsory and the number of candidates must exceed the number of posts (e.g. a minimum of five candidates for four posts). Here again, Fujian has led the way by requiring that more than one candidate must stand for each post (e.g. a minimum of eight candidates for four posts). Fujian and other provinces have also banned voting by proxy, experimented with absentee ballots and made primaries compulsory (O'Brien 2001: 417). Of further note is the right of the electorate (Article 15) to submit to the relevant department reports of any electoral malpractice (e.g. intimidation, bribes or forged ballots), although this power does not extend to the removal or replacement of a VC member (Article 11). According to O'Brien (2004), many village voters now combine their legal rights of protest (also comprising collective petitions and seeking audiences with power holders) with what he describes as "not quite unlawful" actions (e.g. silently marching through village streets with lit candles in broad daylight as a symbol of the "dark rule" of the VC authorities) as a means demonstrating their displeasure with an unpopular leader or VC. Such behaviour (which O'Brien refers to as "boundary spanning contention") is never *patently* in violation of prevailing statutes, although it is often tenuously close to being so.

On a less positive note are the imperfections still associated with VC elections. For example, the provision empowering residents of a particular village to vote or stand for election means that non-residents are logically precluded from doing so (Article 20), disenfranchizing millions in the modern Chinese era of inter-rural migration. Women are under-represented (even in the more progressive areas) despite, or perhaps because of, Article 9 (see earlier) which is ambiguous at best in guaranteeing women "appropriate" representation. According to O'Brien (2001: 419–20), a VC often contains only one woman 'and it is easy to guess her portfolio – the thankless job of enforcing family planning'. Furthermore, as Howell (1998: 99–100) points out, female representation has declined since the mid-1990s following a central directive to combine neighbouring VCs as part of a cost-cutting exercise.

Election malpractice is also a problem. So-called "steering groups", usually headed by the village party secretary and sometimes even containing VC candidates, often dominate the candidate nomination process at the expense of genuine villager participation (Pastor and Tan Qingshan 2000: 494). The procedures for choosing VC candidates from the original nominees are unclear with local party branches often in a position to obstruct the progress of "inappropriate" nominees (Kelliher 1997: 82). The persistent use of mobile ballot boxes in areas that do not require them (this method of voting is meant only for use in isolated regions or to assist the sick and elderly to vote) casts serious doubt over ballot secrecy. In a study of a Liaoning VC election over 90 per cent of the votes were cast in mobile boxes instead of at polling stations (Pastor and Tan Qingshan 2000: 497–8). Perhaps most significantly (although not necessarily a form of election malpractice), research suggests that on important economic matters real decision making authority continues to rest with the local party secretary rather than with the VC (Oi 1996: 136).

Our analysis of VC elections in China brings us logically back to Beetham's electoral mode. As we saw in the Introduction, the dual characteristics underpinning the electoral mode are the enfranchizement of the entire adult population and a genuine choice of political parties at the polls. Clearly, Beetham's model is most applicable to modern day multi-party democracies rather than single party systems like China, but it is nevertheless useful to examine the extent to which VC elections (which claim after all to be democratic within a village context) conform to the electoral mode. In terms of enfranchizement, there are, as we have seen, serious negative consequences deriving from the requirement that only people registered as residents of a particular village are entitled to vote in elections to that VC in that those millions who frequently move to other villages (often in search of work) are prohibited from voting in their "adopted" villages. There are also problems regarding lack of real candidate choice stemming from the domination of the candidate nomination process by the local party secretary and the lack of clarity underpinning the procedures for choosing VC candidates from the original nominees.

Notwithstanding these difficulties and the others noted earlier, within a Chinese context the continuing development and maturity of VC elections represents a notable breakthrough in local democracy. Perhaps the clearest evidence of the legitimacy of these elections lies in the considerable increase in voter participation. Despite the initial lack of voter interest, turn out at the polls improved dramatically once villagers realized that the elections were an ideal way of dislodging corrupt or incompetent leaders. Indeed, Pastor and Qingshan (2000: 504) found that in some villages the turnover of VC personnel after an election was 31 per cent. Other studies have shown that entire teams of VC members have been voted out of office in some areas, especially where economic growth has been unsuccessful. In addition, more and more villagers feel empowered to nominate candidates or even stand for election, and in general the atmosphere surrounding

VC elections is increasingly lively. There has, for example, been a notable increase in campaigning.

But what do VC elections mean for the legitimacy of the CCP, which might seem somewhat remote from the whole process? Whilst the leadership would insist that VC elections are an example of the party functioning as a modern and progressive force, there are, inevitably, motivations of regime legitimacy underpinning the improvements made to VC elections. One of the principal reasons for instituting the elections has been to ensure that corrupt or self-serving local leaders, whose rule may have alienated their constituents, are held accountable at the polls. By facilitating this process, the leadership anticipates that it will take some credit for this, given the problems that official corruption continues to pose for the party (as discussed later). The leadership also hopes that in offering villagers an opportunity to oust unpopular leaders, the electorate will not take to the streets in a protest that might ultimately be directed at the party. As O'Brien (2004: 109) explains, 'by making the lowest level cadres more accountable to the people they rule, Party leaders in Beijing hope to shore up the regime, boost their legitimacy and prevent wayward officials from driving the people to rebellion'.

Some scholars believe there is an inherent danger for the CCP in opening up the democratic process at the VC level in that it may create a "snowball effect" such that democracy sweeps inexorably through all levels of the party-state. China would not be the first country to experience this. Significantly for the CCP, as Chao and Myers (2000) point out, local election activity was the beginning of democratic development in neighbouring Taiwan which ultimately spelled the end of single party rule by the KMT.

## The question of economic legitimacy

Aside from the party's efforts to enhance its legal rational and electoral legitimacy, the popularity of the regime has remained most closely linked to its ability to deliver on the economy, which it has done, on the face of it, with some success. Consistently high annual growth rates (9.1 per cent in 2003 and 9.5 per cent in 2004 and in the first half of 2005) deriving primarily from China's increasing participation in the global economy (culminating in its accession to the World Trade Organization (WTO) in 2001) have continued to raise the living standards of millions of Chinese and have made China one of the world's leading economic powers (Lardy 2002, Zweig 2002). The Chinese economy is now the second biggest in the world (behind America). China is the fourth largest trader in the world and has massive foreign currency reserves (second only to Japan). In this context it might seem incongruous to talk about economic dilemmas challenging party legitimacy. Yet, just as it was during the 1980s, the party has been confronted by an array of pressing economic difficulties which have grown out of the economic reform process and which in each case pose a considerable threat to the party's popularity.

### High level corruption

One such problem has been the persistence of official corruption. We saw in Chapter 5 how the introduction of economic reform led to a sudden rise in corruption. This was caused primarily by the incremental way in which the reforms were implemented, allowing dishonest local officials to take advantage of their positions of power for personal gain. Despite numerous leadership campaigns to deal with the issue (including highly publicized executions, mass expulsions from the party and greater transparency in relation to the financial affairs of officials), instances of corruption have multiplied within party and government circles (Ting Gong 1997, Lu Xiaobo 2000).

One of the reasons for this is the continued concentration of power at the local level providing opportunities for officials to exploit certain processes related to the reforms. Some local officials have been able to use their positions of authority to control the procedure for the allocation of new production or construction contracts and have often accepted (or sometimes demanded) bribes from bidding companies or have established their own companies which then win the tender. One of the most high-profile examples of this form of corruption involved the Mayor of Shenyang, Mu Suixin, who manipulated the tendering process so that his wife's construction company was awarded the contract to build a new ring road around the city and so that his daughter won the RMB 280 million (£20 million) contract to provide new street lighting in the region. Mu was sentenced to death in October 2001, as was his deputy Ma Xiangdong and 15 other senior officials from the province. Similarly, as more and more state assets are privatized, officials have found themselves able to manipulate prices so as to ensure that they, their families or their associates can buy those assets at favourable prices. In this way, as Guo Yong and Hu Angang (2004: 272) point out, the government is in complete control, not as 'the maker of the rules of the game, but also the sportsman competing in the game and the referee for the game at the same time'.

As cases of corruption increased during the 1990s and into the early twenty-first century, they also became (and continue to be) much more high profile. In 1995, the Deputy Mayor of Beijing, Wang Baosen, was accused of stealing around RMB 18 million (£1.3 million) of treasury money, committing suicide on discovering that he was being investigated. In 1998, Beijing party head and Politburo member Chen Xitong (whom we discussed earlier) was sentenced to 16 years in prison (but later released on medical parole) for his role in an RMB 300 million (£21.4 million) embezzlement scandal. In 2000, Vice-Chair of the NPC Cheng Kejie was executed for misappropriating over RMB 40 million (£2.9 million) from the state.

Some of the biggest corruption cases have been linked with large infrastructure or redevelopment projects such as the Three Gorges project to dam the Yangtze River. A 1999 audit for the massive resettlement associated with this project (affecting approximately two million people) showed that over RMB 473 million (£33.8 million) had gone missing, comprising 8.8 per cent of the total resettlement fund. A separate report conducted in July 2000 showed that 97 state officials participated in corrupt activities relating to the project. The construction of the world's largest network of ring roads in Beijing has also been plagued by corruption scandals. Most notably, the man heading up the project, Bi Yuxi, is currently under investigation on suspicion of embezzling RMB 60 million (£4.3 million). There have also been instances of corruption in relation to preparations for the Beijing 2008 Olympics. Official investigations found that between 1999 and 2003, the General Administration of Sports siphoned off RMB 131 million (£9.4 million) earmarked for redevelopment programmes related to the games.

### Local corruption: illegal taxes in rural areas

Highly publicized cases such as these are clearly very damaging to the party's legitimacy as reflected in the results of national surveys frequently carried out on the subject. In addition, it is important to examine the almost daily instances of small time corruption that occur in rural towns and villages, specifically the illegal excising of taxes and fees. According to studies by scholars such as Thornton (2004) and Bernstein and Lu Xiaobo (2003), many rural cadres simply invent often unlikely-sounding new types of fees on a whim, including anything from flood prevention or security fees to sanitation or slaughtering fees. The animosity created by these illegitimate practices has been exacerbated by the increasing use of IOUs by some local authorities to acquire, but never actually pay for grain, together with arbitrary price rises in chemical fertilizers and other production necessities (Wederman 1997).

Violent protest erupts when aggrieved members of the local peasantry witness overtly extravagant consumption by corrupt officials such as lavish banqueting, business class trips abroad and the purchase of expensive new cars. Reported instances of violent outbursts are manifold. In a single incident that took place in August 2000, over 20,000 disgruntled peasant taxpayers from Yuandu (Jiangxi province) stormed government buildings, attacking cadres and confiscating chemical fertilizers and other items in short supply. In November 2004, local police suppressed an uprising of 100,000 farmers in Sichuan. In total, according to Security Minister Zhou Yongkang, some 74,000 protests and riots broke out across China in 2004 involving more than 3.7 million people. This has prompted the authorities to set up riot police units in 36 cities to control any further outbursts.

So what does this rising rural anger mean for CCP legitimacy? Can these protests be accurately portrayed as a direct challenge to the legitimacy of the party or are they more an expression of discontent with local affairs, directed primarily at dishonest local cadres rather than at the party as a whole? For Yep (2002) rural protests are a local matter and do not constitute an immediate problem for the party for at least three reasons. First, Yep suggests that most rural disputes are disorganized affairs and are usually short lived as a result. Second, he argues, there is no real sign of any rural–urban alliance against the party on socioeconomic issues jointly affecting these sectors. This is partly because urban residents prefer to remain aloof from their peasant counterparts and partly because of the restrictions on unauthorized peasant movement to the cities. Finally, Yep (2002: 5) describes peasant demands as largely 'remedial in nature' and concludes that they 'do not constitute a direct and fundamental challenge to the legitimacy of the regime'.

For its part, the CCP leadership in Beijing has been very keen to ensure that any bad feeling arising as a result of local corruption is deflected away from the centre. It has done this by addressing peasant complaints directly by reducing fiscal burdens, extending labour contracts and improving village-level governance (e.g. VC elections). In addition, on several occasions senior party figures have personally intervened to diffuse explosive situations by, amongst other things, authorizing the dismissal or punishment of corrupt local officials, outlawing illegal taxes and repaying IOUs. In this way, not only does the blame stay at the local level but the centre may even enjoy a degree of popularity by being seen as acting decisively against local corruption.

Yet, this could just be a temporary victory for the central authorities. Whilst small rural outbursts may be easy to quell, there has been a clear rise, despite Yep's assertion, in much larger co-ordinated demonstrations (at least *within* the rural sector) which bring together hundreds of thousands of disaffected peasants from neighbouring provinces. During May 1997 over half a million peasants staged simultaneous demonstrations (some riotous) in more than 50 rural counties in Anhui, Hunan, Jiangxi and Hubei provinces. This was the culmination of a series of smaller disturbances which began in late 1996 and which took place in about 40 counties involving almost 380,000 peasants. Likewise, in July and August 1997, over 200,000 farmers from 15 counties in Jiangxi rallied against corrupt local practices (Thornton 2004: 91–2). Any transition from sporadic and isolated outbursts to a more organized and sustained social movement could pose a serious threat to the party's monopoly on power, especially if independent grass roots organizations are established such as the "committees of peasant autonomy" and "peasant autonomous governments" that were set up along the Hubei– Sichuan border in October 1995 (Thornton 2004: 93).

Another concern for the party leadership are reports that local officials have actively participated in rural demonstrations against new tax laws imposed by Beijing. This has been caused ultimately by the market oriented and decentralized nature of the reforms which has closely aligned the financial interests of local cadres to the economic success of the local community such that (perceived) "unreasonable" directives from central government are ignored (see later discussion). According to Thornton (2004: 90), during recent disputes over central tax directives, local officials (along with enterprise managers and administrators) not only came out in support of their discontented local constituents and but even helped organize the protests.

### The growth of unemployment

Just as corruption has impacted on the legitimacy of the party, so too has the rapidly increasing rate of unemployment in China. In rural areas this has stemmed from, amongst other things, a far greater reliance on machinery instead of manual labour and a shift from the huge collective work teams that characterized the Mao era to the much smaller family units which first emerged under the household responsibility system of the late 1970s. As a result, it is estimated that at least six million rural workers become unemployed every year, although the real figure may be even higher than this. Whilst the expansion of TVEs was able initially to soak up surplus labour, the second half of the 1990s saw many TVEs go under as the rural economy suffered retrenchment (Park and Shen 2003) and most experts now suggest that at least 120 million rural labourers are without work for most of the year. Such massive levels of unemployment have led inevitably to a growth in migration as peasants move to urban areas in search of work (known as the "floating population"). In reality, however, most of these people lack the training, education and residents' permits needed to compete for work in the cities and spend much of their time simply drifting from city to city (Solinger 1999).

Urban areas have also been hit by rampaging unemployment. Following a return to the late 1980s' policy of reducing state investment in industry and leaving SOEs to the mercy of the market, millions of urban workers have lost their jobs as scores of SOEs have become insolvent (Steinfield 1998). This situation has been exacerbated by China's accession to the WTO which has forced Chinese companies to compete directly with foreign corporations, in many cases unsuccessfully. Government figures for the urban unemployed are typically at the bottom end of the scale (25 million in 2004) but they only account for those who are registered as jobless. Excluded from the official statistics are, amongst others, laid off workers who are still contractually tied to their work units (possibly receiving limited short-term benefits) and unpaid surplus workers who are technically employed but economically expendable. Neither laid off nor surplus workers are counted as unemployed until they have been out of work for three years uninterrupted. In this context, as Solinger (2001) points out, if you are temporarily re-employed but then end up out of work again you are not officially unemployed, making it, she argues, almost impossible to come to an accurate figure for urban unemployment in China. Those who attempt to do so usually come up with a figure in excess of 100 million (Wolf *et al.* 2003).

One of the hardest hit regions has been the north eastern "rustbelt" of Manchuria, comprising Liaoning, Heilongjiang and Jilin provinces. Once heralded by the CCP as the epicentre of China's oil and steel industry and the driving force behind the socialist economy, these three provinces are now only able to boast the highest unemployment rates in the country. According to an October 2004 World Bank report, Liaoning has an unemployment rate of 17.68 per cent, Heilongjiang has 15.43 per cent and Jilin has 13.88 per cent. Many of the unemployed from this area are middle aged men who feel aggrieved that as young men they devoted their lives to the development of China's industrial base. Now they find that not only have they been cut loose by their erstwhile employers (contradicting the original promise that they each had a "job for life") but also that their employers often fail to deliver on promised redundancy packages. To make matters worse, many of the unemployed are without the social security benefits that they and their families enjoyed for so long (the so-called "iron rice bowl"), notwithstanding the party's limited efforts to develop a social security system (Duckett 2003).

Like their rural counterparts, unemployed urban workers have responded to their predicament by taking to the streets in increasing numbers. According to research conducted by Weston (2004: 67–9) in March 2002 tens of thousands of former oil industry employees gathered at the city of Daqing (Heilongjiang) in protest at mass redundancies and the absence of medical and retirement benefits. A comparable protest took place in Liaoyang (Liaoning) at about this time which was then repeated in Autumn 2002 (in an attempt to coincide with the convening of the Sixteenth National Party Congress in Beijing) and then again during the first half of 2003. Smaller scale demonstrations by redundant workers have occurred in many other provinces including Anhui, Gansu and Hebei.

Although strictly illegal, unofficial trade unions have gradually surfaced in response to the plight of redundant workers. The unemployed of Daqing set up the Daqing Petroleum Administration Bureau and the Retrenched Workers' Provisional Union Committee. In Liaoyang, laid off workers from a number of different factories joined forces under the banner of the Liaoyang City Unemployed and Bankrupt Workers' Provisional Union and in Changchun (capital of Jilin) the Unemployed Toilers' Committee was formed. These and other independent trade unions have attempted to co-ordinate cross-provincial activities as a unified protest against the hopeless position of the unemployed. So far their efforts have been unsuccessful, but as Weston suggests, if they were to take off this would present the party with a real challenge:

> Instead of having to quell disturbances at isolated trouble spots around the country, the powers that be could be faced with a hydra-headed monster able to put forth a strong claim as the legitimate voice of China's working class.
>
> (2004: 69)

Beijing has responded by adopting a divide and rule strategy, encouraging those people still in employment to remain aloof from the protests for fear of losing their jobs (clearly, an implied threat), whilst attempting to convince unemployed participants at the rank and file level that such protests are the root cause of the cancellation of their severance payments. In an effort to deter people from participating in further demonstrations, key labour activists at the highest level have been arrested, although this has sometimes backfired on the party. The arrest in March 2002 of labour leader Yao Fuxin in Liaoyang inspired over 4,000 redundant workers from the Liaoyang Ferralloy Factory (where Yao worked) to join forces with approximately 30,000 supporters who marched to the Liaoyang municipal building in protest at Yao's arrest. The party reacted by arresting three other prominent activists from the area, Xiao Yunliang, Pang Qingxiang and Wang Zhaoming, but this simply accentuated the problem as protestors dubbed the arrestees the "Liaoyang Four" and continued to lobby for their release (Weston 2004: 78). Of the four, Yao and Xiao were indicted for "subversion" in

January 2003 (ten months after first being detained) and sentenced to jail for seven and four years respectively. Pang and Wang were eventually released without charge.

What are the implications of all of this for party legitimacy? Given that many of these protests appear to focus predominantly on local unemployment issues, some scholars have assumed that they do not pose a direct challenge to party legitimacy on a national scale. Indeed, one of the tactics successfully used by the CCP to insulate itself from worker discontent has been to redirect workers' ire to the local enterprises that employ(ed) them. Moreover, in a similar vein to Yep's position on rural discontent, Blecher (2002: 286) points to, and expresses surprise at a lack of real cross-provincial co-ordination at the urban level 'in the face of the fundamental transformations that have so profoundly afflicted so many workers and that threaten so many more'. The reason for this, Blecher posits, is that on the whole urban workers accept the underlying rationale for the reforms, an assessment shared by Lau (1997: 46): 'ideologically, most labour-oriented activists accept the logic of the regime's reforms, with many seeing a private capitalist market economy as "just", to be tempered only by a "humanitarian quality of competition" '.

Yet, the significance of urban unemployment for CCP legitimacy should not be under estimated. In orthodox Marxist terms, as we have seen, the CCP has traditionally presented itself as the vanguard of urban working class interests (the People's Democratic Dictatorship) and has exalted this class as the most progressive force in communist society. In material terms, the millions who make up the urban proletariat were previously rewarded not so much with highly inflated salaries but with the "cradle to grave" benefits as described previously. But by overseeing mass redundancies in this sector, the CCP has effectively severed the link with the working class leaving Solinger (2004: 50) to the logical conclusion that 'the Chinese state has lost its legitimacy for some tens of millions among its old urban proletariat'. The clear irony here is that what was once the original constituency of the party now poses one of the biggest challenges to its very incumbency. As Hays Gries and Rosen (2004: 2) remark 'with millions laid off from state-owned enterprises (SOEs), urban workers, once the pride of Mao's China, have become a specter haunting early 21st century China'.

## Stability as a source of legitimacy

It is perhaps ironic given the considerable insecurity brought about by economic reform, that the CCP has in recent times sought to present itself in a new light as a force for stability. Although this concept is currently in a state of infancy and is still being developed by party theorists and leaders alike, official statements put out by the CCP allude more and more to stability as a new and important mode of regime legitimacy. It is also noticeable that influential semi-official think tanks such as the Chinese Academy of Social Sciences are increasingly discussing and researching this idea.

In simple terms, the party now asserts that its continued incumbency is the only realistic way of ensuring political stability and personal safety during the current transitional period. In so doing, the party seeks to play on deeply felt public fears about social and national fragmentation in China and is quick to draw stark contrast with what it claims (often in exaggerated tones) to be the growing socio-political uncertainty that is prevalent in the post-communist states of Eastern Europe. Significantly, stability in China, it is suggested, is not necessarily a con-sequence of the economic growth and prosperity that China has witnessed over the last two decades or so but rather a *prerequisite* to such factors, a line which has been pursued with some vigour during the Hu Jintao/Wen Jiabao era, to a certain extent contradicting what Jiang Zemin and Premier Zhu Rongji were arguing over during much of the 1990s.

Shue (2004) suggests that the main reason for this shift towards stability as a source of legitimacy stems from a growing inability on the behalf of the party leadership to derive credit for economic improvements in China. In light of the post-Mao decentralization of economic control to the provinces and lower levels of the government apparatus as well as the increased role of the much vaunted "invisible hand" of the market, the party has been almost *forced* to re-consider its role in society and has therefore re-invented itself as a hallbearer of stability. This does not mean, of course, that party leaders blushingly deny any praise due for the success of the reforms. As Shue (2004: 29) notes, 'official trumpeting of glowing statistics remains a part of the trappings of rule in China now, as it was under Mao'. Realistically, however, all the party can really take credit for now is its "enlightened general policies" which provide the necessary framework for economic growth:

> The present regime stakes its legitimacy, as I read it, not on its technical capacity to steer and to grow the economy, but on its political capacity to pre-serve a peaceful and stable social order under which, among other things, the economy can be expected to grow.
>
> (Shue 2004: 29)

In fact, Shue's observation draws on a much broader and fundamental point relating not just to whether the party can take credit for economic reform but whether it actually still *controls* the process. A recurring theme from our earlier discussion of economic reform is the party's efforts to deflect any blame for the failings of the reforms to the local level by blaming corrupt local officials or erroneous local policies. Is the party simply being tactical to cover its own back or is local discontent genuinely caused by local policies and policy makers? Whatever the answer, the increasing loss of economic decision making power to the localities makes it increasingly difficult for the party to pursue a successful policy of economic legitimacy.

At this juncture, it is important to acknowledge an obvious degree of overlap between stability and nationalism as modes of legitimacy. We shall see shortly how, from the early 1990s, the CCP has sought to flag up its nationalist cre-dentials, partly because of the gradual erosion of its Marxist legitimacy. Often, in presenting itself as the only viable force for stability in China, the CCP has sought to appeal directly to the public's fervent nationalist sentiments. As Dickson (2004: 144) points out, 'at a time when it [the CCP] no longer promotes class struggle or other communist goals, it can claim to promote nationalistic aspirations, beginning with maintaining national unity and order'. At the same time, however, much of the official rhetoric on stability is presented as distinct from nationalism, presumably to add a new and distinct source to the regime legitimation process.

## The withering of Marxism

One of the key challenges for the CCP during the post-Mao era has been how to reconcile Marxism, which remains China's official ideology, with the increasing application of what can only be described as capitalist economic methods. We examined in the previous chapter the mid-1980s theory of the Socialist Commodity Economy, and then later Zhao Ziyang's Primary Stage of Socialism which held that the party was guiding China through the penultimate capitalist phase of social development (as set out by Marx) before the inevitable transition towards communism. Neither theory was successful in shoring up the party's ideological credibility amongst the masses and in the end served only to add to the growing schism within the leadership between economic reformers and ideological traditionalists.

### *Criterion of productive forces*

The need for a comprehensive explanation of how capitalism can exist in a Marxist society became even more pressing following the collapse of socialism in Eastern Europe and the Soviet Union and the subsequent intensification of economic reform in China. However, post-Tiananmen efforts to reconcile theory and practice have been equally unconvincing. We saw earlier in this chapter, how in attempting to re-assert his authority over the economy, Deng Xiaoping expounded a theory known as the Criterion of Productive Forces. According to Deng, the only real test of whether a certain aspect of the economy (e.g. privatization) was truly socialist related to what he described as the Three Advantages. These were: (i) whether or not something was advantageous to the development of socialist productive forces, (ii) whether or not something was advantageous to increasing the comprehensive strength of the socialist nation and (iii) whether or not something was advantageous to raising living standards (Fewsmith 1997: 497). For Deng, the post-Mao economic model pursued by the CCP passed each of these three criteria as demonstrated by the phenomenal economic growth that China enjoyed. From this Deng concluded that it remained wholly acceptable and indeed logical to describe the Chinese economy as socialist.

Deng's reasoning on this was extremely simplistic and the theory as a whole constituted a fairly weak explication of how capitalist methods could exist in a nominally Marxist state. In many respects, it resembled Zhao's Primary Stage concept in asserting that just about anything could be called socialist as long as it strengthened the Chinese economy. Indeed, after yet another reconceptualization of China's economy as the Socialist Market Economy during the Fourteenth National Party Congress in 1992 (Kluver 1996: 93–119), the party returned to the Primary Stage idea in 1997 as Jiang Zemin sought to legitimize the process of reforming China's SOEs through the widespread adoption of a shareholding system, arguing (seemingly without a hint of irony) that 'the share-holding question can be used both under capitalism and socialism' (Fewsmith 2001: 192–3).

### The Three Represents

The most recent pronouncement of official CCP ideology was made at the Sixteenth National Party Congress in 2002 in the form of Jiang Zemin's theory of the Three Represents (Bao Tong 2002, Fewsmith 2003b). According to Jiang, the party now represents three forces in Chinese society: "the most advanced social productive forces" (including China's growing urban middle class of entrepreneurs, professionals and high technology specialists), "the most advanced culture" (which now includes foreign and traditional Chinese culture) and "the fundamental interests of the broad masses of the people." On the face of it, this appears to be yet another convoluted justification of the party's continued monopoly on power and on this basis was barely acknowledged at home or abroad. But in fact Jiang's theory is noteworthy. This is because is constitutes a fundamental sea change in relation to what and who the party claims to represent.

The claim to represent the "most advanced culture" is important in that the party has finally moved beyond the anachronistic Maoist view that both foreign and traditional Chinese culture was somehow bourgeois or feudalistic. But of greater significance to our study of legitimacy is the party's formal recognition and acceptance of the new and emerging middle class in China, "the most advanced social productive forces" (which together with the working class comprise "the broad masses of the people"). Consistent with its Marxist roots, the party has traditionally claimed to represent the interests of the proletariat which it defines as, amongst other things, the urban working classes and the peasantry. The post-Mao embrace of the market, however, and the accompanying reconfiguration of China's social structure has made it almost impossible for the party to steadfastly maintain this position given that, in effect, the CCP has *created* China's middle class. By including the middle class as a core part of its constituency, the CCP is finally acknowledging this reality.

At the same time, the party is quick to point out that it has not abandoned its traditional support base. Far from it. According to Zheng Bijian, Vice-President of the Central Party School and one of the principal theoreticians behind the Three Represents, the "most advanced social productive forces" also includes workers and peasants. Whilst some workers have lost their jobs, Zheng notes:

> This does not mean that the Chinese working class has lost its advanced nature, much less that the working class is no longer the foundation of the CCP. Exactly the opposite. In the course of contemporary China's strategic

adjustment of its socio-economic structure and particularly its industrial structure, the overall quality and superiority of the Chinese working class is being raised to a new level.

(Fewsmith 2001: 230)

Despite Zheng's insistence that the party still cares about workers and peasants, there has in recent years been an unmistakeable movement towards accommodating the increasingly large and powerful ranks of the Chinese middle class, principally as a means of co-opting a potential source of opposition *into* the system. In his extensive research on the subject, Dickson (2003, 2004) points to the adoption of a dual strategy by the CCP. The first aspect of this strategy has been the creation of new institutional links with the middle class through the establishment of corporatist organizations (e.g. chambers of commerce, professional organizations, sports and hobby clubs) which represent various professions, especially in industry and commerce (Pei Minxin 1998, Saich 2000). As Dickson (2004: 146) notes, 'they are sanctioned by the state, are granted a monopoly on the interest they represent, at least in their locality, and may even have Party or government officials in their leadership'. The second, more controversial element of this strategy has been to actively recruit entrepreneurs and other professionals into the party. This has seen the percentage of entrepreneurs belonging to party rise from 13 in 1993 to 30 in 2003 (notwithstanding that there was a ban on recruiting entrepreneurs from August 1989 to November 2002).

In light of the party's emphasis on economic reform and modernization, it appears, on the face of it, to be good sense and pragmatic for the party to concentrate on enlisting those people who have primarily been responsible for China's economic growth. But in ideological terms this strategy and the Three Represents as a guiding theory has pushed the party even further from its original Marxist moorings, leaving it in a position where it seems almost ridiculous to describe the CCP as a communist party. As Deng Liqun, the veteran socialist of 1980s fame accurately concludes, the theory of the Three Represents is 'more a slogan for a social democratic party than a communist party' (Wo-Lap Lam 2000).

## The rise of anti-foreign nationalism

In an effort to compensate for the erosion of its Marxist legitimacy, the party has expended much effort on nurturing and propagating its nationalist credentials. For sure, the party has always sought to present itself as the leading (indeed only) nationalist force in Chinese society and has, at times, benefited considerably from nationalist legitimacy, especially during the early post-revolutionary period. The post-Tiananmen era has seen a notable increase in official (and later non-official) expressions of nationalism, particularly with regard to a crude brand of anti-foreign nationalism.

The waning impact of Chinese Marxism is not the only reason for the increased focus on Chinese nationalism. As noted earlier, the lesson learned from the late 1980s economic crisis was that an over-reliance on economic legitimacy created a very tenuous existence for the incumbent regime given the unsettling social and economic side-effects associated with such a fundamental overhaul of the economy and the widespread discontent that arises from this. As such, the stress on nationalism has been part of a concerted effort by the party to expand and diversify the foundations of its legitimacy. It might further be argued that such emphasis is intended to divert attention away from socio-economic inequalities and other domestic problems that have continued to beset the CCP.

Another factor which helps to explain the emphasis on nationalism was the international fallout immediately following the Tiananmen crackdown. Notwithstanding the relatively limited nature of the economic and military sanctions that were imposed on China after the crackdown (Harding 1992), the rhetoric of the international community, especially in the West, was fiercely critical of the party's decision to use military force on its own people. In response, the CCP accused Western nations, (particularly the United States) of covertly liaising with student leaders to bring about the downfall of the CCP, an attempt, it was argued, which formed part of a much broader strategy of trying to "contain" China (see later discussion). It was from this point that the party began to construct its policy on anti-foreign nationalism.

### *The Campaign for Patriotic Education*

A key aspect of the official line on nationalism has been to remind people of past humiliations suffered by China at the hands of foreign powers in an attempt to whip up a sense of public indignation. In May 1990, as part of a joint commemoration to mark the May Fourth Movement (of 1919) and more particularly the 150th anniversary of the Opium War (against the British), Jiang Zemin told over 3,000 attending students that the Opium War symbolized the beginning of China's humiliation by foreign imperialists and that certain Western nations were still intent on humbling and embarrassing China. A month later, under the heading "hold much higher the great flag of patriotism", the *People's Daily* wrote a piece on the Opium War concluding that 'we have to open our country to the world, but we cannot advocate total Westernization and must resist the pressure from the West' (Xu Guangqiu 2001: 156). A few days later, the *Liberation Army Daily* insisted that:

> Since the Opium War, the West has never stopped its aggression against China. After the PRC was established, the West first imposed an economic embargo on China and then isolated and contained the new socialist country in order to overthrow this government in its cradle.
>
> (Xu Guangqiu 2001: 156)

On the back of this and other nationalist proclamations, the party, under the auspices of Jiang Zemin and PSC member Li Ruihuan (a specialist in ideological matters), published a series of papers during the early 1990s which pushed the nationalist line even harder and became part of the official Campaign for Patriotic Education. In the 1991 State Council white paper on human rights, the authors drew close attention to the legacy of foreign imperialism in China in an effort to expose the alleged hypocrisy of those nations that were critical of China's human rights record after Tiananmen:

> The Imperialists massacred people in untold numbers during their aggressive wars. In 1900, the troops of the Eight Allied Powers – Germany, Japan, Britain, Russia, France, the United States, Italy and Austria – killed, burned and looted, raising Tanggu, a town of 50,000 residents to utter ruins, reducing Tianjin's population from one million to 100,000 and killing countless people when they entered Beijing, where more than 1,700 were slaughtered in Zhuangwanfu alone. During Japan's full scale invasion which began in 1937, more than 21 million people were killed or wounded and ten million people mutilated to death. In six weeks beginning on 13 December 1937, the Japanese invaders killed 300,000 people in Nanjing.
> (Information Office of the State Council 1991: 1)

Other, more specifically nationalist publications included the 1991 "notice about conducting the education of patriotism and the revolutionary tradition", which used language of a similarly inflammatory nature to the above and the 1994 "outline for the implementation of patriotic education" which implored local party leaders to strengthen patriotic teachings amongst the masses because 'patriotism has long been the banner for mobilizing and inspiring the Chinese in struggle and represents a dynamic force' (Xu Guangqiu 2001: 156). The Campaign for Patriotic Education was also propagated in secondary schools where children were taught patriotic songs, first year university students were required to take a course in modern Chinese history emphasizing the nationalist achievements of the CCP and students (and workers) were encouraged to visit "patriotic bases" (Xu Guangqiu 2001: 156).

In addition to these domestic initiatives, the party leadership sharpened the tone of its foreign policy in the early 1990s by developing the concept of international containment. This theory held that the United States and other Western powers were covertly working together to prevent China from evolving naturally as a major international force with the ultimate aim of destroying Chinese socialism altogether. Although the Cold War had ended, it was argued, the West remained intent on expanding its power and influence overseas, particularly with regard to China. Indeed, the relaxation of international tensions following the demise of socialism in Eastern Europe and the old Soviet Union had made Western forces even more arrogant and even more determined to constrain China, as evidenced by the more robust Western position on highly sensitive issues of Chinese sovereignty. Growing Western criticism of China's human rights policy in Tibet and its confrontational stance towards Taiwan particularly angered Chinese leaders. The West, especially the United States, was also blamed for the protracted delays to China's accession to the WTO and for its failure to win the bid to host the 2000 Olympic Games, a source of particular anguish for many Chinese. The passing of a US Congressional resolution in July 1993 against China's Olympic bid was seized upon as evidence of a US conspiracy against China.

### The response from the public

As hoped and anticipated, the public responded by rallying behind the new anti-foreign party line. In the intellectual arena, there was a sudden proliferation of anti-Western literature which built further on the containment theory, arguing that the United States remained intent on hegemony. These and other publications were in stark contrast to the more cosmopolitan, pro-Western works of the 1980s which had been critical of traditional Chinese culture and had blamed it for China's slow rate of development during the modern era (Zhao Suisheng 1997, Guo Yingjie 1998). New academic journals and periodicals began to appear which focused exclusively on nationalist topics, most notably a journal called *Strategy and Management* which became extremely popular amongst Chinese scholars. In addition, there was a dramatic increase in "cultural" academies (e.g. Beijing University's Institute of Chinese Culture) and related university courses, reflecting an upsurge of scholarly interest in traditional China.

The new focus on nationalism also elicited a positive response from ordinary citizens. Already predisposed towards strong feelings of sinocentrism, the public was more than happy to embrace the new anti-Western line. This was particularly evident from the results of opinion polls on the subject (of which there have been few given the sensitivity surrounding Chinese foreign policy). In a 1995 poll carried out by the state-controlled *China Youth Daily* (a popular source of youth opinion), over 87 per cent of respondents perceived America as the country which was "least friendly" to China, whilst over 57 per cent professed to feeling more negative towards America than towards any other country in the world (including Japan). Over 85 per cent believed that the United States had intervened in the 1990–1 Gulf War "out of its own interests" (Fewsmith 2001: 155). In a separate poll conducted in 1996 by the Youth Research Centre, over 50 per cent of respondents said that they thought American culture was "empty", that American society had a low morality and that official and police corruption was a serious issue. Over 90 per cent believed that drugs were a big problem in America (Xu Guangqiu 2001: 158).

Japan was also singled out for public criticism at about this time. In a 1996 survey, 84 per cent of respondents said that they associated the word Japan with the 1937 Nanjing massacre (when up to 300,00 Chinese were killed by the Japanese military), whilst 81 per cent immediately thought of China's war of resistance against Japan (1937–45) and Japan's denial of its wartime aggression in China. Another question in the survey asked which twentieth century Japanese person was most representative of Japan; first place (29 per cent) went to Hideki Tojo, the Japanese political and military leader who ordered the attack on Peal Harbour in 1941. When asked to identify a personality trait most closely associated with Japanese people, over 56 per cent chose "cruel" (Fewsmith 2001: 261). In a 2005 survey conducted by the Japanese think-tank Genron NPO (in combination with Beijing University and the *China Daily*) Japan did not fare much better. More than 63 per cent had a "very bad" or "not very good" impression of Japan. A further 93 per cent said Japan should take sole responsibility for the recent strain in Sino-Japanese relations.

In the context of the spring 2005 wave of anti-Japanese protests that swept through China following the publication of a Japanese school text which appears to downplay Japan's wartime legacy in China (see shortly for more), these findings would not be surprising. At the time, however, such strength of feeling against Japan and the United States *was* surprising (apparently even to those who organized the polls) and was not in keeping with the more public positive perception of these countries during the 1980s. This suggests that the party was successful in instigating a strong undercurrent of nationalism in Chinese society.

### *The rise of unofficial nationalism*

Yet, it would be a mistake to assume that the party and its propaganda machine were solely responsible for the growth in Chinese nationalism after Tiananmen. As Hays Gries (2004) points out, nationalism, like any social movement necessarily involves a key role for both leaders and *followers*. Despite popular perceptions in the West that the current wave of Chinese nationalism is purely a state-controlled, "top down" phenomenon, much of the nationalist activity in China has come from independent grass roots movements. This is evidenced by the growth in populist publications on the subject and the increasing use of the internet as a vehicle for discussion, something which the party is finding increasingly difficult to patrol (Deans 2004).

What is crucial about understanding these new groups is that they often express themselves in ways that *challenge* the party's claim to be the sole representative of the national interest by suggesting that the party does not go far enough in sticking up for China and is weak in the face of contending foreign pressures. Ironically, therefore, nationalism has become something of a double-edged sword for the CCP as far as regime legitimacy is concerned. Whilst the original objective was to use nationalism as an alternative source of regime legitimacy, many popular nationalist groups are using nationalism in ways that detract from or even threaten CCP legitimacy.

The first sign of an unofficial nationalist voice came in 1996 during a hostile diplomatic exchange between China and Japan over sovereignty claims to Diaoyu/Senkaku islands, a collection of eight uninhabited rocky outcroppings in the East China Sea between Taiwan and Okinawa (over which Taiwan also claims sovereignty) (Strecker-Downs and Saunders 1998–9, Deans 2000). When a group of young Japanese nationalists landed on the islands and erected a lighthouse as a symbol of Japanese sovereignty, both the Chinese and Japanese governments responded by reinforcing their claims over the islands. This led to a series of spontaneous anti-Japanese demonstrations on Chinese streets which were quickly suppressed by the authorities. Notwithstanding this, a number of internet sites and print publications subsequently appeared which expressed strong anti-Japanese sentiments and suggested that the CCP was too submissive on the Diaoyu/ Senkaku issue. For example, in a highly inflammatory text published in 1997 and entitled *Be Vigilant Against Japanese Militarism!*, the authors declared that 'no Chinese should be willing or dare to relinquish sovereignty over Chinese territory, leaving a name to be cursed for generations' (Zi Shui and Xiao Shi 1997: 78).

The challenge posed by popular nationalism was even more evident with the publication in 1996 of a best selling book called *China Can Say No* (Song Qiang *et al.* 1996). In print just before the Diaoyu/Senkaku dispute, the book was an impassioned backlash against the widely held Chinese perception that America was trying to hold China down and lecture China on morality. In keeping with the party line on the issue, the five authors (each from non-intellectual backgrounds) cited, amongst other things, US sympathy for Tibet and Taiwan as evidence of an anti-China conspiracy in the West. They also launched a vociferous attack on Western denunciations of China's human rights record asking whether the West really had the moral high ground on this issue given its chequered legacy of impe-rialism. Where the book deviated from the party line was in its forthright asser-tion that China should be much more bold and forthright in standing up ("saying no") to America and the West and should even be prepared to bear arms against its foreign oppressors. Although not overtly critical of Chinese foreign policy, there was a clear implication here that the government was too soft in its dealings with the West.

At first the party enthusiastically endorsed the publication of *China Can Say No*. Yu Quanyu (Deputy Chair of China's Human Rights Commission) described the book as closely reflecting popular opinion, whilst several editorials in the state-controlled media praised the works (Fewsmith 2001: 155). When the under-lying tone of the book became apparent the party was forced to back-track, con-demning the piece as an unwarranted attempt to interfere in foreign policy matters. But by this time the book had already sold hundreds of thousands of copies (50,000 copies of the first edition sold out immediately), becoming the single most popular book in China in the 1990s and drawing numerous letters of support from all over China. It also spawned a burgeoning cottage industry of similarly themed (and unimaginatively named) books such as *China Can Still Say No* and *Why Does China Say No?* which were more directly critical of Chinese foreign policy.

The resultant banning of the "say no" series of works and other popular anti-foreign tracts (such as *Be Vigilant Against Japanese Militarism!*) was hardly an unprecedented move by the CCP. It was, however, highly significant in that it exposed a sudden realization that this new wave of popular nationalists had, on the face of it, become *more* representative of public opinion on the question of nationalism than the party itself. This was deemed (rightly so) to constitute a direct threat to the party's nationalist legitimacy.

Subsequent expressions of popular nationalism have been even more pronounced than the "say no" phenomenon and have forced the party to alter its approach from suppressing the demonstrators to accommodating them. This was first evident during the public protests which took place in May 1999 following the American bombing of the Chinese embassy in Belgrade which killed three

Chinese employees. As the US and Chinese governments deliberated over the full extent of any apology to be given by the Clinton administration, street demonstrations erupted in over 100 Chinese cities comprising participants from all generations and social backgrounds. Whilst many protestors were angry with the United States, public attention also focused on the government's apparent unwillingness to confront the United States, preferring, as one protestor claimed, to adopt a policy of "merely lodging fierce protests". The diversity of the participants was further manifested by the 281 condolence letters delivered to the *Guangming Daily* which came from 26 Chinese provinces as well as from outside China. Those sending the letters included students, teachers, members of the party-state and media workers and here again criticism was directed both at America *and* the CCP (Hays Gries 2004: 129–31).

Unable to control the demonstrations (despite a nationally televised plea for calm from Hu Jintao) and afraid that they would rapidly evolve from being anti-US to anti-CCP (in light of the approaching tenth anniversary of Tiananmen), the authorities in Beijing moved quickly to accommodate the protestors by providing a bus service, mainly for students, from the outer regions of the city to the central embassy district. The students were then allowed (albeit closely watched by the police) to walk past the US ambassador's residence, the embassy building and then the chancellery, throwing bricks, ink and faeces as they went. As Fewsmith points out:

> It was certainly better, from the Party's point of view, to have such public anger directed at the United States than to have students throw stones at Zhongnanhai (the compound in which the leadership lives), which they certainly would have done had the Party's reaction been perceived as weak.
>
> (2001: 213)

The anti-Japanese demonstrations of April 2005 also forced the party into a position of compromise with the popular nationalists. The catalyst for the protests was the decision by the Japanese education ministry to approve a revised history textbook which allegedly whitewashes atrocities from Japan's militaristic past. Initially, the CCP sought to co-opt the demonstrators by claiming in the national media to represent the anti-Japanese sentiment that was sweeping through the country. But as the outpouring of public anger escalated to a scale much larger than the 1999 demonstrations and with the anniversary of the May Fourth Movement fast approaching, the party had to resort again to providing buses to transport protestors into city centres, leaving the authorities to look on nervously as some demonstrators attacked Japanese shops, restaurants and cars. In summary, Hays Gries makes the following astute observation:

> The Party's movement away from suppression and toward co-option or acquiescence suggests that a popular nationalism is now emerging in China that increasingly challenges the Party-state. Struggling to keep up with popular nationalist demands, the Party is slowly losing its hegemony over Chinese nationalism.
>
> (2004: 121)

## Fragile legitimacy?

A key objective of the party leadership in the post-Tiananmen era has been to diversify and strengthen the basis of CCP legitimacy. Greater emphasis has been placed on legal rational and electoral legitimacy, especially since the death of Deng, and a new concept of stability is gradually being introduced by the state-controlled media and other sources of communication. Economic performance remains a priority for the party, and as the economy continues to grow at break-neck speed millions of people now enjoy a high standard of living, enhancing the party's economic legitimacy amongst those who have benefited from the reforms. In addition, in light of the gradual attrition of Marxism, the party has sought to rely increasingly on anti-foreign nationalism to boost its support base.

Yet, the legitimacy of the party probably remains as uncertain as ever. Developments in the legal rational and electoral system have not gone far enough to really bolster the party's credibility, and stability, at this stage, is too recent a concept to have had any real effect. Nor has the economy necessarily saved the CCP as the rise in economic performance has also seen a rise in social and economic disparities leading to almost daily instances of unrest in rural and urban areas, a problem exacerbated by a huge increase in corruption. Finally, and per-haps most importantly given the energy expended by the party, the decision to push hard on the nationalist line appears to have rebounded. Struggling to control the strength of nationalist feeling amongst the public, the party could soon find itself in a position where the popular nationalists move from anti-Western demonstrations to anti-CCP demonstrations.

# Conclusion

The incumbency of the CCP has been characterized by an almost relentless struggle to legitimize its monopoly on political power. Virtually from the very moment the PRC was established the party has found it necessary to devise different ways of trying to retain the popular support (or revolutionary legitimacy) that it enjoyed on coming to power. In so doing, as we have seen throughout this book, two quite different modes of legitimacy emerged: a Maoist mode of legitimacy that underpinned Mao's time at the helm and for a short period afterwards and a post-Mao mode of legitimacy that has prevailed since the inception of the economic reform programme in the late 1970s. In summing up we shall assess the efficacy of these alternative modes of legitimacy and examine some of the challenges that the CCP may have to overcome if it is to remain in power indefinitely.

## Maoist mode of legitimacy

The cornerstone of CCP legitimacy during the Mao era was ideology. Without underestimating the utility of nationalism, and to a certain extent tradition, as prototypes of unofficial ideological legitimacy, the official ideology of the CCP under Mao was Marxism. Reinforced by a diverse network of propaganda techniques, the party presented itself as the People's Democratic Dictatorship, an organization which, through its unique understanding of Marxism, was able to rule exclusively and benevolently (drawing partly on the ancient Confucian concept of benevolent government) in the interests of the proletariat and in opposition to the exploitation of the bourgeoisie. The party's long-term goal was the creation of a utopian communist society founded on the principles of equality and freedom.

The sinification of Marxism as applied by Mao led Marxism into new areas. In China's predominantly rural society the proletariat was not an exclusively urban force as Lenin had insisted but was comprised mainly of the peasantry, the majority disenfranchised class. Social class was determined not just by one's socio-economic relationship to the means of production but also by one's class background and even one's state of mind. The revolution did not simply cease upon the victory of the armed struggle but continued well into the post-revolutionary state through a series of smaller grass roots revolutions.

Notwithstanding these (and other) revisions of Marxism the role of the CCP remained the same: to represent and protect proletarian interests and to act as a guiding force, a moral exemplar for that class. It was in performing this role and striving towards the utopian ends of a communist society that the party sought to derive Marxist legitimacy.

The Cultural Revolution all but destroyed the party's credibility as a Marxist organization. By the mid-1970s as the movement subsided it was difficult for the masses to see precisely what good Chinese Marxism, and by implication the CCP, had done for the country. China remained impoverished and underdeveloped despite over two decades of CCP rule. One man, supported by a group of zealous radicals, had totally undermined the country's political system and decision making apparatus. In those places where the party-state had not collapsed completely, it had splintered into hostile rival factions. Far from representing proletarian interests, the party had neglected them altogether. Far from acting as a moral authority for the masses to aspire to, the party had exposed itself as a self-serving elite, preoccupied with petty infighting.

Just as Marxism proved to be inadequate as a legitimizing force for the CCP so too did its reliance on charismatic legitimacy, specifically that relating to Mao Zedong. Within the party leadership Mao's charismatic legitimacy derived from his ability to emerge victorious during times of crisis (e.g. at the 1935 Zunyi conference) and to make the right call on matters of controversy (e.g. China's entry into the Korean War). In this regard, Mao's prestige amongst his colleagues was perfectly genuine. But outside the confines of the party elite where very few people came into contact with Mao it was deemed necessary to propagate the teachings of Mao through the cult of personality (e.g. during study sessions, within the classroom or via emulation campaigns). In this regard, Mao's abilities were often beautified to the extent of pure fabrication.

The problem with seeking to derive legitimacy from charismatic sources, as Teiwes has noted, is the damage it can inflict on the legal rational legitimacy of a given regime. This is because an emphasis on the former is usually made to the detriment of the latter. At various times during his incumbency Mao deliberately took advantage of his charismatic authority in order to force his position on to the party. In so doing he consistently flouted the legal rational norms of democratic centralism. During the mid-1950s debate over rural collectivization Mao went outside the central party apparatus, appealing directly (and successfully) to provincial leaders to ignore central party directives on the issue and adopt his alternative line. At Lushan in 1959 Mao appealed successfully to his leadership colleagues to round on Peng Dehuai simply for exercising his legitimate right to speak out on the excesses of the Great Leap Forward. In launching the Cultural Revolution in an effort to overturn the moderate policies of Liu Shaoqi, Deng Xiaoping and Chen Yun, Mao drew directly on the popularity derived from his cult of personality in forming a powerful *non-party* coalition with the PLA, radical intellectuals and the Red Guards.

As the Cultural Revolution burst into life in 1966 the risks associated with charismatic legitimacy and the cult of personality became alarmingly apparent. Mao as an individual became more legitimate than the party he represented.

With help not just from his Cultural Revolution coalition but also initially from eventual opponents such as Liu Shaoqi and Deng Xiaoping, Mao superseded the party and functioned almost as a separate entity outside of the boundaries of the party, directing his coalition of supporters *against* the party.

The third key tenet of the Maoist mode of legitimacy was mass mobilization. Based on the logic that regime legitimacy would inevitably flow from an all-inclusive approach to China's political and socio-economic development in which the masses would feel as though they were an instrumental part of that development, Mao championed the (non-mutually exclusive) conceptions of the mass line and the mass campaign which in theory afforded the masses a key participatory role in both the formulation and implementation of policy. Such mass activity, Mao believed, would have the added benefit of maintaining the impetus of the 1949 revolution as enshrined in his concept of continuous revolution.

The practical application of Mao's mobilization mode proved to be something of a lottery. The mass campaigns of the early 1950s were arguably successful in legitimizing party rule. During the land reform campaign, for example, poor and landless peasants from all over China were deeply involved in the process of identifying their landlord oppressors and seizing and redistributing the land. Similarly, the "Antis" campaigns which took place in China's cities gave urban residents the opportunity to identify and criticize inept or corrupt officials and people associated with the old KMT regime or other counter-revolutionary organizations. During this crucial early period for the CCP the masses were highly influential in the transformation of both rural and urban society.

But the success of mass politics in China was short lived as marked by the failure of the Hundred Flowers Campaign in 1957. Aimed at giving intellectuals the chance to speak openly on the CCP's record in office in an attempt ultimately to rectify party rule, intellectuals moved beyond the parameters of the permissible by questioning whether the party was competent enough to run the country at all. The subsequent abandonment of the Hundred Flowers (after just five weeks) proved to be a major embarrassment to Mao.

The Great Leap Forward, a much larger exercise in mass mobilization, was an even bigger disaster for the legitimacy of the CCP. In an attempt to boost both agricultural and industrial output simultaneously millions of peasants were put to work on naively ambitious programmes to catch up with the grain and steel production levels of developed countries such as Britain and the United States. But whilst Mao was sincere in his conviction that, correctly mobilized, the masses could conquer any structural impediment to economic development, he was wrong. Mao grossly over-estimated the technical ability and political will of the rural masses and the Leap resulted in China's worst famine on record. This precipitated a process of decline in party legitimacy from which the Mao regime never really recovered.

The calamity of the Great Leap Forward opened up deep divisions within the party leadership over the correct role of the masses. Party moderates such as Liu, Deng and Chen Yun were no longer prepared to contemplate a mass role in Chinese politics. As they steered China towards economic recovery based on the limited application of markets, the masses, they argued, were to be kept firmly in check for fear of disrupting this process. Conversely, Mao lost none of his enthusiasm for mass participation. The Leap failed, Mao argued, not because of any inherent flaw in his model of mass politics but because the masses did not fully understand what was required of them. Their failure to share property with each other or consume in a circumspect manner in the communal kitchens was certainly a cause for concern. However, it simply reinforced the need to educate the masses in the ways of communist society and communal living. This led Mao disastrously towards the Cultural Revolution when the uncontrolled (and probably uncontrollable) participation of the masses brought China to the brink of civil war.

Despite Mao's failings as a political leader and the responsibility he undoubtedly bears for the consequences of mass campaigns such as the Leap and the Cultural Revolution, Mao was acutely aware of the constant need to legitimize CCP rule and much of what he did and said was with that specific objective in mind. Indeed, it is not an over-exaggeration to suggest that Mao's rule was characterized by a succession of "legitimacy gambits". In devising the Hundred Flowers, for example, Mao's principal aim was to combat a perceived decline in party legitimacy as evidenced by the public demonstrations of 1956–7. This was due in part to a process of bureaucratization which saw the party gradually losing touch with the masses and with its socialist origins. By inviting intellectuals to speak out on the party's record in power Mao's aim was to somehow revitalize the party and re-instil it with revolutionary fervour. The Cultural Revolution was launched for similar reasons only this time the situation was deemed to be much more serious. The perceived revisionism that was endemic in every sphere of Chinese political and public life threatened to destroy Chinese socialism altogether and replace it with the kind elitist, bureaucratic party that governed the Soviet Union. The role of the masses was to rectify the party and reverse this process. The Leap was another attempt by Mao to boost the legitimacy of the party. Although the objective was to rapidly accelerate industrial and agricultural production the intention was that this should not occur in vacuum, but should be implemented in a manner that *involved* the masses and made them feel part of the drive to modernize China.

## Post-Mao mode of legitimacy

Mao's death in 1976 and the subsequent rise of Deng Xiaoping allowed the party to jettison the discredited Maoist notions of mass mobilization and the cult of personality (although significantly *not* ideology) and re-invent itself as the party of economic performance. In keeping with its programme of economic reform, the legitimacy of the party was to be measured in economic terms, specifically by its ability to improve the personal wealth and living standards of the individual. The rural landholding system was decollectivized so that farmers could cultivate their own plots of land, some of the produce from which they were permitted to sell in the local market place. Industry was re-organized so that managers had greater decision making powers and workers could earn bonuses. Individual entrepreneurs were encouraged to set up their own private businesses offering consumer goods and services. Trade and investment with overseas companies was embraced as part of the open door policy.

On the face of it, the party's economic reform programme has yielded incredible results with the economy growing at almost 10 per cent per year and China closing in on America as the dominant player in the international market. But whilst the reforms probably saved the party from extinction after the Cultural Revolution they have also spawned a number of unwelcome but inevitable side effects which ironically have served to diminish the legitimacy of the party. Corruption, as we have seen, continues to be hugely detrimental to the party as dishonest officials seek to exploit their positions of power for economic gain. Although high-profile cases are embarrassing for the party the negative impact is just as significant at the local township or village level where instances of corruption leading to public demonstrations take place almost every day. Rising unemployment also cuts deep into the party's popularity. The dismantling of the collectives in rural areas and the reduced ability of the TVEs to provide employment means that an estimated 120 million peasants are currently without work whilst in urban areas the figure is around 100 million. Consequently, although some people in China have become rich many remain destitute.

Another reform-related difficulty for the party has been what to do about its Marxist ideology. Conspicuous by its absence after the death of Mao was any explicit abandonment of Marxism as the country's official ideology and a basis of legitimacy for the CCP. This was because the party simply could not do so. Since the very foundations of party legitimacy derive from its status as the People's Democratic Dictatorship and its claims to understand proletarian interests through its unique comprehension of Marxism, any rejection of Marxism by the party would be tantamount to abandoning its claims to be the sole ruler of China.

Yet, in many ways Marxism has become something of an Achilles heel for the party given the pace and dynamism of economic reform which has moved in a decidedly un-Marxist direction. This has forced the party to come up with some novel reinterpretations of Marxism. The theory of the Socialist Commodity Economy introduced in 1984 was the first real attempt to equate the use of markets with Marxist theory followed in 1987 by the more ambitious Primary Stage of Socialism which claimed that the party was guiding China through the penultimate stage of socialist development, namely capitalism. During the 1990s the party toyed with theories such as the Criterion of Productive Forces and the Socialist Market Economy but in each case the argument, a very weak one, appeared to be the same: as long as an economic model increases production it can be described as a socialist model.

Now it seems that the CCP has virtually given up trying to reconcile the irreconcilable as reflected by Jiang Zemin's theory of the Three Represents. Although the party still presents itself as the representative of the working class it also acknowledges that it represents middle class interests ("the most advanced social forces"). This admission has been a long time coming given that the first signs of an emerging middle class were apparent during the mid-1980s. But in the end the party conceded that it had little option. It *created* China's capitalist middle class through the economic reform process; it could hardly go on ignoring them indefinitely.

Perhaps the question we should ask then is this: so what if the party's Marxist credentials are barely perceptible? Does anyone in China really care anymore? In effect the party's Marxist legitimacy collapsed after the Cultural Revolution and the subsequent embrace of economic reform has made Marxism increasingly irrelevant for the average Chinese man or woman on the street. Topics of discussion amongst the people are not about how Marxism and economic reform can be made more compatible. Public anxieties do not focus on the decline of Chinese Marxism in the modern era of mass consumerism. Instead people are much more interested in discussing business ventures or other financial matters. Concerns are focused much more on making money or in many cases simply making ends meet. No-one refers to anyone else as "comrade" anymore. Lei Feng is now considered by most Chinese to be a faintly amusing relic of a distant communist past.

In light of this, the party has sought to replace Marxism as a basis of ideological legitimacy with Chinese nationalism. With the accent on a form of xenophobic, anti-foreign nationalism as part of the official Campaign for Patriotic Education, party leaders, the state controlled media and other forms of written text (especially prevalent in the classroom) have focused on past humiliations inflicted on China by foreign imperialist powers (e.g. the Opium War). Emphasis has also been placed on the need to build a strong China in order to resist any future foreign domination. Whilst China may no longer be threatened territorially, it is argued, overseas powers led by the United States have attempted to hold China down by interfering in its domestic affairs (e.g. criticism of China's policy on Tibet and Taiwan) and by blocking its integration into the international arena (e.g. China's delayed acceptance into the WTO). In the context of this alleged foreign intransigence the party has presented itself as the sole standard bearer of China's national interests.

But this approach appears to have backfired on the party, not because the public has been disinterested in the renewed stress on nationalism causing the movement to collapse, but because if anything it has been *too* interested in the nationalist cause. In launching the Campaign for Patriotic Education the party may have inadvertently opened a Pandora's Box as evidenced by an increasingly voluble unofficial nationalist voice. Instead of simply supporting the official line on nationalism as the party had hoped, some people in China have been asking whether the CCP is doing *enough* to defend and protect Chinese interests against foreigners, especially Japan and the United States. Of particular concern to the party is that many of these people are organizing themselves and expressing their views over the internet, making it difficult for party censors to prevent the flow of unorthodox views. Ironically, therefore, Chinese nationalism may well be damaging CCP legitimacy rather than fortifying it.

As well as concentrating on economic performance and nationalism (with varying degrees of success) the post-Mao leadership has also sought to develop, or perhaps more accurately *rescue* a degree of legal rational legitimacy. This was imperative after the anarchy of the Cultural Revolution when accepted procedures for making decisions were systematically violated both at the national and regional level. Deng Xiaoping was never properly committed to the (re)construction of a legal rational system. Despite his rhetoric on the necessity of political and constitutional reform, key decisions on policy and the appointment or dismissal of important political figures during the Deng era were usually made secretly by one or two individuals (always including Deng) and then presented to colleagues as a *fait accompli* (e.g. the dismissal of Zhao Ziyang as General Secretary and appointment of Jiang Zemin to that post). Alternatively, decisions were often made by bodies that were not constitutionally authorized to do so and meetings were often conveniently (and unconstitutionally) enlarged to ensure that the requisite decision was reached (e.g. the sacking of Hu Yaobang as General Secretary). Deng did not dominate the political process to quite the same degree as Mao. There was, for example, no cult of personality allowing him to build up his own separate support base outside the party apparatus. But he was invariably the final arbiter on all important decisions.

Deng, like his predecessor, was also prepared to circumvent the party centre altogether if he did not agree with it or found himself in a minority position. This was most evident in 1992 when he gathered political support from outside the party leadership and used it to overturn Li Peng's economic retrenchment policy which was threatening to undermine Deng's entire economic reform programme. In acquiring the support of local leaders, Deng took advantage of his charismatic status as the "founding-father" of modern China, demonstrating again the incompatibility between charismatic legitimacy and legal rational legitimacy.

The post-Deng leadership has shown a much greater commitment to legal rational procedures. Constitutional limits on the length of time for serving in office have generally been adhered to and for the first time in the PRC's history the succession from one paramount leader to another – Jiang Zemin to Hu Jintao – took place in accordance with constitutional parameters rather than as a result of internecine political struggle, although for a while Jiang continued to exercise authority unofficially from behind the scenes. Notwithstanding Jiang's interference, the Hu Jintao regime has developed something of a reputation for transparency in decision making as demonstrated most notably during the campaign to combat the SARS epidemic.

Elections have also been taken much more seriously since the death of Mao with some significant reforms in this area. The direct election of deputies to people's congresses has been extended up the hierarchy to include the county as well as the township level and the procedure for nominating deputies is now much more open to the public. The "fifty per cent rule" means that more than half the electorate must vote if an election is to be valid whilst the successful candidate must receive over half of all votes cast. Reforms to the election of VCs have been even more notable. Compulsory secret balloting and open counts have greatly increased voter privacy. The aggregate number of candidates must exceed the aggregate number of posts for each VC and in some areas (e.g. Fujian) there must be at least two candidates for each post. In addition, voters enjoy the right to lodge complaints about electoral misconduct and this has inspired an increasing number of voters to express their dissatisfaction with unfair procedures or an unpopular VC in ways that are only just within the law.

Part of the rationale for introducing electoral reform, particularly at the VC level, is bound up in a genuine desire to make local politicians more accountable to their constituents and crucially to give voters a chance to eject corrupt officials. This, it is hoped, will deter people from protesting publicly about local corruption and possibly directing their ire at the party leadership in Beijing. The party is also keen to engender a degree of electoral legitimacy from the reforms. Although Beetham's prerequisite bipolar of full enfranchizement and voter choice is more applicable to the multi-party rather than single party system, significant improvements in both these areas albeit within the limited realm of the single party-state have been beneficial for the legitimacy of the CCP.

## Managing the future

Predictions about the future of the CCP are invariably tied up with predictions about the future of China in general given that the party has ruled China for over half a century. Making such predictions, however, is a tricky business and can be embarrassing for those bold enough to do so. Back in 1969 Harrison Salisbury famously prophesied the coming of a full scale war between China and the Soviet Union following years of diplomatic hostility between the CCP and the Communist Party of the Soviet Union. The war never came. Salisbury's howler has not stopped others from subsequently joining in the guessing game. At one end of the scale are those who see communist China as the world's next superpower, usurping the United States some time during the twenty-first century (Overholt 1994, Weidenbaum and Hughes 1996, Burstein and de Keijzer 1998, Murray 1998, Johnston and Ross 1999, Bacani 2003) and possibly even developing into a global hegemonic power (Mosher 2002). Some go so far as to suggest that China's recent emergence on the world scene under the auspices of the CCP will inevitably bring it into direct military conflict with the United States (Bernstein and Munro 1998, Gertz 2000, Timperlake and Triplett 2002) and some even blame China for 9/11 (Thomas 2001, Qiao Liang 2002). In stark contrast, others see a China that is in terminal decline, on the brink of collapse as a result of the social and economic instability thrown up by the post-Mao economic modernization programme (Chang 2001, Pei Minxin 2002, 2003, Naim 2003).

So what are we to make of such forecasts? Are they *all* completely at odds with reality? At the risk of stating the obvious, only time will tell, although it seems to be running out for Bernstein and Munro who predict war between China and the United States during the first decade of the twenty-first century. It is difficult to argue with the perception of China as the next superpower given the torrential speed at which the Chinese economy is growing. The fundamental challenge for the CCP remains *co-ordinating* the economic reform process, an increasingly difficult task given the continued decentralization of economic power. War with America as a consequence of China's burgeoning economic prowess is probably more remote. Although trade differences between the two nations are legion, both sides appear to be committed to diplomatic rather than military solutions, although this could always change if the CCP decides to recover Taiwan using military force.

The "China in crisis" perspective has some merit. As we have seen, the acute anxieties created by the socio-economic side-effects of economic reform have often erupted into public demonstrations and even rioting. The root cause of the 1989 protests was dissatisfaction with the economic reform process. In more recent years, smaller localized protests have taken place in reaction to instances of, amongst other things, corrupt local officials imposing illegal taxes or mass redundancies.

At the moment the CCP appears to have a strategy for dealing with social unrest, albeit largely on a case by case basis. In rural areas the party often intervenes directly when trouble breaks out, rescinding illegal taxes, repaying IOUs or dismissing corrupt officials. In urban areas the party will frequently attempt to curtail protests over unemployment by persuading those people still in a job to remain aloof from the protests whilst arresting those labour activists who organize the demonstrations. Notwithstanding the party's efforts to improve village governance in an attempt to appease the peasant population and introduce a national social security system in the wake of mass redundancies, it still tends to rely more on a reactive rather than preventative approach to reform-related socioeconomic tensions. Is it only a matter of time before the disenfranchized from rural and urban areas join forces? Can the CCP continue to forestall the growth of independent unions indefinitely?

It is not just those who have lost out under the reforms who present problems for the CCP. The party must also adapt to the demands of those who have benefitted from the reforms, namely China's emergent middle class. As we have seen, the party's dual strategy was to co-opt the middle class into the system through a concerted membership recruitment drive and the creation of institutional links with professional organizations and other corporatist bodies. Yet, in the long term this may not be enough and it could only be a matter of time before the middle class start agitating for a more open and inclusive political system. Gilley (2001) believes that such demands are already apparent amongst some rural entrepreneurs who are pushing to extend the democratic process beyond the VC level. Pearson (2001) sees the potential for a democratic movement within the managerial elite of foreign owed companies in China. Guthrie (2001) identifies SOE managers as the most likely source of middle class democratic activism. There is little real evidence at present to suggest any genuine movement for democratic change amongst the middle class. As Goodman (1996, 1999) points out Chinese entrepreneurs and managers currently feel that their interests are better represented *within* the incumbent political system rather than outside it. At the same time, it is worth noting that the South Korean middle class initially supported the authoritarian state until they perceived it as detrimental to their economic interests, at which point they shifted their allegiance towards the Korean democratic movement (Lett 1998, Kim 2000).

Since Tiananmen the party has attempted to diversify the basis of its legitimacy to encompass not just economic performance but also nationalism, stability and to a lesser extent legal rational and electoral legitimacy. With the exception of the concept of stability which is still in infancy, each of these bases carries with it certain difficulties that ironically threaten to detract from the legitimacy of the party. Economic reform has yielded numerous socio-economic side-effects such as unemployment and corruption, nationalism has caused some people to question whether the party is nationalistic *enough* in sticking up for Chinese interests and the tentative steps made in the direction of legal rational and electoral reform may encourage some (e.g. the middle class) to call for more fundamental reforms in these areas. Despite these difficulties, there is nothing which currently suggests that the party's monopoly on power is seriously in jeopardy. As Hays Gries and Rosen (2004: 16) point out, 'the future of the Chinese state may be far from clear, but there is little evidence that it is in imminent peril'. This will only be likely if the party's legitimacy is seriously challenged on most or all of the fronts mentioned earlier rather than just one of them (Perry 1999, Balzer 2004: 249).

# Biography of Chinese leaders

**Bo Yibo (1908–)**

Born in Dingxiang, Shanxi province, Bo joined the party in 1925. An active revolutionary in China's northern border regions, Bo quickly developed a reputation as an economic specialist. After the revolution, Bo played a leading role in formulating China's first Five Year Plan (1953–7) and was appointed Chairman of the State Economic Commission, a key government organization that dealt with central economic planning. Purged during the Cultural Revolution, Bo reappeared after Mao's death in support of Deng Xiaoping's economic reform programme. Yet, like many of the first generation of CCP leaders, Bo became concerned that the reforms were corroding the party's Marxist legitimacy and by the end of the 1980s Bo had become one of the most vociferous critics of the pace and direction of the reforms.

**Chen Boda (1904–89)**

Born in Huian, Fujian province, Chen joined the party in 1924. Acknowledged as an expert in Marxist theory and propaganda matters, Chen served as Mao's personal secretary before the revolution and is believed to have drafted many of Mao's major theoretical speeches and publications. After the revolution Chen became editor of the official party journal *Red Flag* and played a leading role in establishing Mao's personality cult for which he was rewarded with the chairmanship of the CRG in 1966. But as Mao moved away from the radicalism of the Cultural Revolution, Chen found himself at odds with his former patron, especially after allying himself with Lin Biao with whom Mao was in conflict. Purged in 1970, Chen was later accused of being a member of the Lin Biao and Gang of Four cliques for which he received an 18 year prison sentence.

**Chen Yun (1905–95)**

Born in Qingpu (now part of Shanghai), Chen joined the party in 1924 and operated throughout the 1920s as an underground trade union organizer whilst working as a type-setter in Shanghai. After spending time in Moscow, Chen became a specialist in economic affairs and was primarily responsible for the economic reconstruction programme implemented during the early post-revolutionary period. Unafraid to speak his mind, Chen opposed the Great Leap Forward from the very beginning and after the collapse of the Leap in 1960, he was called on to help repair the Chinese economy. Espousing the limited use of local markets to stimulate production as well as material incentives to raise the morale of urban and rural workers, Chen succeeded in stabilizing the economy in the early 1960s. However, with the onset of the Cultural Revolution in 1966, Chen's economic policies were derided as capitalist and Chen disappeared from public view for almost a decade. On returning to the leadership with Deng Xiaoping in 1977, Chen led China into yet another period of economic recovery, although this time without the impending threat of a Maoist backlash. But as the scope of economic reform moved well beyond what Chen had envisaged, he began to feel that the CCP was betraying its Marxist roots. This frequently brought him into conflict with the radical generation of economic reformers such as Hu Yaobang and Zhao Ziyang, and as Chairman of the CAC, Chen became one of the most ardent and active critics of the reforms.

## Deng Xiaoping (1904–97)

A native of Guangan, Sichuan province, Deng (born as Deng Xiansheng) spent his formative years studying in France where he joined the China Socialist Youth League aged 18 years. After returning to China in 1926, Deng joined the Red Army and as Political Commissar of the Second Field Army, he was involved in a number of successful military campaigns against the Japanese army and the KMT. During the early years of the PRC, Deng was a full-fledged Maoist, supporting Mao on a number of issues including the Anti-Rightist Campaign and the Great Leap Forward. Following the failure of the Leap, Deng moved towards the political centre allying himself with the more pragmatic economic policies of Chen Yun and Liu Shaoqi and turning his back on his old mentor. Consequently, Deng became a prime target of Red Guard vitriol during the Cultural Revolution when he was branded "the number two person in authority taking the capitalist road" (behind Liu Shaoqi). Purged in 1966 and sent to work in a tractor factory, Deng's long-standing contacts in the military ensured that he survived the era. With the help of Zhou Enlai, Deng was reinstated as Vice-Premier in 1973 and took over government matters when Zhou became terminally ill, eagerly implementing Zhou's Four Modernizations. Following Zhou's death in 1976, Deng was purged again for allegedly orchestrating the "counter-revolutionary" Tiananmen demonstrations in April of that year. But after a brief spell on the political sidelines, Deng emerged again, dispensing with Hua Guofeng, his main challenger as Mao's successor and spearheading the post-Mao era of economic reform. Domestically, Deng will always be remembered as the "founding-father" of economic reform. Many international observers, however, remember Deng in a more dubious light as the man behind the Tiananmen crackdown of June 1989.

## Hu Jintao (1942–)

Born in Jixi, Anhui province, into a wealthy merchant family, Hu joined the CCP in 1964. After graduating from Qinghua University in Beijing, Hu worked as an engineer in the remote region of Gansu province. In 1982, Hu was appointed to the Secretariat of the Communist Youth League. A few years later he was appointed as Secretary of the Guizhou provincial party and then Secretary of the Tibetan Autonomous Region. In 1992, Hu was catapulted into the PSC at the age of only 49 years old. Hu currently holds the three key posts of President, General Secretary and Chairman of the CMC. His incumbency thus far is largely acknowledged as representing a more politically transparent and legal rational era than anything that came before him.

## Hu Qili (1929–)

A native of Yulin, Shaanxi province, Hu joined the party in 1948. After the revolution, Hu served in a number of capacities including on the Secretariat of the Communist Youth League. Purged during the Cultural Revolution, Hu returned to public office after the fall of Lin Biao as a high ranking official in Ningxia province and then later as Mayor of Tianjin. Hu was promoted to the Politburo in 1985 and then to the PSC in 1987 but was removed from the PSC after 1989 following his sympathetic stance during the Tiananmen demonstrations.

## Hu Yaobang (1915–89)

Born in Hunan province, Hu joined the party in his teens and was one of the youngest participants in the Long March. A few years later, Hu joined the Red Army and became a political officer under the direct authority of Deng Xiaoping. This signalled the start of a close working relationship between the two men. Following the establishment of the PRC, Hu was appointed head of the Communist Youth League, but his opposition to the Anti-Rightist Campaign in 1957 caused him to be purged during the Cultural Revolution. Rehabilitated in 1973, Hu was purged again in 1975 for his liberal attitude towards intellectuals and the education system. Returning again in 1977 during Deng Xiaoping's ascendancy, Hu quickly rose through the ranks and in 1980 he became General Secretary in place of Hua Guofeng. During the 1980s, Hu established himself as a leading economic reformer and became Deng's chosen successor as paramount leader. Along with Zhao Ziyang, Hu championed the replacement of the central plan with the market and argued fervently for the continued decentralization of economic decision making. Hu was also an exponent of limited political reform and became the main patron of the liberal intelligentsia as well as a perceived ally of China's student population. When Hu refused to condemn the pro-reform demands of the student demonstrators in late 1986 he was dismissed as General Secretary and replaced by Zhao Ziyang. Hu's sudden death in April 1989 led to a spontaneous outburst of student mourning and marked the beginning of the 1989 student demonstrations.

## Hua Guofeng (1921–)

Born in Jiaozheng county, Shanxi province, Hua was deeply involved in the military struggle against Japan. After occupying a number of high ranking party positions (e.g. Political Commissar of the Jiaozheng armed forces) Hua was posted to Xiangtan district (Hunan province), home of Mao Zedong. Hua's success in developing the local infrastructure, especially in Mao's home village of Shaoshan, endeared him greatly to Mao and facilitated his rapid promotion to state Chairman following Zhou Enlai's death in January 1976 and party and CMC Chairman after Mao's death in September of that year. But Hua will always be remembered as a political failure. Whilst he was widely acclaimed for ordering the arrest of the much despised Gang of Four, Hua quickly lost power to Deng Xiaoping as a result of his slavish adherence to Mao's seemingly failed legacy. Ridiculed as leader of the "whateverist" faction following his pledge to follow and obey "whatever Mao would have ordered", Hua was easily outmanoeuvred by Deng's superior intellect and political adroitness. By June 1981, Hua had been dismissed from all leadership posts, his political career essentially over.

## Jiang Qing (1913–91)

Jiang was born as Li Yunhe in Zhucheng, Shandong province. A moderately successful actress on the fringes of the Shanghai circuit (under the name Lan Ping), she joined the CCP in 1938 and travelled to Yanan where she met Mao. A year later, she and Mao were married even though Mao was still married to the terminally ill He Zizhen. The party establishment (most notably Zhou Enlai and Deng Xiaoping) distrusted Jiang's motives for marrying Mao and forced her to make a promise that she would refrain from any involvement in politics for 30 years and restrict herself to household chores. But in the 1960s, as Mao searched for allies in the build up to the Cultural Revolution, Jiang became active in cultural affairs. Initially, Jiang channelled her efforts into reforming Beijing opera along more socialist revolutionary lines. However, as a member of the CRG after 1966 and informal head of the Gang of Four, Jiang moved into the political sphere where she used her growing authority to attack and purge senior party officials. In 1969, Jiang was promoted to the Politburo and sought to dominate Chinese politics in the post-Cultural Revolution era. When Mao died in 1976, Jiang lost her most powerful ally and within days she and the other members of the Gang of Four were arrested. Charged with attempting to ferment civil war and planning a coup d'etat, Jiang was sentenced to death in 1981, although this was later commuted to life imprisonment. Speculation still surrounds Jiang's death in May 1991. Some scholars suggest that she died of cancer whilst others believe that she committed suicide whilst out of prison receiving medical treatment.

## Jiang Zemin (1926–)

Born in Yangzhou, Jiangsu province, Jiang joined the party in 1946. A graduate of electrical engineering from Shanghai's Jiaotong University, Jiang served in the

First Machine Building Ministry after the revolution. Relatively unscathed by the Cultural Revolution, Jiang established his political career in the early 1980s when he became involved in setting up SEZs in southern China. After two years as Mayor of Shanghai, Jiang was promoted to the Politburo in 1987 and following the dismissal of Zhao Ziyang in 1989, Jiang became General Secretary. Jiang's rapid ascendancy can be partly attributed to his success in defusing the student demonstrations in 1986 without resorting to military force, and although he supported the implementation of martial law in Beijing, he was not directly associated with the coercion that followed. As Deng Xiaoping's third chosen successor (following the demise of Hu Yaobang and then Zhao Ziyang), Jiang moved carefully during Deng's last years, constructing his own power base, especially within the PLA where he was previously virtually unknown, and in 1994 his formal power increased when he became state President and Chairman of the CMC. Although Jiang was not always portrayed positively by the media, he was undoubtedly successful in the post-Deng era, presiding over the return of Hong Kong (1997) and Macao (1999) to Chinese sovereignty, China's accession to the WTO (2002) and the selection of Beijing as hosts for the 2008 Olympic Games.

### Li Peng (1928–)

Born in Chengdu, Sichuan province, Li joined the party in 1945. After graduating in hydro-electric engineering from the Moscow Power Institute, Li returned to China in 1955. Li then served in various ministerial positions within the government's energy department. After becoming a member of the Central Committee in 1982, Li rose to the Politburo in 1987 when he also became acting Premier. Promoted to Premier in 1988, Li declared martial law during the Tiananmen protests and was instrumental in the dismissal as General Secretary and arrest of Zhao Ziyang. Favouring greater central economic planning and slower economic growth, Li's control was eclipsed by Deng Xiaoping's return to the helm in 1992. Li served as Premier until 1998 when he was constitutionally required to give up the post.

### Li Xiannian (1907–92)

A native of Huangan (now Hongan) Hubei province, Li was one of the foremost military leaders of the revolutionary era, with a string of successful military campaigns to his name. After the revolution, Li moved into civilian politics and was made Minister of Finance in 1954 and later Vice-Premier. Protected by Zhou Enlai during the Cultural Revolution, Li emerged as a key opponent of the radical leftism symbolized by Lin Biao and the Gang of Four. After Mao's death, Li played a leading role in implementing economic reform and in 1983 he was promoted to President, a position which he held until 1988.

### Lin Biao (1907–71)

Born in Wuhan, Hubei province, Lin initially joined the KMT and rose to the position of Company Commander in the KMT military apparatus. Following the split with the CCP in 1927, Lin swapped sides and as head of the communist First Army Group, he defended the Jiangxi Soviet against Chiang Kai-shek's encirclement campaigns. Already renowned for his military expertise, Lin enhanced this reputation during the Chinese civil war by capturing Manchuria from KMT forces and defeating the KMT in both Beijing and neighbouring Tianjin. With help from Mao, Lin was thrust into the centre of Chinese politics in 1959 after replacing Peng Dehuai as Minister of Defence following Peng's dramatic purge at the Lushan conference. From then on, Lin was firmly allied to Mao. In the prelude to the Cultural Revolution, Lin indoctrinated the military with Maoist propaganda and promoted the need for undying loyalty to Mao through the publication of the Little Red Book. But it was Lin's control of the central military apparatus that was crucial in launching the Cultural Revolution, and in 1969 Lin was rewarded for his loyalty when he was officially designated as Mao's chosen successor. Yet, as Mao began to move away from the radical principles of the Cultural Revolution, Lin found himself increasingly isolated and as Zhou Enlai returned to the political forefront, the strength of Lin's political position began to wane. Attempts to cement his succession to Mao only served to alienate Mao and after disappearing from public sight in 1970, Lin died a year later, although his death was not officially announced until 1972. The official line remains that Lin was killed in a plane crash over Mongolia after his assassination attempt on Mao failed, forcing him to flee. The truth may never be known.

## Liu Shaoqi (1898–1969)

Born in Yinshan, Hunan province, into a rich peasant family, Liu joined the party in 1921. During the same year, Liu went to Moscow to study Russian at the University of the Toilers of the East, an experience which marked him out as one of the more Leninist oriented members of the CCP leadership. On return to China, Liu became actively involved in the organization of Chinese urban labour and in 1925 he was appointed head of the newly established All-China Federation of Labour. Liu was also a specialist on ideological matters and in 1939 he published his landmark book *How to be a Good Communist* which identified the traits required to be a model CCP member. After 1949, Liu became one of the foremost leaders of the CCP, participating closely with Mao on a number of political and economic issues. In 1959, Liu succeeded Mao as state Chairman and was widely touted as Mao's chosen successor. After the Great Leap Forward, however, the two men began to drift apart as Liu aligned himself closely with the post-Leap recovery programme favoured by Deng Xiaoping and Chen Yun. Relations with Mao further deteriorated when Liu sought to dilute Mao's SEM and during the Cultural Revolution Liu was identified as the "number one person in authority taking the capitalist road". Stripped of his leadership positions in 1968 and persecuted ruthlessly by the Red Guards, Liu died in a Kaifeng (Henan) prison a year later. Liu was posthumously rehabilitated in 1980.

## Mao Zedong (1893–1976)

Born in Xiangtan, Hunan province, Mao was among the handful of men who gathered in Shanghai to establish the CCP in July 1921. Although he is acknowledged as the founding-father of the PRC, Mao was a relatively unexceptional revolutionary activist during the early years of his political life. In 1927, for example, Mao was held largely responsible for the failure of a peasant rebellion in Hunan, known as the Autumn Harvest Uprising and was dismissed from the Central Committee for his pains. Mao was convinced that the peasantry were a positive revolutionary force and he devoted most of his younger years to the construction of a revolutionary movement in the Chinese countryside. Whilst Mao's uncompromising stance brought him into conflict with Stalin and later Khrushchev, he inspired considerable support at home and after standing firm against pressure for a Soviet style urban based revolutionary strategy during the landmark Zunyi conference in 1935, Mao emerged as the CCP's paramount leader. From then on, Mao became one of the most important revolutionaries of all time, although his tactics of guerrilla warfare that led the CCP to victory belonged as much to Peng Dehuai as they did to Mao. But bureaucratic office did not suit Mao and many observers believe that Mao's best years had been and gone. The facts speak for themselves. In a further attempt to break away from the Soviet model of central economic planning, Mao rushed China into the Great Leap Forward in 1958, an ill-conceived and poorly implemented initiative which sought to rapidly increase production through mass mobilization. The ensuing famine claimed millions of lives. After a brief period on the sidelines, Mao took control again, this time masterminding the Cultural Revolution, a sincere but misguided attempt to stamp out revisionism in the party. The resultant social chaos almost destroyed the CCP and it was thanks only to the PLA that the party survived at all. After Mao died in 1976, the party provided a sanguine assessment of his legacy, concluding that he was 70 per cent "correct" and 30 per cent "incorrect". Since then, however, the party has abandoned Maoism altogether in the quest for a modern, powerful and wealthy society.

## Peng Dehuai (1898–1974)

Like Mao, Peng was a native of Xiangtan, Hunan province. After joining the party in 1928, Peng quickly established himself as an outstanding military leader and is widely recognized, along with Mao, as one of the chief exponents of the tactics of guerrilla warfare which helped the CCP to win power. After leading the troops during the Korean War (1950–3), Peng was promoted to Minister of Defence in 1954. However, following his criticism of Mao's Great Leap Forward at the Lushan conference in 1959, Peng was dismissed from his post and replaced with arch rival Lin Biao. The source of Peng's rivalry with Mao derived ultimately from Peng's belief that the PLA should be modelled on the Soviet Red Army with an emphasis on modern technology and professionalism rather than the politically indoctrinated "army of the people" that Mao preferred. But Peng's proposals for military reform required China to form closer diplomatic ties with the Soviet Union, an option that Mao found repugnant in light of his bitter fall out with Khrushchev. Peng's support for the Soviet Union and his rivalry with Mao made him an obvious target during the Cultural Revolution, and in 1967 he disappeared from public view after being arrested and stripped of his official posts. After years of persecution and solitary confinement, Peng died in 1974. He was posthumously rehabilitated after Mao's death.

## Wang Hongwen (1934–92)

Born in Changchun, Jilin province, Wang was politically unknown until the Cultural Revolution when he impressed Mao as a youthful and working class figure in the 1967 Shanghai Commune. In 1973, aged just 37, Wang was appointed to the PSC and as third-in-command behind Mao and Zhou Enlai. He was widely tipped as a future successor to Mao. But Wang's lack of political experience was soon exposed by his opponents in the leadership and when Mao announced in late 1974 that Deng Xiaoping was to take over the ailing Zhou Enlai's duties as Premier, it was clear that like Liu Shaoqi and Lin Biao before him, Wang had lost Mao's blessing. Arrested in 1976 as a member of the Gang of Four, Wang was sentenced to life imprisonment.

## Yao Wenyuan (1931–2005)

Born in Zhuji, Zhejiang province, Yao is best known as the man who fired the first shot in the Cultural Revolution. Renowned as an incisive literary critic, Yao published a biting critique of the play *Hai Rui Dismissed From Office* written by Wu Han. This precipitated a rectification campaign in art and literature which was quickly broadened to encompass the revisionism perceived to be endemic in the party leadership. During the Cultural Revolution, Yao served as a member of the CRG, helping to instigated many of the Red Guard attacks on senior party leaders. Following the collapse of local authority in Shanghai, Yao and his colleague Zhang Chunqiao attempted unsuccessfully to set up the Shanghai Commune. As the Cultural Revolution subsided, Yao's influence and power began to wane, and after attempting (and failing) to continue with the radical policies of the movement, Yao was arrested as a member of the Gang of Four. He was later sentenced to 20 years in prison.

## Zhang Chunqiao (1917–2005)

Zhang was a native of Juye, Shandong province. During the 1930s, he worked as a writer in Shanghai, joining the party in 1938 after the landmark Yanan conference on art and literature. After the revolution, Zhang became a prominent journalist in Shanghai where he took charge of the *Liberation Army Daily*, and it was from his Shanghai base that he helped Mao launch the Cultural Revolution in 1966. A leading organizer of the Shanghai Commune and a member of the CRG, Zhang made his name during the Cultural Revolution and was duly promoted to the PSC in 1973. In January 1975, Zhang became Deputy Prime Minister but was later arrested as a member of the Gang of Four. Initially sentenced to death, Zhang's sentence was later commuted to life imprisonment.

## Zhao Ziyang (1919–2005)

A native of Huaxin, Henan province, Zhao joined the party in 1938. Immediately after the revolution, Zhao became heavily involved in the implementation of land reform in Guangdong province where he later became party First Secretary. Persecuted by the Red Guards during the Cultural Revolution, Zhao returned to active politics in the 1970s and was again involved in agricultural reform, this time in Sichuan province, one of the first areas to implement the household responsibility system that became national policy a few years later. In 1980, Zhao replaced Hua Guofeng as Premier and became a leading proponent of radical economic reform. In 1987, Zhao became General Secretary, following the sacking of Hu Yaobang, and thus became Deng Xiaoping's second chosen successor. Within two years, however, Zhao was removed from the post. Blamed for the socio-economic circumstances that precipitated the 1989 demonstrations, Zhao became a convenient scapegoat for Deng. After the Tiananmen crackdown, Zhao was placed under house arrest where he remained until his death.

## Zhou Enlai (1898–1976)

Born in Huaian, Jiangsu province into a wealthy gentry family, Zhou joined the party in 1922 whilst studying in France where he set up the Paris based Chinese Communist Youth Group. On return to China, Zhou was appointed to the political department of the Whampoa Military Academy under the auspices of KMT leader Chiang Kai-shek, but after the split with the KMT in 1927, Zhou was forced underground, rejoining Mao and his colleagues in time for the Long March. During the Yanan era, Zhou established himself in a diplomatic capacity as he sought to broker a deal with the KMT government and after the revolution he was duly appointed as Minister for Foreign Affairs. Zhou excelled in this position, establishing diplomatic ties with a number of developing nations in Africa and Asia and laying the foundations for US President Richard Nixon's landmark visit to Beijing in 1972. Zhou was also forced to mediate in China's domestic affairs. As Mao sought to radicalize the Cultural Revolution, Zhou played a delicate balancing act attempting to protect the main targets of the movement whilst somehow remaining (or appearing to remain) loyal to Mao. As Mao retreated from extreme radicalism in the early 1970s, Zhou played a leading role in the rehabilitation of purged party members and was principally responsible for Deng's Xiaoping's reappearance in 1973. His role as mediator during the Cultural Revolution earned him numerous admirers in China and when the public were not allowed to publicly mourn his death in January 1976, spontaneous demonstrations broke out in Tiananmen Square.

## Zhu Rongji (1928–)

Born in Changsha, Hunan province, Zhu joined the party in 1949. A graduate of electrical engineering from Beijing's Qinghua University, Zhu worked as an economic advisor to the State Planning Commission until he was purged during the Anti-Rightist Campaign for criticizing Mao's "irrational high growth" policies. Rehabilitated in 1962, Zhu returned to the State Planning Commission until he was purged again during the Cultural Revolution. Rehabilitated for a second time in 1975 with the help of Deng Xiaoping, Zhu kept a relatively low profile until the early 1980s when Deng finally consolidated his power base. After a spell as an economic advisor to the State Economic Commission, Zhu replaced Jiang Zemin as Mayor of Shanghai in 1987 and it was during this time that he established himself as an adept economic reformer through his transformation of the city's telecom, urban construction and transportation sectors. Promoted to Vice-Premier of the State Council in 1991, Zhu was responsible for cooling China's overheated economy with measures including cutting interest rates, devaluing China's currency and reforming the tax system, whilst also maintaining a relatively high economic growth rate. After becoming Premier in 1998, Zhu developed a more ruthless reputation as a reformer, overseeing massive redundancies in China's bloated bureaucracy and highly inefficient state sector. Zhu also privatized state-owned housing, providing Chinese residents with an opportunity to purchase their own apartments at subsidized prices.

# Bibliography

Bacani, D. (2003) *The China Investor: Getting Rich with the Next Superpower*, New York: John Wiley and Sons.

Bachman, D. (1986) 'Differing visions of China's post-Mao economy: the ideas of Chen Yun, Deng Xiaoping and Zhao Ziyang', *Asian Survey*, 26, 3: 292–321.

Bachman, D. (1988) 'Varieties of Chinese conservatism and the fall of Hu Yaobang', *Journal of Northeast Asian Studies*, Spring edn: 22–46.

Balzer, H. (2004) 'State and society in transitions from communism: China in comparative perspective', in P. Hays Gries and S. Rosen (eds) *State and Society in 21st Century China: Crisis, Contention and Legitimation*, New York: Routledge.

Bao Tong. (2002) 'Three represents: marking the end of an era', *Far Eastern Economic Review*, 5 September.

Barme, G. (1997) 'History for the masses', in J. Unger (ed.) *Using the Past to Serve the Present: Historiography and Politics in Contemporary China*, New York: M. E. Sharpe.

Baum, R. (1964) ' "Red and expert": the politico-ideological foundations of China's Great Leap Forward', *Asian Survey*, 4, 9: 1048–57.

Baum, R. (1971) 'The Cultural Revolution in the countryside: anatomy of a limited rebellion', in T. Robinson (ed.) *The Cultural Revolution in China*, Berkeley, CA: University of California Press.

Baum, R. (1975) *Prelude to the Revolution: Mao, the Party and the Peasant Question, 1962–1966*, New York: Columbia University Press.

Baum, R. (1997) 'The road to Tiananmen: Chinese politics in the 1980s', in R. MacFarquhar (ed.) *The Politics of China: The Eras of Mao and Deng*, Cambridge: Cambridge University Press.

Becker, J. (1996) *Hungry Ghosts: Mao's Secret Famine*, New York: Free Press.

Beetham, D. (1991) *The Legitimation of Power*, London: Palgrave.

Bennett, G. and Montaperto, R. (1972) *Red Guard: The Political Biography of Dai Hsiao-ai*, New York: Anchor Books.

Bernstein, R. and Munro, R. (1998) *The Coming Conflict with China*, New York: Vintage Books.

Bernstein, T. (1977) *Up to the Mountains and Down to the Villages: The Transfer of Youth from Urban to Rural China*, Connecticut: Yale University Press.

Bernstein, T. and Lu Xiaobo. (2003) *Taxation Without Representation in Contemporary Rural China*, Cambridge: Cambridge University Press.

Blecher, M. (1986) *China: Politics, Economics and Society*, London: Pinter.

Blecher, M. (2002) 'Hegemony and workers politics in China', *China Quarterly*, 170: 283–303.

Bonavia, D. (1984) *Verdict in Peking: The Trial of the Gang of Four*, London: Burnett Books.

Breslin, S. (1996) *China in the 1980s: Centre–Province Relations in a Reforming Socialist State*, London: Macmillan.

Breslin, S. (1998) *Mao*, London: Longman.

Bridgham, P. (1973) 'The fall of Lin Piao', *China Quarterly*, 55: 427–49.

Brodsgaard, K. (1981) 'The democracy movement in China, 1978–79: opposition movements, wall poster campaigns and underground journals', *Asian Survey*, 21, 7: 747–74.

Burstein, D. and de Keijzer, A. (1998) *Big Dragon: China's Future: What It Means for Business, the Economy, and the Global Order*, New York: Simon and Schuster.

Byrd, W. and Lin, Q. (eds) (1990) *China's Rural Industry: Structure, Development and Reform*, New York: Oxford University Press.

Chan, A. (1985) *Children of Mao: Personality Development and Political Activism in the Red Guard Generation*, Seattle, WA: University of Washington Press.

Chang, C. (1985) 'The Hainan vehicle trafficking scandal', *Issues and Studies*, 21, 9: 5–7.

Chang, G. (2001) *The Coming Collapse of China*, New York: Random House.

Chao, L. and Myers R. (2000) 'How elections promoted democracy in Taiwan under martial law', in L. Diamond and R. Myers (eds) *Elections and Democracy in Greater China*, Oxford: Oxford University Press.

Cheek, T. (1997) *Propaganda and Culture in Mao's China: Deng Tuo and the Intelligentsia*, Oxford: Oxford University Press.

Chen, J. (ed.) (1970) *Mao Papers: Anthology and Bibliography*, London: Oxford University Press.

Cheng, C. (ed.) (1966) *The Politics of the Chinese Red Army: A Translation of the Bulletin of Activities of the People's Liberation Army*, Stanford, CA: Hoover Institution Publications.

Cotton, J. (1984) 'The intellectuals as a group in the Chinese political process', in D. Goodman (ed.) *Groups and Politics in the People's Republic of China*, Cardiff: University College Cardiff Press.

Deans, P. (2000) 'Contending nationalisms in northeast Asia and the Diaoyu/Senkaku dispute', *Security Dialogue*, 31, 1: 119–31.

Deans, P. (2004) 'The internet in the People's Republic of China: censorship and participation', in J. Abbott (ed.) *The Political Economy of the Internet in Asia and the Pacific: Digital Divides, Economic Competitiveness and Security Challenges*, Westport, CT: Praeger Publishers.

Deng Xiaoping. (1984) *Selected Works of Deng Xiaoping, 1975–1982*, Beijing: Foreign Languages Press.

Denitch, B. (ed.) (1979) *Legitimation of Regimes: International Framework for Analysis*, London: Sage.

Dickson, B. (2003) *Red Capitalists in China: The Party, Private Entrepreneurs and Prospects for Political Change*, Cambridge: Cambridge University Press.

Dickson, B. (2004) 'Dilemmas of party adaptation: the CCP's strategies for survival', in P. Hays Gries and S. Rosen (eds) *State and Society in 21st Century China: Crisis, Contention and Legitimation*, New York: Routledge.

Dietrich, C. (1998) *People's China: A Brief History*, New York: Oxford University Press.

Ding Xueliang. (1994) *The Decline of Communism in China: Legitimacy Crisis, 1977–1989*, Cambridge: Cambridge University Press.

Ding Yi. (1990) *Xuexi Lei Feng* (Study Lei Feng), Beijing: Central Publishing House.

Dirlik, A. and Meisner, M. (eds) (1989) *Marxism and the Chinese Experience*, London: M. E. Sharpe.

Dittmer, L. (1974) *Liu Shao-ch'i and the Chinese Cultural Revolution: The Politics of Mass Criticism*, Berkeley, CA: University of California Press.

Dittmer, L. (1988) 'Reform, succession and the resurgence of mainland China's old guard', *Issues and Studies*, 24, 1: 96–113.

Dittmer, L. (1989) 'The Tiananmen massacre', *Problems of Communism*, 38, 5: 2–15.

Domes, J. (1968) 'The Cultural Revolution and the army', *Asian Survey*, 8, 5: 349–63.

Domes, J. (1970) 'The role of the military in the formation of revolutionary committees: 1967–68', *China Quarterly*, 44: 112–45.

Donnithorne, A. (1959) 'Background to the people's communes: changes in China's economic organization in 1958', *Pacific Affairs*, 32, 4: 339–53.

Duckett, J. (2003) 'China's social security reform and the comparative politics of market transition', *Journal of Communist Studies and Transition Politics*, 19, 1: 80–101.

Eastman, L. (1984) *Seeds of Destruction: Nationalist China in War and Revolution, 1937–1949*, Stanford, CA: Stanford University Press.

Elklit, J. (1997) 'The Chinese village committee electoral system', *China Information*, 11, 4: 1–13.

Endicott, S. (1988) *Red Earth: Revolution in a Sichuan Village*, London: I. B. Tauris.

Feng Chen. (1995) *Economic Transition and Political Legitimacy in Post-Mao China: Ideology and Reform*, New York: State University of New York Press.

Fewsmith, J. (1997) 'Reaction, resurgence and succession: Chinese politics since Tiananmen', in R. MacFarquhar (ed.) *The Politics of China: The Eras of Mao and Deng*, Cambridge: Cambridge University Press.

Fewsmith, J. (2001) *China Since Tiananmen: The Politics of Transition*, Cambridge: Cambridge University Press.

Fewsmith, J. (2003a) 'The sixteenth National Party Congress: the succession that didn't happen', *China Quarterly*, 173: 1–16.

Fewsmith, J. (2003b) 'Studying the three represents', *China Leadership Monitor*, Fall edn.

Fontana, D. (1982) 'Background to the fall of Hua Guofeng', *Asian Survey*, 22, 3: 237–60.

Franke, W. (1963) 'The role of tradition in present-day China', *Modern World*, 4: 75–92.

Fu Xiaolan and Balasubramanyam, V. (2003) 'Township and village enterprises in China', *Journal of Development Studies*, 39, 4: 27–46.

Fu Zhengyuan. (1991) 'Continuities of Chinese political tradition', *Studies in Comparative Communism*, 24, 3: 259–79.

Garside, R. (1981) *Coming Alive!: China After Mao*, New York: McGraw-Hill.

Gertz, B. (2000) *The China Threat: How the People's Republic Targets America*, Washington: Regnery Publishing.

Gill, G. (1982) 'Personal dominance and the collective principle: individual legitimacy in Marxist–Leninist systems', in T. Rigby and F. Feher (eds) *Political Legitimation in Communist Systems*, London: Macmillan.

Gilley, B. (2001) 'The Yu Zuomin phenomenon: entrepreneurs and politics in rural China', in V. Bonnell and T. Gold (eds) *The New Entrepreneurs of Europe and Asia: Patterns of Business Development in Russia, Eastern Europe and China*, New York: M. E. Sharpe.

Gillin, D. (1964) 'Peasant nationalism in the history of Chinese communism', *Journal of Asian Studies*, 23, 2: 269–89.

Gittings, J. (1966–7) 'The Chinese army's role in the Cultural Revolution', *Pacific Affairs*, 39, 3–4: 269–89.

Gittings, J. (2005) *The Changing Face of China: From Mao to Market*, Oxford: Oxford University Press.

Goldman, M. (1981) *China's Intellectuals: Advice and Dissent*, Cambridge, MA: Harvard University Press.

Goldman, M. (1994) *Sowing the Seeds of Democracy in China*, Cambridge, MA: Harvard University Press.

Gong Wenxiang (1989) 'The legacy of Confucian culture in Maoist China', *Social Science Journal*, 26, 4: 363–74.

Goodman, D. (1981) *Beijing Street Voices: The Poetry and Politics of China's Democracy Movement*, London: Marion Boyars.

Goodman, D. (ed.) (1989) *China's Regional Development*, London: Routledge.

Goodman, D. (1996) 'The People's Republic of China: the party-state, capitalist revolution and new entrepreneurs', in R. Robson and D. Goodman (eds) *The New Rich in Asia: Mobile Phones, McDonalds and Middle-class Revolution*, London: Routledge.

Goodman, D. (1999) 'The new middle class', in M. Goldman and R. MacFarquhar (eds) *The Paradox of China's Post-Mao Reforms*, Cambridge, MA: Harvard University Press.

Grafstein, R. (1981) 'The failure of Weber's conception of legitimacy: its causes and implications', *Journal of Politics*, 43: 456–72.

Gray, J. (1990) *Rebellions and Revolutions: China from the 1800s to the 1980s*, Oxford: Oxford University Press.

Guo Baogang. (2003) 'Political legitimacy and China's transition', *Journal of Chinese Political Science*, 8, 1/2: 1–25.

Guo Yingjie. (1998) 'Patriotic villains and patriotic heroes: Chinese literary nationalism in the 1990s', *Nationalism and Ethnic Politics*, 4, 1/2: 163–88.

Guo Yong and Hu Angang. (2004) 'The administrative monopoly in China's economic transition', *Communist and Post-Communist Studies*, 37, 3: 265–80.

Guthrie, D. (2001) 'Entrepreneurial action in the state sector: the economic decisions of Chinese managers', in V. Bonnell and T. Gold (eds) *The New Entrepreneurs of Europe and Asia: Patterns of Business Development in Russia, Eastern Europe and China*, New York: M. E. Sharpe.

Habermas, J. (1975) *Legitimation Crisis*, Boston, MA: Beacon Press.

Hamrin, C. (1984) 'Competing "policy packages" in post-Mao China', *Asian Survey*, 24, 5: 487–518.

Hamrin, C. (2001) 'Inching towards open politics', *China Journal*, 45: 123–9.

Han Suyin. (1976) *The Wind in the Tower: Mao Tse-tung and the Chinese Revolution, 1949–1976*, London: Cape.

Hao Chang. (1971) *Liang Chi-chao and the Intellectual Transition in China: 1890–1907*, Cambridge, MA: Harvard University Press.

Harding, H. (1992) *A Fragile Relationship: The United States and China Since 1972*, Washington, DC: Brookings Institution Press.

Harding, H. (1997) 'The Chinese state in crisis', in R. MacFarquhar (ed.) *The Politics of China: The Eras of Mao and Deng*, Cambridge: Cambridge University Press.

Harding, N. (1983) *Lenin's Political Thought: Theory and Practice in the Democratic and Socialist Revolutions*, New Jersey: Humanities Press.

Hays Gries, P. (2004) *China's New Nationalism: Pride, Politics and Diplomacy*, California: University of California Press.

Hays Gries, P. and Rosen, S. (2004) 'Popular protest and state legitimation in 21st century China', in P. Hays Gries and S. Rosen (eds) *State and Society in 21st Century China: Crisis, Contention and Legitimation*, New York: Routledge.

Held, D. (1989) *Models of Democracy*, Cambridge: Polity Press.

Hinton, H. (ed.) (1980) *The People's Republic of China, 1949–1979: A Documentary Survey*, Wilmington: Scholarly Resources.

Hinton, W. (1996) *Fanshen: A Documentary of Revolution in a Chinese Village*, New York: Vintage Books.

Houn, F. (1961) *To Change a Nation: Propaganda and Indoctrination in Communist China*, Michigan: Michigan State University.

Howell, J. (1998) 'Prospects for village self-governance in China', *Journal of Peasant Studies*, 25, 3: 86–111.

Hsu, R. (1988) 'Economics and economists in post-Mao China', *Asian Survey*, 28, 12: 1211–28.

Information Office of the State Council. (1991) *Zhongguo de Renquan Zhuangkuang* (China's Human Rights Situation), Beijing: Central Literature Publishing House.

Jacobs, J. (1991) 'Elections in China', *Australian Journal of Chinese Affairs*, 25: 171–99.

Jin Qiu. (1999) *The Culture of Power: The Lin Biao Incident in the Cultural Revolution*, Stanford, CA: Stanford University Press.

Johnson, C. (1962) *Peasant Nationalism and Communist Power: The Emergence of Revolutionary China, 1937–1945*, Stanford, CA: Stanford University Press.

Johnston, A. and Ross, R. (eds) (1999) *Engaging China: The Management of an Emerging Power*, London: Routledge.

Joseph, W. (1986) 'A tragedy of good intentions: post-Mao views of the Great Leap Forward', *Modern China*, 12, 4: 419–57.

Jung Chang. (1991) *Wild Swans: Three Daughters of China*, London: Flamingo.

Jung Chang and Halliday, J. (2005) *Mao: The Unknown Story*, London: Jonathan Cape.

Kane, P. (1988) *Famine in China, 1959–61: Demographic and Social Implications*, London: Macmillan.

Kelliher, D. (1997) 'The Chinese debate over village self-government', *China Journal*, 37: 63–86.

Kelly, D. (1987) 'The emergence of humanism: Wang Ruoshui and the critique of socialist alienation', in M. Goldman with T. Cheek and C. Hamrin (eds) *China's Intellectuals and the State: In Search of a New Relationship*, Cambridge, MA: Harvard University Press.

Kim, S. (2000) *The Politics of Democratization in Korea: The Role of Civil Society*, Pittsburgh, PA: University of Pittsburgh Press.

Kissinger, H. (1979) *White House Years*, Boston, MA: Little, Brown and Company.

Kluver, A. (1996) *Legitimating the Chinese Economic Reforms: The Rhetoric of Myth and Orthodoxy*, New York: State University of New York Press.

Knight, N. (1983) 'The form of Mao Zedong's "signification of Marxism"', *Australian Journal of Chinese Affairs*, 9: 17–33.

Kwong, J. (1988) 'The 1986 student demonstrations in China: a democratic movement?', *Asian Survey*, 28, 9: 970–85.

Landsberger, S. (1989) 'The 1989 student demonstrations in Beijing: a chronology of events', *China Information*, 4, 1: 37–63.

Landsberger, S. (1995) *Chinese Propaganda Posters: From Revolution to Modernization*, Amsterdam: Pepin Press.

Lane, C. (1984) 'Legitimacy and power in the Soviet Union through socialist ritual', *British Journal of Political Science*, 14, 2: 207–17.

Lardy, N. (1994) *China and the World Economy*, Washington, DC: Institute for International Economics.

Lardy, N. (2002) *Integrating China into the World Economy*, Washington, DC: Brookings Institution Press.

Lau, R. (1997) 'China: labour reform and the challenge facing the working class', *Capital and Class*, 61: 45–80.

Lee, P. (1987) *Industrial Management and Economic Reform in China: 1949–1984*, New York: Oxford University Press.

Lee Travers, S. (1985) 'Getting rich through diligence: peasant income after the reforms', in E. Perry and C. Wong (eds) *The Political Economy of Reform in Post-Mao China*, Cambridge, MA: Harvard University Press.

Lett, D. (1998) *In Pursuit of Status: The Making of South Korea's 'New' Middle Class*, Cambridge, MA: Cambridge University Press.

Leys, S. (1977) *The Chairman's New Clothes: Mao and the Cultural Revolution*, London: Allison and Busby.

Li Zhisui. (1996) *The Private Life of Chairman Mao*, New York: Random House.

Lieberthal, K. (1995) *Governing China: From Revolution Through Reform*, New York: W. W. Norton.

Lieberthal, K. (1997) 'The Great Leap Forward', in R. MacFarquhar (ed.) *The Politics of China: The Eras of Mao and Deng*, Cambridge: Cambridge University Press.

Lippit, V. (1975) 'The Great Leap Forward reconsidered', *Modern China*, 1, 1: 92–115.

Lippit, V. (1977) 'The commune in Chinese development', *Modern China*, 3, 2: 229–55.

Liu Guoguang and Wu Jinglian. (1979) 'The relationship between planning and the market as seen by China in her socialist economy', *Atlantic Economic Journal*, December edn.

Liu Shaoqi. (1980) *Three Essays on Party Building*, Beijing: Foreign Languages Press.

Lomax, B. (1984) 'Hungary: the quest for legitimacy', in P. Lewis (ed.) *Eastern Europe: Political Crisis and Legitimation*, London: Croom Helm.

Lu Xiaobo. (2000) *Cadres and Corruption: The Organizational Involution of the Chinese Communist Party*, Stanford, CA: Stanford University Press.

Luo Ziping. (1990) *A Generation Lost: China Under the Cultural Revolution*, New York: Henry Holt and Company.

Lyman Miller, H. (2002) 'The succession of Hu Jintao', *China Leadership Monitor*, 1, 2: 1–8.

Lynch, D. (1999) *After the Propaganda State: Media, Politics and 'Thought Work' in Reformed China*, Stanford, CA: Stanford University Press.

Lynch, M. (1998) *The People's Republic of China Since 1949*, London: Hodder and Stoughton.

MacDougall, B. (1980) *Mao Zedong's Talks at the Yanan Conference on Literature and Art: A Translation of the 1943 Text With Commentary*, Ann Arbor, MI: University of Michigan Press.

MacFarquhar, R. (1974) *The Hundred Flowers Campaign and the Chinese Intellectuals*, London: Octagon Press.

MacFarquhar, R. (1983) *The Origins of the Cultural Revolution: The Great Leap Forward*, Oxford: Oxford University Press.

MacFarquhar, R. (1997) 'The succession to Mao and the end of Maoism', in R. MacFarquhar (ed.) *The Politics of China: The Eras of Mao and Deng*, Cambridge: Cambridge University Press.

Mackerras, C. (1984) 'Party consolidation and the attack of spiritual pollution', *Australian Journal of Chinese Affairs*, 11: 175–85.

Maier, J. (1990) 'Tiananmen 1989: the view from Shanghai', *China Information*, 5, 1: 1–13.

Mannheim, K. (1949) *Ideology and Utopia*, New York: Harcourt, Brace and Co.

Martin, H. (1982) *Cult and Canon: The Origins and Development of State Maoism*, New York: M. E. Sharpe.

Meany, C. (1991) 'Market reform and disintegrative corruption in urban China', in R. Baum (ed.) *Reform and Reaction in Post-Mao China: The Road to Tiananmen*, London: Routledge.

Misra, K. (1998) *From Post-Maoism to Post-Marxism: The Erosion of Official Ideology in Deng's China*, London: Routledge.

Mosher, S. (2002) *Hegemon: China's Plan to Dominate the World*, SanFrancisco, CA: Encounter Books.

Mozingo, D. (1983) 'The Chinese army and the communist state', in V. Nee and D. Mozingo (eds) *State and Society in Contemporary China*, Ithaca, NY: Cornell University Press.

Munro, D. (1977) *The Concept of Man in Contemporary China*, Ann Arbor, MI: University of Michigan Press.

Murray, G. (1998) *China the Next Superpower: Dilemmas in Change and Continuity*, London: Palgrave Macmillan.

Naim, M. (2003) 'Only a miracle can save China', *Financial Times*, 15 September.

Nathan, A. (1986) *Chinese Democracy: The Individual and the State in Twentieth Century China*, London: Tauris.

Nathan, A. and Link, P. (ed.) (2001) *The Tiananmen Papers*, New York: Public Affairs.

Naughton, B. (1989) 'Inflation and economic reform in China', *Current History*, September edn.

Naughton, B. (1990) 'Economic reform and the Chinese political crisis of 1989', *Journal of Asian Economics*, 1, 2: 349–61.

Naughton, B. (1995) *Growing Out of the Plan: Chinese Economic Reform, 1978–83*, Cambridge: Cambridge University Press.

Nolan, P. and Dong Fureng. (eds) (1990) *The Chinese Economy and its Future*, Cambridge: Polity Press.

O'Brien, K. (1990) *Reform without Liberalization: China's National People's Congress and the Politics of Institutional Change*, New York: Cambridge University Press.

O'Brien, K. (1994) 'Implementing political reform in China's villages', *Australian Journal of Chinese Affairs*, 32: 33–59.

O'Brien, K. (2001) 'Villagers, elections, and citizenship in contemporary China', *Modern China*, 27, 4: 407–35.

O'Brien, K. (2004) 'Neither transgressive nor contained: boundary spanning contention in China', in P. Hays Gries and S. Rosen (eds) *State and Society in 21st Century China: Crisis, Contention and Legitimation*, New York: Routledge.

Oi, J. (1996) 'Economic development, stability and democratic village self-governance', in M. Brosseau, S. Pepper and Tsang Shu-ki (eds) *China Review 1996*, Hong Kong: Chinese University of Hong Kong Press.

Oi, J. and Rozelle, S. (2000) 'Elections and power: the locus of decision making in Chinese villages', *China Quarterly*, 162: 513–39.

Oksenberg, M. (1976) 'The exit pattern from Chinese politics and its implications', *China Quarterly*, 67: 501–18.

Oksenberg, M. and Sai-cheung Yeung. (1977) 'Hua Kuo-feng's pre-Cultural Revolution Hunan years, 1949–1966: the making of a political generalist', *China Quarterly*, 69: 3–53.

Onate, A. (1978) 'Hua Kuo-feng and the arrest of the Gang of Four', *China Quarterly*, 75: 540–65.

Overholt, W. (1994) *The Rise of China: How Economic Reform is Creating a New Superpower*, New York: W. W. Norton.

Park, A. and Shen, M. (2003) 'Joint liability lending and the rise and fall of China's township and village enterprises', *Journal of Development Economics*, 71, 2: 497–531.

Pastor, R. and Tan Qingshan. (2000) 'The meaning of China's village elections', *China Quarterly*, 162: 490–512.

Pearson, M. (2001) 'Entrepreneurs and democratization in China's foreign sector', in V. Bonnell and T. Gold (eds) *The New Entrepreneurs of Europe and Asia: Patterns of Business Development in Russia, Eastern Europe and China*, New York: M. E. Sharpe.

Pei Minxin. (1998) 'Chinese civic associations: an empirical analysis', *Modern China*, 24, 3: 285–318.

Pei Minxin. (2002) 'China's governance crisis', *Foreign Affairs*, September/October.

Pei Minxin. (2003) 'Contradictory trends and confusing signals', *Journal of Democracy*, 14, 1: 73–81.

Pepper, S. (1999) *Civil War in China: The Political Struggle, 1945–1949*, Boston, MA: Rowman and Littlefield.

Perry, E. (1994) 'Shanghai's strike wave of 1957', *China Quarterly*, 137: 1–27.

Perry, E. (1999) 'Crime, corruption and contention', in M. Goldman and R. MacFarquhar (eds) *The Paradox of China's Post-Mao Reforms*, Cambridge, MA: Harvard University Press.

Powell, R. (1965) 'Commissars in the economy: the "Learn from the PLA" movement in China', *Asian Survey*, 5, 3: 125–38.

Pusey, J. (1969) *Wu Han: Attacking the Present Through the Past*, Cambridge, MA: Harvard University Press.

Putterman, L. (1985) 'The restoration of the peasant household as farm production unit in China: some incentive theoretical analysis', in E. Perry and C. Wong (eds) *The Political Economy of Reform in Post-Mao China*, Cambridge, MA: Harvard University Press.

Pye, L. (1971) 'Mass participation in communist China: its limitations and the continuity of culture', in J. Lindbeck (ed.) *China: Management of a Revolutionary Society*, Washington: University of Washington Press.

Pye, L. (1976) *Mao Tse-tung: The Man in the Leader*, New York: Basic Books.

Qian Yingyi. (1999) 'The process of China's market transition (1978–98): the evolutionary, historical and comparative perspectives', *Stanford Working Papers*, April: 1–34.

Qiao Liang. (2002) *Unrestricted Warfare: China's Master Plan to Destroy America*, Washington, DC: Pan American Publishing Company.

Rigby, T. (1980) 'A conceptual approach to authority, power and policy in the Soviet Union', in T. Rigby, A. Brown and P. Reddaway (eds) *Authority, Power and Policy in the USSR*, London: Macmillan.

Rigby, T. (1982) 'Political legitimacy, Weber and communist mono-organisational systems', in T. Rigby and F. Feher (eds) *Political Legitimation in Communist Systems*, London: Macmillan.

Robinson, T. (1971) 'The Wuhan incident: local strife and provincial rebellion during the Cultural Revolution', *China Quarterly*, 47: 413–38.

Robinson, W. (1996) *Promoting Polyarchy: Globalization, US Intervention and Hegemony*, Cambridge: Cambridge University Press.

Rosen, S. (1982) *Red Guard Factionalism and the Cultural Revolution in Guangzhou (Canton)*, Boulder, CO: Westview Press.

Rosen, S. (1990) 'The Chinese Communist Party and Chinese society: popular attitudes towards party membership and the party's image', *Australian Journal of Chinese Affairs*, 24: 51–92.

Saich, T. (1984) 'Party consolidation and spiritual pollution in the People's Republic of China', *Communist Affairs*, 3, 3: 283–9.

Saich, T. (1990) 'The rise and fall of the Beijing people's movement', *Australian Journal of Chinese Affairs*, 24: 181–208.

Saich, T. (1991) 'Urban society in China', *Nordic Proceedings in Asian Studies*, 2: 558–99.

Saich, T. (1995) 'Writing or rewriting history?: The construction of the Maoist resolution on party history', in T. Saich and H. van de Ven (eds) *New Perspectives on the Chinese Communist Revolution*, New York: M. E. Sharpe.

Saich, T. (1996) *The Rise to Power of the Chinese Communist Party: Documents and Analysis*, New York: M. E. Sharpe.

Saich, T. (2000) 'Negotiating the state: the development of social organizations in China', *China Quarterly*, 161: 124–41.

Saich, T. (2001) *Governance and Politics of China*, London: Palgrave.

Salisbury, H. (1969) *The Coming War Between Russia and China*, London: Pan.

Salisbury, H. (1989) *Tiananmen Diary: Thirteen Days in June*, New York: Little Brown and Company.

Scalapino, R. (1972) 'The transition in Chinese Party leadership: a comparison of the eighth and ninth Central Committees', in R. Scalapino (ed.) *Elites in the People's Republic of China*, Seattle, WA: University of Washington Press.

Schaar, J. (1970) 'Legitimacy in the modern state', in P. Green and S. Levinson (eds) *Power and Community*, New York: Pantheon Books.

Schram, S. (1971) 'Mao Tse-tung and the theory of permanent revolution: 1958–69', *China Quarterly*, 46: 221–44.

Schram, S. (ed.) (1979) *Mao Tse-tung Unrehearsed: Talks and Letters: 1956–71*, Harmondsworth: Penguin.

Schram, S. (ed.) (1987) *Foundations and Limits of State Power in China*, Hong Kong: Chinese University Press.

Schram, S. (1989) *The Thought of Mao Tse-tung*, Cambridge: Cambridge University Press.

Schurmann, F. (1968) *Ideology and Organization in Communist China*, Berkeley, CA: University of California Press.

Schwartz, B. (1964) *In Search of Wealth and Power: Yen Fu and the West*, Cambridge, MA: Harvard University Press.

Selden, M. (1971) *The Yenan Way in Revolutionary China*, Cambridge, MA: Harvard University Press.

Shambaugh, D. (1989) 'The fourth and fifth plenary sessions of the 13th CCP Central Committee', *China Quarterly*, 120: 852–62.

Shambaugh, D. (2001) 'The dynamics of elite politics during the Jiang era', *China Journal*, 45: 101–11.

Shapiro, J., Worster, D. and Crosby, A. (2001) *Mao's War Against Nature: Politics and the Environment in Revolutionary China*, Cambridge: Cambridge University Press.

Shi Tianjian. (1999) 'Village committee elections in China: institutional tactics for democracy', *World Politics*, 51, 3: 385–412.

Shirk, S. (2001) 'Will the institutionalization of party leadership survive the 2002–03 succession?', *China Journal*, 45: 139–42.

Shue, V. (2004) 'Legitimacy crisis in China?', in P. Hays Gries and S. Rosen (eds) *State and Society in 21st Century China: Crisis, Contention and Legitimation*, New York: Routledge.

Shum Kui Kwong. (1988) *The Chinese Communists' Road to Power: The Anti-Japanese National United Front*, Oxford: Oxford University Press.

Solinger, D. (1999) 'China's floating population: implications for state and society', in R. MacFarquhar and M. Goldman (eds) *The Paradox of China's Post-Mao Reforms*, Cambridge, MA: Harvard University Press.

Solinger, D. (2001) 'Why we cannot count the unemployed', *China Quarterly*, 167: 671–88.

Solinger, D. (2004) 'The new crowd of the dispossessed: the shift of the urban proletariat from master to mendicant', in P. Hays Gries and S. Rosen (eds) *State and Society in 21st Century China: Crisis, Contention and Legitimation*, New York: Routledge.

Song Qiang, Zhang Zangzang and Qiao Bian. (1996) *Zhongguo Keyi Shuo Bu* (China Can Say No), Beijing: New World Publishing House.

Starr, J. (1986) ' "Good Mao, bad Mao": Mao studies and the re-evaluation of Mao's political thought', *Australian Journal of Chinese Affairs*, 16: 1–22.

Stavis, B. (1978) *The Politics of Agricultural Mechanization in China*, New York: Cornell University Press.

Stavis, B. (1988) *China's Political Reforms*, New York: Praeger.

Steinfield, E. (1998) *Forging Reform in China: The Fate of State Owned Industry*, New York: Cambridge University Press.

Strecker-Downs, E. and Saunders, P. (1998–9) 'Legitimacy and the limits of nationalism: China and the Diaoyu islands', *International Security*, 23, 3: 114–46.

Sullivan, L. (1986–7) 'Leadership and authority in the Chinese Communist Party: perspectives from the 1950s', *Pacific Affairs*, 59, 4: 605–33.

Teiwes, F. (1984) *Leadership, Legitimacy and Conflict in China: From a Charismatic Mao to the Politics of Succession*, New York: M. E. Sharpe.

Teiwes, F. (1997) 'The establishment and consolidation of the new regime: 1949–57', in R. MacFarquhar (ed.) *The Politics of China: The Eras of Mao and Deng*, Cambridge: Cambridge University Press.

Teiwes, F. and Sun, W. (1995) 'From a Leninist to a charismatic party: the CCP's changing leadership: 1937–45', in T. Saich and H. van de Ven (eds) *New Perspectives on the Chinese Communist Revolution*, New York: M. E. Sharpe.

Terrill, R. (1984) *The White-Boned Demon: A Biography of Madame Mao Zedong*, New York: William Morrow.

Teufel-Dreyer, J. (1996) *China's Political System: Modernization and Tradition*, London: Macmillan.

Thaxton, R. (1983) *China Turned Rightside Up: Revolutionary Legitimacy in the Peasant World*, New Haven, CT: Yale University Press.

Thomas, G. (2001) *Seeds of Fire: China and the Story Behind the Attack on America*, Arizona: Dandelion Books.

Thornton, P. (2004) 'Comrades and collectives in arms: tax resistance, evasion and avoidance strategies in post-Mao China', in P. Hays Gries and S. Rosen (eds) *State and Society in 21st Century China: Crisis, Contention and Legitimation*, New York: Routledge.

Thurston, A. (1984–5) 'Victims of China's Cultural Revolution: the invisible wounds, Part I', *Pacific Affairs*, 57, 4: 599–620.

Thurston, A. (1985) 'Victims of China's Cultural Revolution: the invisible wounds, Part II', *Pacific Affairs*, 58, 1: 5–27.

Timperlake, E. and Triplett, W. (2002) *Red Dragon Rising: China's Military Threat to America*, Washington: Regnery Publishing.

Ting Gong. (1997) 'Forms and characteristics of China's corruption in the 1990s', *Communist and Post-Communist Studies*, 30, 3: 277–88.

Townsend, J. (1967) *Political Participation in Communist China*, California: University of California Press.

Walder, A. (1978) *Chang Ch'un-ch'iao and Shanghai's January Revolution*, Ann Arbor, MI: University of Michigan.

Weatherley, R. (1999) *The Discourse of Human Rights in China: Historical and Ideological Perspectives*, London: Macmillan.

Weatherley, R. (2002) 'Harmony, hierarchy and duty-based morality: the Confucian antipathy towards rights', *Journal of Asian Pacific Communication*, 12, 2: 245–67.

Weber, M. (1964) *The Theory of Social and Economic Organization*, edited by T. Parsons, New York: The Free Press.

Wederman, A. (1997) 'Stealing from the farmers: institutional corruption and the IOU crisis', *China Quarterly*, 152: 802–38.

Wei Jingsheng. (1997) *The Courage to Stand Alone: Letters from Prison and Other Writings*, New York: Viking.

Weidenbaum, M. and Hughes, S. (1996) *The Bamboo Network: How Expatriate Chinese Entrepreneurs are Creating a New Economic Superpower in Asia*, New York: Simon and Schuster.

Weston, T. (2004) 'The iron man weeps: joblessness and political legitimacy in the Chinese rust belt', in P. Hays Gries and S. Rosen (eds) *State and Society in 21st Century China: Crisis, Contention and Legitimation*, New York: Routledge.

White, G. (1993) *Riding the Tiger: The Politics of Economic Reform in Post-Mao China*, Stanford, CA: Stanford University Press.

White, S. (1986) 'Economic performance and communist legitimacy', *World Politics*, 38, 3: 462–82.

Whiting, A. (1960) *China Crosses the Yalu: The Decision to Enter the Korean War*, New York: Macmillan.

Whitson, W. (1969) 'The field army in Chinese communist military politics', *China Quarterly*, 37: 1–30.

Whitson, W. and Wang Chen-hsia. (1973) *The Chinese High Command: A History of Communist Military Politics, 1927–71*, New York: Praeger.

Whyte, M. (1979) 'Small groups and communication in China: ideal forms and imperfect realities', in G. Chu and F. Hsu (eds) *Moving a Mountain: Cultural Change in China*, Honolulu: University Press of Hawaii.

Wietzman, M. and Xu Chengguang. (1994) 'Chinese township and village enterprises as vaguely defined co-operatives', *Journal of Comparative Economics*, 18, 2: 121–45.

Wilson, D. (1982) *The Long March 1935: The Epic of Chinese Communism's Survival*, Harmondsworth: Penguin.

Wilson, I. and You Ji (1990) 'Leadership by lines: China's unresolved succession', *Problems of Communism*, 39, 1: 28–44.

Wo-Lap Lam, W. (2000) 'Deng Liqun attacks the theory of the three representatives', *South China Morning Post*, 19 July 2000.

Wolf, C., Yeh, K. Eberstadt, N. and Lee, S. (2003) *Fault Lines in China's Economic Terrain*, Rand Online.

Womack, B. (1982) 'The 1980 county-level elections in China: experiment in democratic modernization', *Asian Survey*, 22, 3: 261–77.

Wong, C. (1985) 'The second phase of economic reform in China', *Current History*, September: 260–3.

Wong, J. and Zheng Yongnian. (2001) *The Nanxun Legacy and China's Development in the Post-Deng Era*, Singapore: Singapore University Press.

Wylie, R. (1980) *The Emergence of Maoism: Mao Tse-tung, Ch'en Po-ta and the Search for Chinese Theory, 1935–45*, California: Stanford University Press.

Xu Guangqiu. (2001) 'Anti-Western nationalism: 1989–1999', *World Affairs*, 163, 4: 151–62.

Yahuda, M. (1972) 'Kreminology and the Chinese strategic debate: 1965–66', *China Quarterly*, 49: 32–75.

Yao Ming-le. (1983) *The Conspiracy and Death of Lin Biao*, London: Collins.

Yep, R. (2002) 'Maintaining stability in rural China: challenges and responses', paper presented to Chatham House, London, May, 1–22.

You Ji. (1991) 'Zhao Ziyang and the politics of inflation', *Australian Journal of Chinese Affairs*, 25: 69–91.

Yu, F. (1964) *Mass Persuasion in Communist China*, New York: Praeger.

Zagoria, D. (1962) *The Sino-Soviet Conflict: 1956–61*, Princeton, NJ: Princeton University Press.

Zhao Dingxin. (2001) *The Power of Tiananmen: State-Society Relations and the 1989 Beijing Student Movement*, Chicago, IL: University of Chicago Press.

Zhao Suisheng. (1993) 'Deng Xiaoping's southern tour: elite politics in post-Tiananmen China', *Asian Survey*, 33, 8: 739–56.

Zhao Suisheng. (1997) 'Chinese intellectuals quest for national greatness and nationalistic writings in the 1990s', *China Quarterly*, 157: 725–45.

Zheng Shiping. (1997) *Party vs. State in Post-1949 China: The Institutional Dilemma*, Cambridge: Cambridge University Press.

Zheng Shiping. (2003) 'Leadership change, legitimacy, and party transition in China', *Journal of Chinese Political Science*, 8, 1/2: 47–63.

Zi Shui and Xiao Shi. (1997) *Shi Jingti Riben Diguo Zhuyi!* (Be Vigilant Against Japanese Militarism!), Beijing: Jincheng Press.

Zweig, D. (2002) *Internationalizing China: Domestic Interests and Global Linkages*, Ithaca, NY: Cornell University Press.

# Index

Note: Page numbers in italics indicate figures.

For Product Safety Concerns and Information please contact our EU
representative GPSR@taylorandfrancis.com
Taylor & Francis Verlag GmbH, Kaufingerstraße 24, 80331 München, Germany

www.ingramcontent.com/pod-product-compliance
Lightning Source LLC
Chambersburg PA
CBHW050434280326
41932CB00013BA/2117